DESIGN AND ETHICS

Design spans many spheres of everyday life, and an approach that considers its ethical dimension can help contribute to environmental, social and economic sustainability.

The authors represented in this book recognise design as a practice that can transform human experience and understanding, expanding its role beyond stylistic enhancement. The traditional roles of design, designer and designed object are redefined through a new understanding of the relationship between the material and immaterial aspects of design where the product and the design process are embodiments of ideas, values and beliefs.

This book presents a multi-disciplinary collection of writing with authors reflecting on design as a process in which ethics and social responsibility are paramount. With contributions from fields as diverse as architecture, fashion, urban design, philosophy and education, this book presents innovative ways of thinking about and doing design.

Emma Felton is Research Fellow and Coordinator of the Widening Participation Program in the Creative Industries Faculty, Queensland University of Technology. She has a PhD in Human Geography and has worked as a lecturer in media and cultural studies and as a senior manager in e-learning. She has also worked as a consultant in the fields of education and cultural planning.

Oksana Zelenko is a design researcher and academic at the Creative Industries Faculty, Queensland University of Technology (QUT). Oksana has recently completed her PhD on the use of new media and Interaction Design to promote children's resilience. She has worked as the interface designer and researcher on ARC-funded projects, including developing a world first in online visual counselling as part of the QUT Online Visual Counselling Tools project. Oksana's broader practice includes the design of interactive and educational programmes for cross-cultural training of medical staff working in remote regions across the Pacific, development of interactive modules for the Queensland Government and, more recently, the design of rich media resources for training health workers at World Vision, China.

Suzi Vaughan is Deputy Vice-Chancellor, Teaching and Learning at Queensland University of Technology. She has 15 years' experience of teaching and leadership in higher education both in the UK and Australia, and is the recipient of a number of teaching excellence awards in recognition of her work in fashion education and academic leadership. In 2008, she was a member of the expert reference group for the Federal Government Review of the Australian textile, clothing and footwear industry. Her current research interests are in teaching and learning in higher education, particularly with respect to authentic learning, first-year experience and the pedagogies of studio-based learning.

DESIGN AND ETHICS

Reflections on practice

Edited by
Emma Felton, Oksana Zelenko and Suzi Vaughan

Routledge
Taylor & Francis Group
LONDON AND NEW YORK

First published 2012
by Routledge
2 Park Square, Milton Park, Abingdon, Oxon OX14 4RN

Simultaneously published in the USA and Canada
by Routledge
711 Third Avenue, New York, NY 10017

Routledge is an imprint of the Taylor & Francis Group, an informa business

British Library Cataloguing in Publication Data
A catalogue record for this book is available from the British Library

Library of Congress Cataloging in Publication Data
Design and ethics: reflections on practice/edited by Emma Felton, Oksana Zelenko, and Suzi Vaughan.
p. cm.
Includes bibliographical references and index.
1. Design – Moral and ethical aspects. I. Felton, Emma. II. Zelenko, Oksana. III. Vaughan, Suzi. IV. Title: Reflections on practice.
NK1520.D455 2012
174′.97 – dc23 2011038597

ISBN: 978-0-415-68812-3 (hbk)
ISBN: 978-0-415-68813-0 (pbk)
ISBN: 978-0-203-12397-3 (ebk)

Typeset in Bembo and Stone Sans
by Florence Production Ltd, Stoodleigh, Devon

MIX
Paper from responsible sources
FSC www.fsc.org FSC® C004839

Printed and bound in Great Britain by
TJ International Ltd, Padstow, Cornwall

CONTENTS

ILLUSTRATIONS

Figures

Tables

CONTRIBUTORS

Leslie F. Becker is currently Director of Design and former Chair of Graphic Design at California College of the Arts, San Francisco. In addition to graphic design studies, she teaches Visual Studies courses that address the ethical and social effects of design on popular culture. A practising designer for over thirty years, Leslie works in areas such as corporate graphics, signage systems and furniture. She has presented papers at design conferences and universities such as Tsinghua University, Beijing, Harvard University and University College, Dublin. In 2010, Leslie lectured for one week to design educators as a guest of the Chinese Ministry of Education. Her writing has appeared in multiple design magazines and texts. She holds a BFA from The Cooper Union for the Advancement of Science and Art, an MA in Design and a PhD in Architecture/Theory and Methods from UC Berkeley. Her research area is design and ethics.

Laurie Buys is Professor at the School of Design, Creative Industries Faculty, at Queensland University of Technology. She is an experienced social science researcher and research manager, who frequently collaborates with scientists from various disciplinary backgrounds on complex research initiatives. Her main research interests fall under the broad headings of social sustainability and social gerontology, focusing specifically on issues associated with community engagement, corporate social responsibility, sustainable buildings and active ageing.

Paula Dunlop lives and works in Brisbane, Australia. She is currently undertaking a PhD at Queensland University of Technology investigating dressmaking, remaking and ethics in fashion design from a practitioner's perspective.

Emma Felton is Research Fellow and Coordinator of the Widening Participation Program in the Creative Industries Faculty, Queensland University of Technology. She has a PhD in Human Geography and has worked as a lecturer in media and cultural studies and as a senior manager in e-learning. She has also worked as a consultant in the fields of education and cultural planning.

Karen Fiss is Professor of Design at California College of the Arts. Her research examines the history of 'nation branding' in the production of visual culture, from the rise of the nation-state to its current role in shaping the social, artistic and built environment of emerging economies. Her most recent book is *Grand Illusion: The Third Reich, the Paris Exposition, and the cultural Seduction of France*, published by the University of Chicago Press (2010). The study examines related developments across fine arts, film, architecture and mass pageantry in order to illuminate the role of National Socialist propaganda in the French decision to ignore Hitler's war preparations and pursue an untenable policy of appeasement. She also recently co-edited, with Hazel Clark, a special volume of the journal *Design Issues* on globalization, post-colonialism and design (summer 2009).

Tony Fry is a professor, design educator, award-winning designer and writer. Tony heads the Design Futures Program of Griffith University's Queensland College of Art (QCA). This radical program offers postgraduate students cutting-edge opportunities to learn how to engage with thinking and practice that can advance sustainable futures. He also leads QCA's Creative Industries, Development and Timor-Leste project, which is funded by an AusAID Australian Development Research Award. This project is helping establish a design-based creative industry education institution in East Timor based on principles of sustainability, economic viability and employment generation. Tony is the author of numerous articles and nine books – the latest being *Design as Politics,* published by Berg, 2010.

John Hartley, AM, is Distinguished Professor of Queensland University of Technology's Creative Industries Faculty, of which he was the founding dean in 2000. He was an ARC Federation Fellow (2005–2010). Previously, he was Founding Head of the School of Journalism, Media and Cultural Studies at Cardiff University in Wales. The author of over 20 books and 200 papers in the fields of communication, cultural, media and journalism studies, his most recent books are: *Communication, Cultural and Media Studies: The key concepts* (Routledge, 2011), *Digital Futures for Cultural and Media Studies* (Wiley-Blackwell, 2012) and *The Uses of Digital Literacy* (UQP/Transaction, 2009). He is Editor of the *International Journal of Cultural Studies* (Sage). His current research interests are in the role of consumer co-creation as 'micro-productivity' and social learning in digital media, and in 'cultural science' – the convergence of arts and science in the study of cultural and economic systems.

Stephen Loo is Professor of Architecture at the School of Architecture & Design, University of Tasmania. He has taught at the University of South Australia, University of Sydney and University of Adelaide. Stephen is a registered architect and a Member of the Australian Institute of Architects, in which he is a Councillor of the Tasmanian Chapter and Chair of the Education Committee. He is a the founding partner of the architectural, design and interpretation practice, Mulloway Studio. Stephen's research is located at the intersections of philosophy, architectural theory, contemporary visual art and experimental digital practice, in particular on the relationships between architecture, urbanism and citizenship.

Noëmi Manders-Huits is Assistant Professor in Applied Ethics at Delft University of Technology. With a background in philosophy and business administration, she studies the ethical dimensions of new media and information technologies. She has particular interest in privacy and identity, ethics of technology, access to knowledge and value-conscious design. In addition, she is Managing Editor of the Springer journal *Ethics and Information Technology*.

Wendy Miller is Senior Research Fellow in the Faculty of Built Environment and Engineering at Queensland University of Technology. She has many years' experience in the renewable energy industry and in school, community and technical education. Her research interests encompass zero-energy communities, performance of advanced buildings and building materials, and energy systems planning and performance. She has a particular interest in exploring the connections between technology, the professions that implement technologies and the ultimate end users.

Justin O'Connor is Professor in the Creative Industries Faculty, Queensland University of Technology, Brisbane, Australia, and visiting Chair, Department of Humanities, Shanghai Jiaotong University. Until September 2008, he was Professor of Cultural Industries at the School of Performance and Cultural Industries, University of Leeds. Between 1995 and 2006, Justin was Director of Manchester Institute for Popular Culture at Manchester Metropolitan University. He was involved in policy development for the cultural and creative industries in Manchester and in a number of European and Russian cities. He has just completed a lengthy report for the Australia Council on Arts and Creative Industries and is advising the city governments of Qingdao and Shanghai, China, on creative clusters. He is an international cultural policy expert for UNESCO and is working with Qingdao city to become a 'City of Music' under that organization's accreditation scheme.

Alice Payne is a fashion and textile designer, currently undertaking doctoral research at Queensland University of Technology (QUT). Her research explores the Australian mass-market fashion design process in the context of sustainability, with an emphasis on privileging designers' voices. Alice holds honours degrees in Visual Arts (University of Sydney) and in Fashion and Textile Design, University of Technology Sydney (UTS). Her recent design work has explored design processes and systems, resulting in the ThinkLifecycle website and content management system. Her collection of modular garments was exhibited in

Materiality in Gaffa Gallery, Sydney, in 2008. She was also a finalist in the 2006 Lancome Fashion Design Awards. Alice is a tutor at QUT in Fashion History and Theory, and a past tutor at UTS, in fashion design studio.

Gavin Sade is a designer in the field of interactive computational media, with a background in music and sonology, and is currently the Undergraduate Study Area coordinator for Animation, Interactive and Visual Design in the Creative Industries Faculty at Queensland University of Technology. He has previously been Head of Communication Design and coordinated postgraduate course work programmes in Communication Design. Since 1997, Gavin has written, coordinated and run both undergraduate and postgraduate classes on Media Technology, Interaction Design, Physical Computing, Virtual Reality, Contemporary Issues in Design and Technology, Game Design and Web Development. Between 1999 and 2003, Gavin was a member of the Transmute Collective. In 2003, he formed Kuuki, a creative media group, which has exhibited works nationally and internationally.

Paul Sanders is Professor and Head of the School of Design in the Faculty of Creative Industries, Queensland University of Technology (QUT). He has published in international journals in the fields of architecture and urban design, and specializes in the field of urban morphology. He has extensive design experience through built work, as well as international design competitions.

Shannon Satherley is a lecturer in Landscape Architecture at Queensland University of Technology, and has been involved in landscape architecture education in theory and practice since 2003. Shannon's teaching is focused on the creation of externally engaged learning environments fostering active and interactive student and community learning. She has a strong related research focus investigating issues surrounding the balance between the processes and the outcomes of external student design projects. Shannon is also currently researching a PhD investigating the effects of landscape design on the manifestation of cultural values in deindustrialized landscapes.

Kuniko Shibata, PhD, is Visiting Research Fellow of the Centre for Transdisciplinary Gender Studies at the Humboldt University of Berlin, and a URP Research Fellow of the Urban Research Plaza at Osaka City University in Japan. She has a PhD in Regional Planning on the history of the public interest in Japanese planning development in 2007 from the Department of Geography and Environment at the London School of Economics and Political Science in the UK. Her academic research has focused on the relationships between planning, politics and the economy, including an analysis of regulatory framework, and the ideologies and roles of planning institutions in relation to the modern state development. She is currently working on the research project, 'Mainstreaming Gender in European Cities: Comparative Studies of Urban Policy Development under Multi-level Governance'.

Suzi Vaughan is Deputy Vice-Chancellor, Teaching and Learning at Queensland University of Technology. She has fifteen years' experience of teaching and leadership in higher education both in the UK and Australia, and is the recipient of a number of teaching excellence awards in recognition of her work in fashion education and academic leadership. In 2008, she was a member of the expert reference group for the Federal Government Review of the Australian textile, clothing and footwear industry. Her current research interests are in teaching and learning in higher education, particularly with respect to authentic learning, first-year experience and the pedagogies of studio-based learning.

Marci Webster-Mannison commenced her architectural career in 1979. After three decades working in architectural practice in Noosa Heads, Sydney, Canberra, regional NSW and Brisbane, Marci joined the University of Queensland in 2008 and is the Director of the University's Centre for Sustainable Design. Marci is known for state-of-the-art, ecologically inspired architecture as a practising architect, speaker and writer. Among over twenty state, national and international awards for her architecture, Marci received a Special Jury Award (RAIA) for her contribution to the advancement of architecture and commitment to environmentally sensitive design in 2001.

Oksana Zelenko is a design researcher and academic at the Creative Industries Faculty, Queensland University of Technology (QUT). Oksana has recently completed her PhD on the use of new media and Interaction Design to promote children's resilience. She has worked as the interface designer and researcher on ARC-funded projects, including developing a world first in online visual counselling as part of the QUT Online Visual Counselling Tools project. Oksana's broader practice includes the design of interactive and educational programmes for cross-cultural training of medical staff working in remote regions across the Pacific, development of interactive modules for the Queensland Government and, more recently, the design of rich media resources for training health workers at World Vision, China.

Michael Zimmer, PhD, is Assistant Professor in the School of Information Studies at the University of Wisconsin–Milwaukee, and Co-Director of the Center for Information Policy Research. With a background in new media and internet studies, the philosophy of technology and information ethics, Zimmer studies the ethical dimensions of new media and information technologies, with particular interest in privacy, social media, internet research ethics and value-conscious design.

ACKNOWLEDGEMENTS

We are very grateful to Professor Phil Graham, Institute of Creative Industries and Innovation, Queensland University of Technology, for his support and enthusiasm for the project, and for assisting in facilitating the initial concept. Our thanks also go to the internal and external reviewers for giving their time and expertise to review individual contributions. The book's progress was enhanced primarily by the excellent editorial assistance of Jessica Rodgers, and at other stages by Gretchen Coombs and Sandra Kafrouni. All three were a pleasure to work with.

PART I

Perspectives on design and ethics

1

FRAMING DESIGN AND ETHICS

Oksana Zelenko and Emma Felton

Design is undergoing a reconceptualization triggered by debates about its potential to instigate meaningful social, cultural and environmental change. Simultaneously, design and the allied design-based industries are experiencing a vigorous ascendancy across many spheres of life. While our collective aesthetic is finely tuned to contemplate and consume all things designer, innovations in digital media are generating new dimensions in the design realms – spawning new industries and aesthetic developments. From designer kitchens and clothes to technology and landscapes, our senses have become hard-wired to appreciate the nuances and aesthetics of the visual.

At the same time, a growing consensus about environmental fragility, and how practices of production and consumption are contributing to an unsustainable future, underpins a discourse that sees the potential of design to be transformative or 'redirective' (Fry 2009). There is little disagreement that we are witnessing an 'ethical turn' occurring in professional and allied practices, including the design fields. This reconceptualization extends design's role – and that of practitioners' responsibility – beyond stylistic enhancement, or the quest for optimal product solutions, to account for the aesthetic dimensions of human experience and consequences of creative decision-making underpinning design processes. The traditional roles of design, designer and designed object are thus redefined through new understandings of the relationship between the material and immaterial aspects of design, where the design product and process are understood as embodiments of ideas, values and beliefs. This notion brings to the fore central questions around social responsibility, sustainability and consideration for the life of the object beyond the design studio.

The practice of ethics as a mode of being shaped by socially determined attitudes and beliefs is positioned beyond any single disciplinary perspective. Taking a cross-disciplinary approach to ethics requires a recognition of the plurality of opinions, practices and socio-cultural perspectives, and the opportunity to open established value systems to questioning and renegotiation. This approach to ethics can be regarded as one of *critical ethics* (Colebrook 1999) where key questions about *who* creates the codes, *how* and in what context, shape the debate. In this sense, *critical ethics* is a *dynamic* ethics based in awareness and responsibility and representative of the flux, context and negotiation in process. It is through this lens that we hope you will view *Design and Ethics: Reflections on practice* as a multidisciplinary approach to the topic, which paradoxically does not diminish the primacy of any individual disciplinary specialization, but rather, by virtue of juxtaposition with other disciplines, amplifies and increases the visibility of viewpoints. The aim is to create a space for critical engagement in which contrasting, contradictory views are a necessary part. The value of the cross-disciplinary approach is in the intersections between disciplines that are not necessarily evident from publications based in a single discipline.

The pressures of finding sustainable solutions to complex problems increasingly requires practitioners to operate beyond their disciplinary specialization. This process demands a pedagogical framework that has a strong ethical foundation enabling practising and prospective professionals to cultivate an awareness of, and critical engagement with, value systems, professional codes and social standards. Many contributors to this volume, who are both design practitioners and educators, endorse an ethics of design in their pedagogical practice, illustrating the limitations and potential for this approach.

The chapters collected here are multidisciplinary excursions in and around the two triggers of 'design' and 'ethics', in which ethics is interpreted in ways that transcend the specificity of disciplines and practices. The chapters are organized in five parts, with this, the first chapter in Part I, offering a traditional philosophical framework that serves to anchor the diversity of perspectives and disciplines presented on the topic. The collection then moves through the practices of interaction and visual design, architecture, urban planning and fashion, and concludes with a provocation on the potential of design's future. Each disciplinary cluster attempts to create vignettes of practitioners' reflections on practice alongside theoretical perspectives from non-practitioners, allowing the reciprocity and dynamics shaping theory and practice to become more apparent. From a practitioner's perspective, ethics as applied to the various design fields is both a process of constant negotiation that recognizes the inherent messiness of collaboration and consensus as well as a mechanism for addressing these complexities. In efforts to ensure sustainable outcomes in design practice, as writers and practitioners point out, the authority of, and commitment to, a sustainable future is paramount.

The ethical concerns positioned at the intersection of design practice and design pedagogy are charted in Stephen Loo's chapter, 'Design-*ing* ethics: the good, the bad and the performative', which presents a layered ordering of the complex philosophical terrain that spans the field of design and moral theory. Incorporating traditional forms of philosophical enquiry, the first order utilizes Aristotelian and deontological approaches in a way that frames the design and educative process in an ethical context. The second order looks to the designer as human citizen beyond disciplinary or professional boundaries, while the third order charts the triadic relationship between human subjects, constructed objects and the environment.

In this framework, Loo interrogates the ontological status of design as it relates to ethical considerations, the importance of which, for Loo, lies in design's function as a mediator of 'people-to-people relations'. The difference between 'good design' and the more contested idea of 'ethical value' presents an epistemological conundrum for educators and practitioners alike. Because ethics in moral theory is more likely to involve concepts of the 'good' and the 'right', it follows that design tends to become defined as 'ethically sound', which assumes particular functional qualities such as accessibility, usefulness and safety, all of which arrive from a moral imperative. The circularity of this way of thinking, for Loo, requires us to think differently about ethics and design, towards the idea of design as *performative* ethics. This requires the designer to re-evaluate actively and constantly their role in the design process.

Drawing on her experience as a practitioner and educator in 'Design, ethics and group myopia', Leslie F. Becker would endorse the idea of performative ethics, although she expresses this idea in the context of critical reflection, for practitioners and educators. Professional practitioners tend to produce group affinities and myopia – shared assumptions and values – that create certainties and biases, which reproduce ideas about what is 'right action', but in actuality can often be an impediment to ethical action. Becker's thirty years' experience brings to her chapter a varied and rich tapestry of trends in design practice and thinking that are both perennial and evolving. Becker suggests that, despite the recent ascendancy of ethics in the public sphere and across the disciplines, an improvement in human and environmental flourishing is not yet evident. Debates about the value of art and culture, and ergo, design to society are perennial. Justin O'Connor takes this up in his discussion on the repositioning of art and culture in the framework of 'creative industries' – a term that first appeared in the mid 1990s and arose from the United Kingdom's Labour government and is now more widely adopted in other countries. In 'From allure to ethics: design as a "creative industry"', O'Connor suggests that the creative industries' framework, as a strategy for economic and commercial development, positions 'design' so that it becomes a broker for art and industry – and that this has implications for design to function in an ethical capacity.

In other contemporary reconceptualizations of design, Karen Fiss, at the start of Part II, questions the recent claims of design to instigate significant change, especially in relation to projects deemed socially responsible. Socially responsible projects frequently involve intercultural negotiation and, in the case of graphic design, the question of cultural difference produces its own set of ethical considerations. In 'Hybridity, hegemony and design in a globalized economy', Fiss asks how designers establish relationships with collectives and populations they seek to help or collaborate with, when those populations are more often than not disadvantaged and culturally Other. Fiss shows how Bhabha's concept of 'hybridity', a dynamic and contingent process of representation involving peripheral cultures merging with dominant cultures, is appropriated for the benefit of corporate branding strategies.

Increasingly, advancement of human values forms an integral part of evaluation frameworks assessing the ethical and moral consequences of technology design. In 'Values and pragmatic action: the challenges of engagement with technical communities in support of value-conscious design', Noëmi Manders-Huits and Michael Zimmer argue for a pragmatic framework that ensures design of technological systems includes, from the onset, sufficient consideration of ethical and moral consequences of their design. Discouraged by the outcomes of two attempts to engage groups of practitioners in setting up a framework that corresponds to the real-world design context, they identify three key challenges to a successful implementation of a value-conscious design project, and present a scenario for addressing them in the design of web applications that preserve user privacy.

Metaphor and analogy are tools of the visual designer and can be useful to help us reconceive everyday practices and hard-held beliefs. Gavin Sade's 'Designing well: sustain-able Interaction Design and vegetarianism' draws on vegetarianism as the analogy for shifting our understanding of discourses in ethics and sustainability as they relate to Interaction Design. Sade critiques models of sustainable practice and unpacks the extent to which they emphasize awareness and consciousness-raising – these being the key design goals necessary for instigating social change. Vegetarianism, Sade holds, is a useful mechanism for reconceptualizing design practice as it relates to the production, consumption and sustainability of energy and energy sources.

The growing significance of grass-roots approaches to Interaction Design foregrounds participatory design (PD) as a vehicle for recognizing users' contributions, visibility and responsibilities in the design process. First, the potential of participatory design methods to empower children as practitioners forms the central argument of Oksana Zelenko's 'Design and ethics in digital mental health promotion', in which she suggests democratic design methods are a necessary foundation of an ethical framework for the development of strength-based digital resources promoting children's resilience. The chapter explores the implications of introducing a digital humanities methodology into a health-promotion context by drawing parallels between the experiential dimension of both resilience learning and design practice, and investigating the impact this has on the dynamics between designer, participants and the resulting form of the designed object. Zelenko uses a case study of engaging primary school children in designing interaction and interfaces for a set of resilience tools to demonstrate PD's potential to foster resilience learning through enabling agency, dialogue and self-reflection.

In 'Interaction Design, mass communication and the challenge of distributed expertise', John Hartley urges for the development of a new 'user ethic' to support a distributed model of expertise that encompasses a diversity of knowledge sources comprising the practice of designing interaction. The user ethic, Hartley argues, shifts the dynamic of power between designer and user from an expert-led to a participatory model – a dynamic that is contradicted in the field of mass communication but has shaped the 'expert-in-charge' models of practice symptomatic of industrial-age consciousness. Hartley suggests that an expert-led, one-to-many model of communication is irrelevant to DIY culture and user-led innovation, and argues for distributed expertise as the driver of a new paradigm of knowledge growth, one based on increased user agency and a consequent re-envisioning of Interaction Design as productivity design.

Moving from the digital, visual domain to the bricks and mortar of the built form, the next four chapters are underpinned by an awareness of both environmental and social vulnerability, at a time when people live in an increasingly populous and complex world. A common marker and catch-cry of life in the twenty-first century is that now, for the first time in history, more than half the world's population live in cities. Questions of sustainability, population management and environmental degradation are the subject of policy and debates worldwide, with the disciplines of urban planning and architecture playing a central role in the future of our cities. Historical evidence points to the rational ethos underpinning the planning of urban space and the built environment, with critiques suggesting that human interaction in place and space can frequently be overlooked by an over-emphasis on the rational. Emma Felton, in 'Living with strangers: urban space, affect and civility', draws our attention to the emotional life of urban citizens, and proposes that greater consideration to the affective dimension of public life might help produce more convivial and democratic public spaces. Increasing urbanization across the world is placing greater pressure on cities and citizens. Felton describes the second-tier city of Brisbane, Australia, like many other cities, as undergoing rapid transformation that requires people to live in different ways in denser, more culturally diverse urban environments where tolerance and civility in public spaces requires daily negotiation.

Paul Sanders, Shannon Satherley and Kuniko Shibata parallel the current attention on ethics in urban design with the historical development of modern planning and citizenship rights among disadvantaged populations in modern industrial cities. Key individuals have driven reform movements throughout history and advanced the cause for more equitable and just cities. In 'Built environment, design and ethics: the social responsibility of educational institutions', the authors see education grounded in an ethical framework as central to pursuing this agenda in contemporary times, by focusing the curriculum on professional ethics in relation to design practices. Through the example of a design project in which students were engaged in remote communities in Australia, the authors conclude that, with real-life application, it is possible to demonstrate the importance and processes for projects that attend to disadvantaged sectors of the population.

Marci Webster-Mannison brings a pragmatic account from a practitioner's perspective of the inherent tensions in the collaborative process for a built design project that has a strong environmental ethos and is located in a rural campus of an Australian university. In 'Rethinking practice: architecture, ecology and ethics', Webster-Mannison draws on her experience as an architect of many years to discuss the limitations of integrating an ecologically sustainable approach into design and construction. The close relationship between architects and the construction and real-estate industry is almost symbiotic and, while it can be mutually beneficial for all participants, it can also present a barrier for the development of environmentally responsible buildings. Drawing on her experience in rural Australia, Webster-Mannison concludes that new understandings about ecocentric architecture are possible.

In 'Sustainable housing: family experiences with supply chain ethics,' Wendy Miller draws our attention to the role of human relationships within the built design process, from the less understood perspective of the end-users' experience of the design and build process. Through in-depth interviews with families involved in the development of homes in an Eco-village, it is evident that the conflicting values of those involved requires careful negotiation in order to achieve the kind of outcomes that can truly be regarded as environmentally sustainable.

As Part III on the built environment testifies, the sustainability of the natural and built environment is the focus of much public attention and debate, coordinated around the central issue of climate change. While governments across the world have reached varying levels of consensus on the call for action, the micro-level details of environmental sustainability present the greatest challenge. In Part IV, the use of environmental resources for manufacturing and production raise yet another set of concerns and discourses that are typically industry specific. Moving from the environment around us to the clothes we produce from that environment, Paula Dunlop's 'Fashion, ethics, ethos' opens the section by framing the notion of ethos as a contextual anchor that firmly positions practice within the complexity of historic-socio factors underpinning the creation of a garment. Understood as a location, ethos, she argues, is critical to facilitating a reframing of domestic dressmaking from an outcome-based practice to one that is situated, experienced and 'always in the making'. By establishing this ontological lens, Dunlop further explores the broader implications of such a shift on the changing role of designer as a singular authoring power in the design process and on bringing to the forefront the factors shaping the designed object.

In 'Nourishing or polluting: redefining the role of waste in the fashion system', Alice Payne complements Dunlop's emphasis on contextual complexity and discusses the broader cultural shifts that impact on the value of garments in the production cycle. Payne proposes a sustainable model of practice in the West that requires an inversion of the role attributed to waste and a subsequent rewiring of the value chain in garment production, thus aligning the ethics of practice to maximizing assimilation of waste into the creative process. The regenerative function attributed to waste, Payne argues, has the potential to reframe the industry because it extends the locus of moral judgement to include the ethics of creative decision-making. In this, both chapters link the ethic of fashion design practice beyond its apparent physicality to the ephemeral origins of creative decisions that shape practice.

In Part V, Tony Fry's afterword to the book offers a reflection that transcends the disciplinary boundaries established through the organization of chapters. As such, it presents a further provocation beyond those made by the contributors, and it is an appeal to the reader to reconsider the potential of design as central to a sustainable future. It is an ethical imperative that highlights the urgency of reconsidering the very notion of sustainability as it relates to practice (and vice versa), bringing forth the idea of design as a powerful force that shapes not only the materiality of our environment but our very being, predisposing us to conceive of design as a form of *futuring* – as opposed to defuturing or unsustainable – practice.

References

Colebrook, C. (1999) *Ethics and Representation: From Kant to poststructuralism*, Edinburgh: Edinburgh University Press.

Fry, T. (2009) *Design Futuring: Sustainability, ethics and new practice*, Sydney: University of New South Wales Press.

2

DESIGN-*ING* ETHICS

The good, the bad and the performative

Stephen Loo

Introduction

There is little disagreement that many disciplines are witnessing an 'ethical' turn. The raised awareness of environmental degradation and climate change, inequalities in wealth distribution and persisting conflict around the world have caused individuals who are practitioners in different disciplines to question their ethical obligations, not merely to those close to them, but to global Others whom they cannot fully define. The question of ethics is a question that defines the values that an individual would live by in order to increase the possibility of generating common 'good' with others, and in corollary, eschew 'bad' relations that reduce their capacities as human beings. Complicating this definition is a burgeoning ecological understanding that extends human obligation to non-human entities, namely to the environment and its myriad of life forms, whether geographically proximate or dislocated. Here, ethical thinking and action towards the environment as non-human Other questions the subscription to human moral imperatives of thinking and doing 'right' or 'wrong'.

Design disciplines are not exempt from this phenomenon. After all, design and designers are implicated in the generation and materialization of much of what can loosely be considered the artificial or constructed environment. From nanomachines to giant skyscrapers, including the crossover realms of human technology and 'natural' biology, design as a mode of thinking and practice has been instrumental in modifying the nature of inter-human and environmental relations. More significantly, design has charted new human relations to the non-human, non-sentient, non-living and technologically mediated realm of objects and constructed environments.

Orders of ethical consideration

It is already clear in this chapter that the ethical turn in design is not straightforward. This complexity can generally be described through three orders of ethical considerations in design. In the first order, ethical thinking needs to be problematized in design because design mediates people-to-people relations. Here, the more 'traditional' forms of philosophical ethics may apply. The consequentialist or utilitarian approach would assert that human actions are right or wrong depending on their consequences, and are based on the total good or harm they produce. Alternatively, the deontological approach urges us to consider ethics as based on the type of action, where a wrong action consists of a moral violation, while an action is right if it subscribes to an accepted moral code. Lastly, ethical thinking may be based on the concept of virtue arriving from Aristotelian ethics whereby actions are governed by moral requirements or minimum character traits that are socially valued, such as truthfulness, humility or concern.

As in all disciplines, the designer is an ethical subject at two levels. First, as a practitioner, a person who acts professionally in the name of a discipline, or whose actions can be described as subscribing to the commonly understood tenets that identify a discipline. In the present argument, a designer is an ambassador for the moral obligations of the disciplines of design. Disciplinarity affects thinking and action by providing frameworks for how we are able to see and organize what we are able to say. As such, thinking and acting from within a discipline are subject to ethical consideration because values themselves are formulated and articulated through the discursive regularities of disciplines. Second, the designer is a human citizen outside disciplinary qualifications, where she or he is subject to more general, and perhaps universally accepted, values that govern relations with other human citizens. According to Phillipe d'Anjou (2010: 358), using Sartrean existentialism and quoting Simone de Beauvoir, 'humans can make ethical choices without the need of normative systems; the ethical rests at the very core of the individual's existence; he/she knows what is right or wrong.' To d'Anjou, individual freedom is the ability to choose, and this is innate within human nature.

In the second order of ethical consideration, design is almost always implicated in modifications to the natural environment through practices of compartmentalization, division and attenuation, which increase particular parts in the environmental balance (for example, emissions and by-products of design processes and outcomes), and depletes other parts, say, that of natural resources. Concerns surrounding design's impact on the biophysical realm, including natural ecosystems, spawned a generation of approaches under the ambit of 'environmental ethics', which are often mistakenly made synonymous with the much used but highly abused notion of 'sustainable design'. The impact of design on the environment forces designers to confront their practices and the effects these have on other human beings in the short term – for example, in their designs for environmental comfort, sense of belonging, representation of identity, and so forth – and on the health and sustainability of natural ecosystems in the global environment in the (not so) long term.

Environmental ethics promotes an understanding of design ethics as ontologically embedded within the dyad of the designer and the designed, where the concern is in what things that emerge out of this circle of relation do, and what values they hold. To Tony Fry, in this hermeneutic circle, design continues 'de-signing' towards new ways of looking at the world, and is therefore a sustainable practice in itself (Fry 1999: 6).

In the third order of ethical consideration, design most specifically necessitates ethical frameworks pertaining to the relations between human subjects and constructed objects and environments. The presence of material manifestations and physical outcomes in the design discipline is that which pushes traditional approaches to ethics to their limits. What measures can an approach to ethics take in human comportment to designed objects? Warwick Fox asks, in his seminal *A Theory of General Ethics*, whether this approach relies on an internal value of the object – an inherent goodness or badness – without resorting to subjectivist claims of preference or aesthetic judgements (Fox 2006: 12). Does the context of the designed object play a role here, and how does an ethical approach get any purchase on this issue of contextuality, especially in the relations between object and object, relations that are necessarily outside of the anthropocentric realm? The latter points to a relational aesthetics (Bourriaud 2002), or perhaps an ecology of objects (Bennett 2001). Cameron Tonkinwise (2004) believes that things embody an ethics in the sense of an ethos of things, while Michael Ostwald adopts Berys Gaut's theory of 'ethicism' which 'holds that a work is ethically meritorious (or defective) insofar as it manifests ethically admirable (or reprehensible) attitudes' and that 'ethicism relies on a broad and inclusive view of aesthetics that values the artistic or architectural merits of a structure that are personified in its appearance [aesthetics]' (Gaut in Ostwald 2004: 202). To Ostwald, the frame of reference for 'ethical aesthetics' is an 'internal coherence' of the object given by the concepts of the good (as having some value) and the just (as being right) (Ostwald 2004: 203–204).

To consider ethics within, or through, the realm of objects alone borders on phenomenological aesthetics, where concepts such as the 'thing-ness of things' augurs an openness for human beings to think and be; designed objects provide an ontological substrate for the possibilities of being human. Aesthetics is no longer the external formal qualifications that are then interpreted or read by the human subject as good or bad, but that the potential for subjectivity itself is given by aesthetic conditions and by virtue of humans *being-there* in situational encounters with designed objects. Drawing on the work of Heidegger, design theorists such as Fry, Tonkinwise and Adrian Snodgrass and Richard Coyne (2006) speak about design as a process or *praxis* that does not propose nor proceed towards representing ethical values in objects, but an ontological design-ing of the world in which the relations between the designer and the design cannot be unravelled.

The relations between aesthetics and ethics are beginning to show *partial* configurations of both object and subject; neither is there in full. There are hints that conventional epistemologies in which a clear distinction between what is inside (human perception, knowledge and instincts leading to moral values, etc.) and what is outside (design objects, spaces and environments leading to knowable aesthetic dimensions) is eroded. The aesthetic regime that is being alluded to here is one where design is no longer defined within ways of doing or criteria of inclusion and exclusion allowing human judgement, but as a mode of what Jacques Rancière calls 'sensible being' specific to design that is both identical with but differs from itself (Rancière 2009: 65–66) – a regime of aesthetics to which I will return at the end of this chapter.

Epistemological conundrums in design ethics

Owing to the complex interrelationships between shifting fields of knowledge that range from psychosocial states of human subjects to the ontological condition of objects, and to self-organizing natural ecologies of the biophysical world, considerations of design and ethics inevitably run into epistemological conundrums. For example, in a single research project on design and ethics, there is likely to be a requirement at the outset to relate the readily conceived idea of 'good' design to a more slippery idea of ethical value. And the research may then have to differentiate what good design is specific to its field from the myriad of other spheres of design, each with their own disciplinary articulations that arise, not only from their community of practitioners, but from the scale of work that can be anything between the design of biomedical instruments to design of the built environment, before relating it to ethics. The research may then face a task of negotiating huge epistemological differences when formulating what constitutes ethical design in/as physical and material objects as opposed to design as a participatory process, as well as ethics in professional or commercial design practice as opposed to that in educational institutions. Finally, the project may need to call for an ethico-aesthetic paradigm that is able to deal with the range of stakeholders, from disciplinary peers with a common language to consumers with an aesthetic desire, and to the passer-by or general public with no specific interest in the design but who are nevertheless impacted by it.

Finding new connections across the fields of ethics, design objects, natural and built environments, commercial practice, educational institutions, stakeholders and the public is certainly important and commendable work, but not straight-forward. Although there may seemingly be shared language, concepts, values, methods and desired outcomes in all these fields, they arrive from very specific disciplinary knowledge structures, emergent from different historical and contextual conditions. For a start, the relationship between 'good' design and ethics relies upon careful negotiation of the territories between the 'good' and ethics, and between design and ethics, as the study of the relations between ethics and design is often complicated by a circular argument. Ethics – at least in normative ethics or moral theory – is generally argued to involve both a theory of the 'right' and of the 'good'. The right relates to knowledge of a moral imperative and involves metaphysical ideas of justice, virtue and ethos, whereas the good can be defined in terms of value based on a 'positive' benefit defined by action, as in 'good design' – the criteria for which comes, in a circular fashion, from knowledge of, and feeling for, the 'right'. That is, 'good' design is generally defined as 'ethically sound', which is assumed to mean accessible, useful and safe, all of which arrive from a moral imperative that stems from a metaphysical knowledge of the right – and around it goes.

As a way to break the circularity, the proposition of 'how is design a "reflection" of values and ethos?' cannot be answered by uncritically saying that it is so because the design functions well, is accessible to, and suits the needs of its users. Even before qualifying 'functioning well' versus 'functioning badly', we need to ask, why is functionality a criterion for the establishment of moral imperatives in design in the first place? Usefulness is inherent in the epistemology, if not the etymology, of design. The idea of function and accessibility are metaphysical conditions that have organized ways of thinking design, in the West at least, and made possible the rise of design as a discipline in itself. Functionality and accessibility are so close to the possibility of design that they are constantly forgotten and rarely questioned concepts. Design is always design-*for*. It is a projective practice, outwards to its context and its human benefactors. In corollary, design's inherent value, is based on its suitability to context as thought through its fitness to the human body and senses, and/or the environment to which it is useful and for which it 'serves'.

Can design, through the contiguity with an investigation of ethics, be thought of otherwise to avoid the risk of subjective assertions of the good based on epistemological structures already present in design thinking and knowledge; structures that ultimately organize how we can articulate the notion of ethics in the first place and brackets the various justifications admissible for the ethical judgement in design? Can we reverse the way the proposition is posed, namely 'how does design provide new and specific ways to ask the questions of what is right and wrong, and good and bad?' What kinds of moral judgements can be made of design, through design as a practice, with its often-undeniable connection to concrete materiality? Do such judgements have a similar epistemology to those in philosophy, or law, or literature, or business, which generally deal with non-material disciplinary outputs when compared with design? In short, can design provide a contribution to the field of ethics?

Ethics and aesthetics: art and design

Allow me a proposition through substitution, using an extremely problematic, if not dangerous, example: the politics of aesthetics in art. Rancière in his *Aesthetics and its Discontents* (2009: 26–27) explains that art, using the example of an ancient Greek statue referred to by Friedrich von Schiller, is much more than a demonstration of the power of a creative genius over the medium. Owing to the 'free appearance' of the statue that manifests its essential characteristic of divinity through its 'idleness' and 'indifferency', the statue in its autonomy is arguably liberated from use value or even a concern for the phenomenological effects of the material. The work of the creative genius is rather in the modification of the sensory milieu, or what Rancière calls the distribution of the sensible, in a way that is foreign to ordinary forms of sensory perception; that is, it suspends the ordinary connections between appearance and reality, form and matter, activity and passivity, and understanding and sensibility (Rancière 2009: 30).

Can design be thought of in the way of the Greek statue? After all, the statue demonstrates a genealogy of a mimesis and, in the parlance of design, precedents and exemplars supported by an epistemology that values mastery of the past to progress the future. Mimesis involves 'not the obligation of resemblance . . . but a principle of division within human activities, one that delimits a specific domain enabling objects to be subsumed under concepts and classes of objects to be compared' (Rancière 2009: 66). Through mimesis, what is art can be separated from non-art, which sounds remarkably applicable to the process by which (good, and therefore just) design is separated out from non (poor) design.

Yet the aesthetic definition of the statue as an art object, or what makes it an art object, holds within its ontology a paradox. The aesthetic value of art lies in an affirmation of autonomy, striving to say how it is not an expression of what has come before. Aesthetic identification of art is paradoxically defined as the lack of distinguishing characteristics or, more specifically, a constant passing between the art form as autonomous and the life forms of which they are expression. Such an epistemology, if applied to design, would make ethics design not based on purely expressive qualities that are the progenitors of moral values, but the fibrillation between expression and formal autonomy, between functionality and dissonance. The proposal I put forward here is that a design becomes ethical because it performs the *distribution of the sensible*, supporting possibilities for life opened up in this space of indeterminacy.

Ethics and life caught in a professional groove

Another necessary segue: while design disciplines can be generally characterized through their material outputs in the form of designed objects, spaces and environments, they are also represented by a unique professionalism that is inscribed by the seemingly opposing forces of capital and social good, of individual creativity and the collective labour of a team. We often hear that the design profession is constantly falling short of their ethical mission, in the wake of their neglect to address social justice and upholding public interest in the built environment'. This is synonymous with the perceived gap between the technical-aesthetic and social-political, and differences in ethical responsibilities between corporate practices and the largely publically funded (at least in Australia) educational institutions with their socially relevant civic missions, and with a different capacity to undertake projects of high social need.

While it is hard to argue against the common view that the commercial realities mitigate deeper engagement with social and political factors at the expense of technical and aesthetic concerns, it is equally hard to argue that a conception of ethics, and of ethical design, can be straightforwardly compared between professional practice and education. To see ethics as a depiction or demonstration of the metaphysical 'spirit' of the good or right in the activities of the professions or at educational institutions short-changes the definition of ethics itself.

What I have been arguing towards here is a position that ethics is not something that can necessarily be seen as outside of the very acts that make up design practices in the professional and educational worlds. The shape of ethical considerations is intrinsic to the practices themselves – they are different for professional practice and design education. Objects and activities that result from the disciplinary practices are ethical because they contribute differently to the shape of the human being 'to come' and, as Giorgio Agamben calls it, their 'coming communities' (Agamben 1993). And the form of ethics that arises out of these practices are specific – they make particular contributions to help human beings to find/make places in the chaos that is our world. It is important to note here that this paradigm dramatically changes the relationship between design and ethics. It is no longer the case that 'all human beings are entitled to good design', but that design, enacted through certain professional practices, is no longer limited to a concern for one type of person or community, but is a mechanism that is located at the centre of human life – that is, design as a human practice is so pervasive that it has the effect of defining how we live, what we can say, do or feel.

In *Science and the Modern World*, the mathematician-philosopher Alfred North Whitehead warned of the dangers in what he called 'professionalism': 'Another great fact confronting the modern world is the discovery of the method of training professionals, who specialize in particular regions of thought and thereby progressively add to the sum of knowledge within their respective limitations of subject' (Whitehead 1953: 244).

The danger lies not in the sharpening of concepts and specialization of skills, nor the maintenance of disciplinary boundaries, but rather that these activities are carried out at the expense of a more general productive experience of life. Within professions, we would find a high degree of articulation of a particular way of thinking and method of practice: 'Each profession makes progress but it is progress in its own groove' (Whitehead 1953: 245). When the possibilities of variations wear out, we are left with a 'staleness' and a reduction of appreciation (of life) perpetuated by repetition of the known. While the authority of a particular set of understandings restricts the definition of a profession into a groove, the issue becomes ethically problematic when this authority limits the way life itself is defined.

Whitehead advocates a convergence of professionally driven epistemologies. This task of coordination or convergence is to resist the misplaced authority of the professions. Convergence does not mean smooth clear connections, and the objects of knowledge that arise out of professional convergences cannot be defined in isolation from their external relational continuity, namely how they behave together. The central mechanism in this process of experience is creativity, in which an act of approximation transforms the potentiality of nature into actuality and leads to new singular unities of experience. The convergence of contradictory understandings without dialectical resolution to a point or instant is an occasion of the creative advance. This is where life exists and from which it stems. Novelty and life exist in the interstices of stable (professional) understandings or laws. In this way, Whitehead's philosophy does not eschew stable or known laws and their techniques of production because abstraction and repetition of such laws are the conditions for the enjoyment of novelty, and thus the actualization of self-creation, or life.

In differential engagements between entities, manifest in practices, perceptions and mediations, whose definitions can only be partial, we can say that life is always already in excess, in what Isabelle Stengers calls an 'ecology of practices'. Ecology 'is about how different forms of knowledge and cultural practices work, it is also the relation between what is happening and the way it defines itself in relation with others, or the way it represents those others. It is not concerned with individuals but practitioners' (Stengers 2002: 262).

From this argument about the relationship between ethics and life, aesthetic considerations do not need to be downplayed in favour of the social and political. Besides arguments that the aesthetic is always political (Rancière 2009) and social (Bourriaud 2002), design projects that posit an alternative conception of the aesthetic – perhaps those that are process-oriented, or with material and immaterial outcomes that provide orientation, and therefore definition, for what else is possible in life – are primarily ethical.

Design as performative ethics

This analysis of the relationship between ethics and aesthetics works to frame an alternative 'ethico-aesthetic' paradigm (Guattari 1995) in design practice. The argument thus far is that in design, through its *processes* of investigation, new ethical functions for design can be sought, as well as how design is itself a form of ethical investigation (Levine *et al.* 2004) that can be demonstrated. More specifically, it philosophically reconsiders the location of the designer as the creative agent and source of aesthetic judgement. In doing so, the arguments reconsider ethics in design away from one based on moral code – whether the resultant design as a material and poetic production is desirable or undesirable – informed by a priori functional, environmental, social or conceptual criteria.

Certainly, the ethical imperative in aesthetic judgements remains: the designer assesses, critiques and selects iterations on the aesthetic grounds based on traditional representational categories such as beauty (whether transcendental or culturally imbued), function (including efficiency and economics) and, recently, sustainability. The processual approach to ethics, however, makes contingent the human designer as the primary source of judgement and the source of ethics. A first hypothesis here: if through its processes of the distribution of sense immanent to aesthetic judgement extends the territories within which human life is defined, and working through different systems, concepts and values that in turn create new freedoms (Guattari 2000) and enchantments (Bennett 2001), design extends its ethical function. Design is a practical ethics, one that arrives through the unfolding of an aesthetic practice. And because such aesthetic practices in design lead to re-enchantments of thinking and being (Guattari 1995), it can be argued that the resultant conception of ethics is beyond an a priori humanist definition.

So what constitutes ethical practice in design? The conceptual framework of this ethics in design – a practice that involves complex systems and that has as its trademarks irreducible indeterminacy, incompleteness and plurality of process, rather than the surety of resultant form and principles – must then be distinct from a predetermined moral or professional code that arrives from 'external' evaluations. The latter is an ethics applied to architectural projects after the event (Levine *et al.* 2004), as a matter of consensus, settled by certain interests and balances of power that will be used afterwards to explain or justify the ethical judgement (Stengers 2005).

Current research, of which this chapter is a part, frames ethics as *immanent* to a question of choice, and as an uncategorical opening up of possibilities. Ethics becomes less a matter of enforcing a moral test than encouraging the testing of the practices at hand in different situations that answer contingent problems, to actively seek divergence from current conventions for the possibility of other 'technics of life' (Murphie 2005) at each aesthetic moment. As such, design contributes to shaping a paradigm within ethical philosophy because design philosophy is faced with the unmistakable materialization of its fundamental tenets (the relations between inside and outside, ideas and expression, the right and the good, etc.), but one that defies immediate codification and that forces it to take flight into experimentation.

Ethical judgement is not based on clear material manifestations, but arrives from working through already ongoing processes, to mine them for other divergent relations. Design is therefore a specific 'evental' site that may give rise to situation-transforming procedures that build conviction and fidelity of future judgements. Therefore, the key contribution such thinking about design and ethics offers, is that it prepares a philosophical framework for aesthetic practice as practical ethics. A processual approach to ethics through design is a fundamental innovation in ethical philosophy.

References

Agamben, G. (1993) *The Coming Community*, trans. Michael Hardt, Minneapolis: University of Minnesota Press.

Bennett, J. (2001) *The Enchantment of Modern Life: Attachments, crossings and aesthetics*, Princeton, NJ: Princeton University Press.

Bourriaud, N. (2002) *Relational Aesthetics*, trans. Simon Pleasance and Fronza Woods, Paris: Les presses du reel.

d'Anjou, P. (2010) 'Toward an horizon in design ethics', *Science and Engineering Ethics*, 16(2): 355–370.

Fox, W. (2006) *A General Theory of Ethics: Human relationships, nature, and the built environment*, Massachusetts: MIT Press.

Fry, T. (1999) *A New Design Philosophy: An introduction to defuturing*, Sydney: UNSW Press.

Guattari, F. (1995) *Chaosmosis: An ethico-aesthetic paradigm*, trans. Paul Bains and Julian Pefanis, Sydney: Power Publications.

Guattari, F. (2000) *The Three Ecologies*, trans. Ian Pindar and Paul Sutton, London: Athlone Press.

Levine, M., Miller, K. and Taylor, W. (2004) 'Introduction: ethics and architecture', *The Philosophical Forum*, 35(2): 103–115.

Murphie, A. (2005) 'Differential life, perception and the nervous elements: Whitehead, Bergson and Virno on the technics of living', *Culture Machine*, 7. Available at: www.culturemachine.net/index.php/%20cm/article/viewArticle/32/39 (accessed 23 June 2011).

Ostwald, M. (2004) 'Freedom of form: ethics and aesthetics in digital architecture', *The Philosophical Forum*, 35(2): 201–220.

Rancière, J. (2009) *Aesthetics and Its Discontents*, trans. Steven Corcoran, Cambridge: Polity Press.

Snodgrass, A. and Coyne, R. (2006) *Interpretation in Architecture: Design as a way of thinking*, London: Routledge.

Stengers, I. (2002) 'A "cosmo-politics"? Risk, hope, change', in Zournazi, M. (ed.) *Hope: New philosophies for change*, Sydney: Pluto Press.

Stengers, I. (2005) 'Deleuze and Guattari's last enigmatic message', *Angelaki*, 10(2): 151–167.

Tonkinwise, C. (2004) 'Ethics by design, or the ethos of things', in *Design Philosophy Papers*. Available at: www.desphilosophy.com/dpp/dpp_journal/back_issues/paper4_Tonkin Ethics/dpp_paper4.html (accessed 22 March 2009).

Whitehead, A. N. (1953) *Science and the Modern World*, Cambridge: Cambridge University Press.

3

DESIGN, ETHICS AND GROUP MYOPIA

Leslie F. Becker

Design then (without ethics), design now (with ethics)

The increasingly unexamined and popular use of the term 'ethics' begs for critical examination within our own community of designers. If one of our more recent currencies as designers is to consider ourselves ethical practitioners, how do we carve out the time for rigorously reflecting upon held a priori assumptions? And may some form of less-than-egregious collusion be implied by the 'we' of a group? How do we manage to view ourselves with a degree of objectivity – the way in which a photograph of the self in stark daylight reveals a reality we often manage to keep at a distance? My project here is to interrogate assumptions about ethics that are lodged in, and biased by, group affinities, making a case for designers to revisit our certainties. Rather than rely on opinion, a systemization of thought process is sought through which a group can navigate complex and often thorny issues. A detailed method of ethics is beyond the scope of this chapter, but an initial attempt to acknowledge our relatively unexamined assumptions about what constitutes right action is understood to be a sociological problem of groups. It may be difficult to define a group because so many forms of groups exist, but early and simplified definitions by social psychologists include 'a face-to-face aggregation of individuals who have some shared purpose for being together' (Sommer 1969: 58). Bias is not assumed to be inherently evil, but rather unconscious. As cognitive linguist George Lakoff notes, 'At present white men hold top positions throughout our society. They are the ones doing the judging. As honestly as they may do that judging, the values by which they judge will almost inevitably be the largely unconscious values of their own subculture' (Lakoff 1996: 224). Sociologists, anthropologists and ethnographers have written extensively about what they have observed as constitutive of a group, especially its behaviours, rituals and the transmission of social attributes that identify it. Christian ethicist Reinhold Niebuhr comments on the strength of social cohesion in large groups (such as nations), while acknowledging the thesis 'that group relations can never be as ethical as those which characterize individual relations' (Neibuhr 1932: 83). Others believe that intersubjectivity exists within the goals and aspirations of members of a group. A group may be defined in terms of its shared policy interests (Sagoff 1986: 313). Philosophers themselves can be thought of as the constituents of groups that have adhered to a particular philosophical position regarding a method of ethics. Consequentialists, for example, constitute one group of philosophers who subscribe to the position that whatever maximizes the good is the way we measure right action. The attributes of a group reflect a bias or loyalty that reveals one's status to be either part of a group or not.

Ultimately, we ought to formulate an enquiry that works to dislodge designers from our comfort zones and unpack the ramifications of embedding ourselves simultaneously and sequentially in groups that not only replicate, but actually magnify, unexamined assumptions that we are 'right' and that we know in some intuitive way what constitutes 'right action'. This involves carving out reflective time to examine our multiple and simultaneously inhabited identities. These identities may be local or global, real or virtual, as we live at the intersection of art and commerce yet tend to keep an eye on social and political causes. With few exceptions, our responses to social problems too often have been to create design for designers that simply points to a problem. Graphic designer Milton Glaser's twelve steps (ranging from minor to major violations) of his own 'willingness to lie' through design action are both comprehensible and obvious to most students and practitioners (in Heller and Vienne 2003: x–xi). However, he offers no framework for assessment.

My questions emerge from multiple positions that I inhabit. As a design educator and practitioner for more than thirty years, I bring a lived history to my current set of queries and reflections on ethics that have been brought into sharper focus through my research into formal methods of ethics. The mutually informing positions of practitioner and educator offer me a way to understand the enormity of the impact of my own Bauhaus-influenced design education that took place at a particular time and place, having been trained under the influence of high modernism in general, and in New York and the 1960s in particular. Over my three decades of teaching design, I witnessed a major shift away from the focus of my own education that prepared me to master formal design issues and skills. We were expected to be inventive within rigid aesthetic confines, still believing that we could (re)present the world in a never-before-seen way.

In a recent video, modernist designer Massimo Vignelli reaffirmed his long-held position, widely known among designers, that only a few type families were ever needed. However, in contrast to his earlier claim that there were only six good typefaces, he slightly expanded his earlier point of view, implying that he was being 'generous' by saying that there may be a dozen good families. 'Good' is used here as an absolute declaration of value of the typography independent of contextual use (Vignelli 2010). For many decades, design publications and juried annuals reinforced this universal aesthetic through an almost clinical disconnect from anything that could be read as personalization. Professors and students from the Bauhaus (at Illinois Institute of Technology, Yale, Cooper Union) populated the most influential design schools in the United States, transmitting their brand of design to a next generation of students who eventually began to teach, using orthogonal twentieth-century technologies that frequently dictated the resulting visuals. (A contemporary parallel is found in the relationship between means of production and visual results, using the computer's *absence* of those constraints.) Paul Rand extolled the creative potential of the grid in his famous essay, 'Design and the play instinct' (Rand 1985: 189–201). And Herbert Bayer's 1961 poem, 'Homage to Gropius' captured the modernist zeitgeist:

but the world of machine production
with its innate facts and functions
was already colouring the future . . .

there was a unifying air – the spirit of a group

Bayer references 'an invaluable heritage of timeless principles' (Bayer 1967: 10). Assumptions about timelessness and universality, now on much less terra firma, were carried into practice to address client need. One could argue that although the vehicles for delivery of messages have changed dramatically, the primordial design task has not: it has always been, and remains, to distinguish one's messages from the detritus of others. The effects of the relatively univalent 1960s' design pedagogy were difficult to discern until twenty years later when the modernist canon began to crack. Design theory, issues of alterity, and even evidence of regionalism in design annuals invaded the perceived certainty of the modernist canon, yet the formalism of mid-twentieth-century European pedagogies lingers to this day. In the 1980s, the confluence of radically new technologies that made it easy to manipulate type and images, David Carson's deliberate scrambling of modernist design in his six issues of *Beach Culture* magazine during the 1980s, and even the seepage into the broader academic culture of Foucault's challenges to certainty and power destabilized the formal certainty of modernist design. British designer Neville Brody, speaking at the 1989 AIGA (American Institute of Graphic Arts) conference in San Antonio, Texas, discouraged designers from using what he referred to as a supermarket cart for typography. Brody challenged designers to resist tossing existing typefaces into their work, but rather to invent, rethink or simply 'think', as he typographically warned the audience.

Modernist graphic design choices became aestheticized, *learned* archetypes: Helvetica and simplified Platonic geometries were corporate; black-and-white photography implied seriousness of content and journalistic authority; and red was revolutionary. Recent and complex arrays of colours, forms and typographies, resulting in part from deconstrained technologies, typically were perceived as interpretive and personal, and therefore not universally valid (not universalizable). Not only had we learned to make images within modernist confines, we also learned to read them within these confines. With near-absolute trust in what we learned, we applied this knowledge in practice and, as some of us began to teach, generally attempted to transfer it, often wholly intact, to the next generation of design students with little self-reflection about its ongoing value(s). Sadly, many remained generally unaware of the founding utopian modernist vision that catapulted modernist *style* into such enormous twentieth-century prominence in the West. *Our* group shared urban, European, design knowledge. Those émigrés from the Bauhaus (and later the Swiss institutions such as the Kuntsgewerbeschule Basel), having lived through the horrors of war in Europe, as faculty at major universities (i.e. Josef Albers at Yale, Gyorgy Kepes at Illinois Institute of Technology and later Massachusetts Institute of Technology) and art schools (i.e. Hannes Beckmann at The Cooper Union) influenced design pedagogy for decades. The formal knowledge transmitted to students was evident in the edited volumes by Kepes that included *Education of Vision* (1965) and *Josef Müller-Brockmann: Pioneer of Swiss Graphic Design* (Müller 1995). 'His [Brockmann's] attitude is unswerving . . . based on integrity, on a sense of social and cultural responsibility, and on the designer's uncompromising professional ethic' (Müller 1995: 38). Reference made to his 'profound knowledge of the design repertory' (Müller 1995: 39) implies a relatively fixed visual toolkit. This Swiss aesthetic persisted for several generations of designers and, until the appearance of digital media in the latter part of the twentieth century, the ability to produce design(ed) work resided mostly within the proprietary domain of those trained in design (including the ability to set type, specify type and prepare mechanical artwork for print reproduction). The physical aspects of producing any sort of design work required a highly specific, technical knowledge and meant that design was, prior to the digitization of production, a highly undemocratic activity.

The explicit (transferable and repeatable) aspect of current design pedagogy continues much as it did in the mid-twentieth century, although stylistic changes occur regularly and mimetic cycles seem to be shorter and slightly more diverse because of the technologies that multiply and provide increasing numbers of surfaces and applications for viewing. One notable difference between design content then and now is the introduction into the design glossary, and the increased use of, the term 'ethics' as we discuss design activity and the product of that activity. The term had little, if any, presence in the design academies of the twentieth century, perhaps with the exception of Adolf Loos who implied a failure in ethics in 1908 in his now (in)famous essay 'Ornament and crime' stating that ornamentation was evidence of the moral depravity of those responsible for such (criminal) embellishments (Loos 2003). Once inside the academy, we were subsumed by the unexamined 'of course-ness' of what we were taught to make and how we were taught to think about what we made.

Recent manifestations of interest in ethics

The twenty-first century has seen an explosion in ethics-related writing, often attached to interest in professional codes, intellectual property law, and an increase in presumptiveness about what constitutes virtuous behaviours as various types of formal mastery are somewhat marginalized. Codes of ethics, renewed interest in political activism and sustainability currently preoccupy designers, and are seen in writing, conference themes and, increasingly, within pedagogy – especially as educational institutions seek relationships with corporations and look to protect the interests of their students and faculty. De-emphasis on the visual accommodates ethics, design strategy and design thinking, and refocuses discourse on topics such as professional codes, like the AIGA's *Design Business and Ethics*. This writing does little to protect human flourishing and much to protect professional profitability, despite AIGA's stated mission that 'includes educating designers, clients and the public about ethical standards and practices governing design' (AIGA 2001: cover). David Vogel, political scientist and professor of business ethics at the Haas School of Business at the University of California, Berkeley, is one of many who has looked at, and written about, corporate social responsibility in recent years. In particular, Vogel raises questions about whether or not virtue pays, and concludes that the evidence does not suggest increased profitability within socially responsible corporations (2005: 45). Few designers, however, have taken the time to discover with any rigour what ethics actually is. We seem to have transferred the certainty of modernism to a different and generally less-vetted certainty about 'right action'.

Group myopia and the absence of challenge

Often defined through the use of words such as 'aggregated', 'relatedness' and 'similar', a group is typically a myopic entity, its members blinded by some commonality and shared goals. Although congruity is not always negative, because general agreement often provides a degree of efficiency, the failure to see alternatives to a commonly held point of view is potentially problematic. Any group tends to be attentive to what is in front of it and not distracted, influenced or challenged by what is off to the side, even if what is off to the side yields fruitful challenges and finer-grained information. As sociologist and philosopher Georg Simmel noted, once we get beyond the initial unselected group that we think of as family, we tend to inhabit groups based upon 'purpose, on factual considerations . . . on individual interests' (Simmel 1955: 129).

Once reasonably formalized, groups tend to be sites of unexamined assumptions, most often based on some mutual interest or need: 'When we believe that something is factually true or morally good, we also believe that another person, similarly placed, should share our belief' (Harris 2010: 14). We can imagine the deliberate act of choosing to join a group, but once aligned, the reflective space seems to decline. Our intra-group affinities are both powerful and invisible. Scholars from diverse disciplines have made important observations about groups and their tendencies to act in unison. Since the flourishing of guilds in the Middle Ages, which often had compulsory membership, groups have formed with protective agendas (Weber 1958: 165). Herbert Simon, economist and sociologist, in his study of behaviour in organizations, discussed the issue of loyalty, stating, 'It is a prevalent characteristic of human behaviour that members of an organized group tend to identify with that group' (Simon 1945: 12). Additionally, he asserted that the anticipated outcomes of a decision were taken with respect to the effect on the particular group and its salient identity. Loyalty is an important adhesive for the group. Economist Kenneth Boulding looked at the scale of organizations and the need 'to keep large purposes before the minds of small people' (Boulding 1963: 161).

As members of the AIGA, we make decisions that are good for design in general and identify (within the context of that larger group) as designers, although different communities of interest within the AIGA reflect multiple sub-loyalties. Loyalty may even extend to an interest in the health and survival of the group itself (Simon 1945: 115, 205). Philosopher Hannah Arendt, in her examination of labour, casts activity in the political sphere:

> Specialization of work and division of labour have in common only the general principle of organization, which itself has nothing to do with either work or labour but owes its origin to the strictly political sphere of life, to the fact of man's capacity to act and to act together and in concert.
>
> (Arendt 1958: 123)

She asserts that it is the finished product that is guided by specialization and is distinct from the interchangeable nature of division of labour (which we can assume is the antithesis of the condition of producing designed artefacts, or what Arendt might classify as work) (Arendt 1958: 123). Designers, too, can be assumed to protect their political interests. Ethicist and professor of religion Roger Betsworth offers the position that we seem to inhabit cultural images of ourselves and the world: 'We have become those who represent and express the culture itself; we are the ones who teach the next generation the language in which it will think' (Betsworth 1990: 18). Eventually, these images, he suggests, guide actions (Betsworth 1990: 18). These images are not only transmitted but often shared. Bourdieu observes that the ways in which a group represents itself contributes to its reality (Bourdieu 1991: 133). He writes of 'professionals capable of manipulating ideas and groups at one and the same time' (Bourdieu 1991: 182).

Within any group, special interests may emerge from particular relationships (such as familial) and challenge otherwise generally coherent values. We are embracing, when we give preference to someone close to us, what philosophers term 'agent relative positions'. For example, we may, if faced with having to choose to save one of several people who are in equal peril, choose to aid someone who has a special relationship to us. Certainly, this is an example of a specific group in which scale matters. Other groups may form as a result of shared professional expertise (such as the AIGA) or hobbyist interests such as bird watching. Some group affinities we 'inherit' from our parents – especially religious (tacit and explicit), and often political (mostly tacit) affiliations. Even rejections of these inheritances can be construed as constrained in the sense that they often manifest as diametric oppositions to early parental influence. We do not think of some of our quotidian affinities as belonging to groups, although often they have a strong coherence of values. What, for example, is your news source? In the United States, Fox News is associated with the right end of the political spectrum while National Public Radio and *The New York Times,* likely to be a coincident group, are associated with progressive politics. Are you part of a virtual group (often age-related) that gets its news from Jon Stewart? The point is that we listen, watch and read that which reinforces our pre-existing values and entertain opposing values only when we are challenged or operating in a consciously critical mode.

If we look at design practitioners, it is reasonable to expect that many have attended design school. Often the programmes are located within a college of art and design (as opposed to others that may be subsets of university art departments). Further, these colleges tend to be situated in diverse urban environments from which they draw a largely practitioner faculty. Even the broader rings of those concentric geographic sets that any individual inhabits mostly share similar political and social attitudes, views and values that are often attached to the particularity of the geography and its scale. Those who gravitate towards art and design schools typically have been raised in politically and socially liberal families, arriving with a healthy dose of anti-establishment thinking. It is precisely this likelihood of homogeneous values within the art and design school environment that demands criticality and a willingness to entertain opposing social and political viewpoints. Judging empirically from the nature of involvement in causes (for example, anti-war, AIDS activism and environmental issues) that appear regularly in poster competitions and the self-selected content of student projects, it is reasonable to assume a degree of coherence in (progressive) values within art school populations (though this does not imply that groups do not experience divergence). For an investigation to be rigorous and arrive at some ethical resolution (even the word 'resolution' implies a form of confrontation having existed), it must be interrogated, questioned and called to defend itself in a systematic way. Rigour in design thinking is not new. In the 1960s, designer and theorist Horst Rittel discussed a category of 'wicked problems' to address the difficulties in defining complex and non-linear design problems that could not simply proceed in a step-by-step manner (Buchanan 1992: 15). The rigour required to synthesize complex factors noted by Rittel may be extended to ethical problems that go unchallenged and maintain a potentially artificial coherence among like-minded individuals.

In design, for example . . .

Although the following examples may be useful as case studies for design and ethics, they are offered here specifically to extend my general claim of group bias to design culture. The increasingly unexamined and popular use of the term 'ethics' begs for a more critical examination. Shared assumptions about issue X or interest Y often serve as motivating factors to initiate the formation of a group or to propel someone to join a group. If you were a graphic designer working in 2008 in an urban centre in the United States, then it was assumed by your peer design community that you were: supporting Barack Obama, concerned about the evils of Bush's war, and willing to pay taxes if those taxes were to be applied to social programmes for the disenfranchised. You probably approved of the now famously idealized 'HOPE' illustration of Barack Obama created by Shepard Fairey, despite accusations that Fairey was not the originator of the image. The image that brought Fairey such wide recognition was allegedly taken from a 2006 photograph taken by Mannie Garcia who was employed by Associated Press (AP) at the time the image was shot (Kaplan 2010). This is a Fair Use case, and the profits Fairey earned from using the AP photograph as the basis for his artwork without permission from AP brought invoking the Fair Use claim into question. If one could substantiate that Obama was elected in part because of the power of this image, a consequentialist Democrat would argue that how the image was obtained was of no ethical import. For the consequentialist, if the result of the action yields the greatest good, then the action is a right action.

Within graphic design classrooms (temporary groups) many professors currently offer their students choice of content when assigning a project because we slid, long ago, into the belief that politically and socially relevant content helps to deepen the generally unarticulated, but frequently referenced, 'citizenship' component of design education. Years ago I asked students in my class at California College of the Arts to select a political or social cause about which they felt strongly and to create a persuasive graphic that might encourage the viewer either to align with the message or, preferably, to take action. Of the eighteen students, all but one chose issues that were routinely seen as part of a progressive political or social agenda. A single student, however, chose to defend an individual's right to bear arms. We had the expected design critique addressing audience and intent, the power of metaphor, and the formal success or failure of typography and form. The student's classmates were unnerved by his atypical political stance. I asked the student if we might talk briefly after class. As I mentioned to the class, our critiques were not evaluating a point of view, but rather how effectively this view was presented. When talking alone with the student, initially I reiterated that I fully supported each student's right to choose a topic, but reminded him that his task would be made even more difficult because of a climate in the classroom that was politically antagonistic. To convince this group of the legitimacy of his opinion through strong graphic work would be much more difficult than the tasks facing his classmates who constituted a group holding generally shared political leanings. The rest of the class faced the more predictable critical questions around formal, visual choices. They were preaching to the (group) choir.

This situation offered me a clear view of the dynamics of groups and their behaviour. It provided a wonderful learning opportunity and opened the possibility of a fine-grained navigation for all of us. I, in particular, felt enlightened by having the discussion expand far beyond the expected parameters of a relatively straightforward design assignment. It took me outside of the multiple, and in this case, concentric decreasing frames bounded by groups such as United States/West Coast/San Francisco/art and design school/graphic design programme/course.

Why ethical decisions require a method

Neuroscientist Sam Harris notes, 'the inseparability of reason and emotion confirms that the validity of a belief cannot merely depend on the conviction felt by its adherents; it rests on the chains of evidence and argument that link it to reality' (Harris 2010: 126–127). Returning to the case of Fairey's Obama illustration, as designers we might make an assumption that many of us wanted to see Obama elected and many of us assumed that the poster was a mobilizing (though unverifiable) factor in the election. This wish may even behave as an example of an agent-relative position, or designers looking to themselves as the problem solvers. Even if the assumption is hypothetical, we might assume that the circulation of the image actually resulted in Obama's win and that this win was all that mattered. The ends, in this case, have justified the means. How is reasoning processed and framed? Consequentialism, as a method of ethics for determining right action, appeals to many, and perhaps especially to designers, because it seems so very tangible. Aggregating the good lends the method an aura of scientific validity because it requires of us that our decision be governed by whatever action will produce the greatest good, seeming to provide a rather clear metric. The reasoning may include the acknowledgement that Obama must win because he is the best candidate and any actions that bring about this result (an election win) are ethical. Not unlike doctrinaire religions that have a seemingly black-and-white moral clarity to them, consequentialism is a scientific poser. Invoking this method as one that yields a clear metric (despite the frequent difficulties of what constitutes accurate measurement) results in a generally easy preference for consequentialism. If, for example, Fairey did use the photograph of Obama without permission, can we then say that the 'successful' outcome of the election (hypothetically connected to the success of the image) nullifies what may have constituted a questionable (or perhaps even illegal) use of an image? The lawsuit between AP and Fairey has been partially settled (with neither party agreeing that they were in error), but the case involving use of the 'HOPE' image in Fairey's clothing line still remains unresolved (Fairey 2011). If we disregard Fair Use law, what other laws are we willing to overlook in favour of other particular outcomes of aggregated good? The Fair Use discussion, of course, is taking place within the broader a priori acceptance of capitalism and its concomitants of ownership, privatization and intellectual property. The entire enquiry could be widened to interrogate the capitalist system itself. However, for practical reasons, I am drawing a line around the current economic and legal system.

Generally, unexamined assumptions represent a form of (sometimes specious) tacit knowledge, the sort of knowledge that is absorbed from family, religious values and the surrounding culture. We do not invoke a conscious meta-perspective of what we know and we have no explicit rules for passing it on to others. Tacit knowledge is acquired by doing and copying, and often cannot be made explicit in the sense that it is difficult to transfer in writing. Yet we *perform* what unreflectively seems to constitute right action whenever we are confronted with an ethical dilemma or are required to render a moral decision. Although a method may be insular and favoured over another by a particular group, each individual needs to have some conscious and deliberate knowledge about a method of ethics that informs decisions about right action. After evaluating the practicality of various methods of ethics (in work that contains far greater detail and exceeds the scope of this writing), a hybrid method based on communicative ethics and casuistry may be most productive in design pedagogy and practice.

Communicative ethics offers a functional approach that could be used in the studio environment in which students produce graphic images. Derived from Kant's categorical imperative (and grossly oversimplified here, to that which is rational/universalizable is moral), Frankfurt School philosopher Habermas argued for discourse as a means to resolve complex issues. His text would be particularly useful within a design curriculum because Habermas offers explicit and understandable 'rules' for participating in discourse. Interested in the development of competency in communication that would allow individuals to engage in rational discourse, Habermas claimed that it was 'real argument [that] makes moral insight possible' (Habermas 1990: 62). His conditions were based on motivating the other actors to rational speech, rather than to influence. Contemporary feminist philosopher Seyla Benhabib further refines communicative ethics and rejects ethical formalism by asking more postmodern questions about authority and who gets to decide who should be heard. Benhabib, therefore, by providing a discursive space for those typically marginalized by (the traditions of) analytic philosophy, also situates argumentation as a replacement for Kantian universalizability (Benhabib 1990: 331). Benhabib focuses on the following question:

> Instead of asking what I as a single rational moral agent can intend or will to be a universal maxim for all without contradiction, the communicative ethicist asks: what principles of action can we all recognize or agree to as being valid if we engage in practical discourse of a mutual search for justification?
>
> (Benhabib 1990: 336)

Her break with Habermas is a partial one, but for our purpose is most distinctive in her understanding of who meets the criteria to have a voice. She clearly understands universalism in moral theory as constituting 'equal worth and dignity' for all human beings (Benhabib 1992: 185). Benhabib's philosophical critique of what Habermas proposes tends towards circularity, meaning, as she describes it, that the 'normative content precedes the moral argument itself' (Benhabib 1990: 338). Of course, every deliberation must be seeded by something to which a group can begin to respond, something that can be construed as normative.

Casuistry is an old Christian theological method that fell out of favour hundreds of years ago because it was seen as manipulative during the Counter-Reformation. It has enjoyed a rather strong resurgence among professional ethicists (particularly biomedical ethicists) because it is rather pragmatic and recognizes ambiguities in any case that concerns moral right actions (Preston 1991: 94). It is, at its root, a case-based method that establishes paradigmatic cases to guide professional casuists in making determinations, in concert with those affected by and involved with an ethical question under review, about what the case at hand is like. If, in fact, those trained in casuist methods do not see a likeness to existing cases (which actually help decipher thinking about the dilemma at hand and its resolution – because in casuistry resolving an ethical question is a moral requirement), a new paradigm is established. For design, this would require the development of a set of design-based paradigmatic cases. As a method it guides enquiry, discussion and resolution, and provides each discipline, through the recording of cases, with its own ethical case history for purposes of future reference in deciphering similarity.

A segment of undergraduate or graduate studio time could be devoted to ethics discussions that are held on a regular basis following assigned readings both in communicative ethics and casuistry. Participants in a studio course would be granted a good deal of freedom to make decisions in concert with faculty to determine which projects merit ethics evaluation and who should be sitting at the table when a particular project is reviewed (classmates, studio faculty, philosophy faculty and content mentors, for example). Design pedagogy could evolve a method for interrogating the image so that it becomes second nature to continue this group process in practice in much the same way that formal design skills are carried from pedagogy into practice. The recommendation of working within a method of ethics will require a group to be diversely constituted as it conducts investigations, including those with non-aligned positions that are worthwhile and relevant to the dilemma at hand. The proposed method of interrogating an image is intended to infuse the site of image production with a form of reflection about how an image might be received. Although anticipatory, this reflection is based on an accretion of knowledge from having vetted not only the (often) corporate conditions surrounding a current design project, but other antecedent and concurrent images, and how they have behaved in circulation.

Over time, a new body of paradigmatic, case-based knowledge would emerge that is particular to design. Case studies would be recorded for future reference, and design faculty who have developed an expertise in this method would become proficient in helping to constitute relevant groups to examine ethical questions and guide a process, part of which would involve deciphering the likeness of a case at hand to a previously established paradigmatic case. Several important design-specific ethical questions may arise. Who may determine that an image is problematic and worthy of investigation? Who should participate in the investigation? To what is this case similar and how was that prior case resolved? The first two questions are derived from recent iterations of communicative ethics and the last question is derived from casuistry. An assumption must be made from the beginning of the investigation that some form of rational language is shared among the participants despite potentially discrepant points of view about the nature of a problem and how to resolve it, both of which should be deciphered during the process of investigation.

Recent pairings of ethics and sustainability are evident in the formation of designer-focused and populated groups such as The Designers Accord (www.

designersaccord.org) or The Living Principles, with its broader mission of 'creative action for collective good' (www.livingprinciples.org). The *First Things First Manifesto*, originally written in 1964 and resuscitated in 2000, brought to the forefront the sometimes uncomfortable relationship between design and commerce, although it did little to alter behaviours and some of the recent signers acknowledged its limitations (McCarron 2001: 118–123). Sustainable behaviours in design practice *may* constitute an ethical choice, but ethics is not intrinsically synonymous with sustainability or any other content. Properly practised, ethics is the application of a philosophical method and not a personal point of view. The ability to take right action and, most importantly, the ability to base that action on an intellectual understanding of a well-thought out method for deciphering what constitutes right action is the goal. Working with, and making explicit, a method of ethics means that you are closer to being able to answer the question, 'How do you know what constitutes right action?' by escaping from the bias of your group.

References

AIGA (2001–2003) *Design Business and Ethics*, New York: AIGA.

Arendt, H. (1958) *The Human Condition*, Chicago, IL: University of Chicago Press.

Bayer, H. (1967) *Herbert Bayer: Painter, designer, architect*, New York: Reinhold Publishing Corporation.

Benhabib, S. (1990) 'Afterward: communicative ethics and current controversies in practical philosophy', in S. Benhabib and F. Dallmayr (eds) *The Communicative Ethics Controversy*, Cambridge, MA: MIT Press.

Benhabib, S. (1992) *Situating the Self*, New York: Routledge.

Betsworth, R. (1990) *Social Ethics: An examination of American moral traditions*, Louisville, KT: Westminster/John Know Press.

Boulding, K. (1963) *Conflict and Defense: A general theory*, New York: Harper Torchbooks.

Bourdieu, P. (1991) *Language and Symbolic Power*, Cambridge, MA: Harvard University Press.

Buchanan, R. (1992) 'Wicked problems in design thinking', *Design Issues*, 8(2): 5–21.

Fairey, S. (2011) 'The Associated Press Case Update'. Available at: http://obeygiant.com/headlines/the-associated-press-case-update (accessed 2 April 2011).

First Things First Manifesto (1964) London: Ken Garland.

Habermas, J. (1990) 'Discourse ethics: notes on a program of philosophical justification', in S. Benhabib and F. Dallmayr (eds) *The Communicative Ethics Controversy*, Cambridge, MA: MIT Press.

Harris, S. (2010) *The Moral Landscape: How science can determine human values*, New York: Free Press.

Heller, S. and Vienne, V. (eds) (2003) *Citizen Designer: Perspectives on design responsibility*, New York: Allworth Press.

Kaplan, D. (2010) 'Judge in AP-Shepard Fairey Fair Use Suit Suggests Settlement'. Available at: http://paidcontent.org/article/419-judge-in-ap-shepard-fairey-fair-use-suit-suggests-settlement/ (accessed 2 December 2010).

Kepes, G. (1965) *Education of Vision*, New York: George Brazzilier.

Lakoff, G. (1996) *Moral Politics: How liberals and conservatives think*, Chicago, IL: University of Chicago Press.

Loos, A. (2003) 'Ornament and crime' in C. Gorman (ed.) *The Industrial Design Reader*, New York: Allworth Press.

McCarron, C. (2001) 'First things first: a second look', in D. K. Holland (ed.) *Design Issues: How graphic design informs society,* New York: Allworth Press.
Müller, L. (1995) *Josef Müller-Brockmann: Pioneer of Swiss graphic design*, Baden: Verlag.
Niebuhr, R. (1932) *Moral Man and Immoral Society*, New York: Charles Scribner's Sons.
Preston, R. (1991) 'Christian ethics', in P. Singer (ed.) *A Companion to Ethics*, Oxford: Blackwell Publishers.
Rand, P. (1985) 'Design and the play instinct', in P. Rand (ed.) *A Designer's Art*, New Haven, CT: Yale University Press.
Sagoff, M. (1986) 'Values and preferences', in *Ethics: An international journal of social, political, and legal philosophy*, 96(2): 301–316.
Simmel, G. (1955) *Conflict and the Web of Group Affiliations*, New York: Free Press.
Simon, H. (1945) *Administrative Behavior: A study of decision-making process in administrative organization*, New York: Free Press.
Sommer, R. (1969) *Personal Space: The behavioral basis of design*, Englewood Cliffs, NJ: Prentice-Hall.
Vignelli, M. (2010) 'We Use Way Too Many Fonts' with Massimo Vignelli. Available at http://bigthink.com/ideas/19591 (accessed 28 March 2011).
Vogel, D. (2005) *The Market for Virtue: The potential and limits of corporate social responsibility*, Washington, DC: Brookings Institution Press.
Weber, M. (1958) *The City*, New York: Collier Books.

4

FROM ALLURE TO ETHICS

Design as a 'creative industry'

Justin O'Connor

I

In this chapter I want to look at the question of design and ethics in a situation where design as a set of related economic practices has been repositioned as a key identifier for a new kind of ideas-driven industry – the creative industries. Previously marginal to cultural policy in the form of applied arts, in the creative industries agenda design became a privileged meeting place, or indeed broker, for art and industry, economy and commerce. I want to explore the new kinds of ethical challenges this brings.

The term 'creative industries', introduced by the UK government's Department of Culture, Media and Sport (DCMS 1998) – developing themes from the Australian government's *Creative Nation* report of 1994 – has generally been viewed in three ways. First, as a merely pragmatic policy-driven change of terminology for a sector previously known as cultural industries; second, as reflective of an economic (Banks and O'Connor 2009), informational (Garnham 2005; Pratt 2005), or neoliberal (Miller 2009) emphasis at the expense of the cultural dimension; or third, as designating a new kind of creative economy that goes beyond both 'the arts' and the cultural industries (Hartley 2005). One crucial strand running through these debates has been about definitional boundaries – just what kinds of activities does 'creative industries' designate and how do these differ from the cultural industries? These boundaries have, on occasion, stretched to all those activities that involve creativity, or intellectual property, or ideas, or novelty and so on – suggesting a creative economy (Howkins 2001) that in some East Asian formulations include bio-tech and nanotechnology, research and development, business consulting, and many others. However, in most countries that have adopted the creative industries agenda, and for many academic writers, the key differentiator between these and the cultural industries (which may or may not include the arts) is the inclusion of design (cf. O'Connor 2011).

In their 1998 *Creative Industries Mapping Document*, the DCMS added software, fashion, architecture and computer games to the traditional list of the arts and cultural industries (the latter including publishing, television and radio, music recording and film). For Nicholas Garnham (2005) and David Hesmondhalgh (2007), two key critics of the creative industries concept, the cultural industries involve the production of symbolic texts; they argue that although fashion, architecture and other design fields involve symbolic meaning, this element does not constitute the main inputs or function for these industries (cf. O'Connor 2010). This distinction – between a primary and secondary relationship to symbolic, aesthetic, artistic and/or cultural inputs – is common in taxonomies of the arts, the cultural, and the creative industries (O'Connor 2011). Indeed, as we shall see, it reflects a separation between art and craft, between pure and applied, that goes back to the Renaissance. But although, for some, this leaves art and cultural industries in a distinct, more purely cultural space than these more applied creative industries, for others, the creative industries idea represents a blurring or abolition of boundaries – between art and industry, between culture and economics, and even between art and life.

The most immediate implications of such a blurring is first, that 'culture' is no longer a pure expenditure but now a generator of employment and wealth creation in its own right; second, the sorts of skills or capacities associated with artistic and cultural production – now labelled 'creativity' – can become crucial inputs and catalysts across the economy as a whole (Cunningham 2006). Accordingly, the separation between art and industry, particularly pronounced in Anglo-Saxon countries, can now give way to their integration (Hartley 2008). This argument comes variously from notions of 'post-Fordism' and the 'information economy', in which large-scale factory-centred industry based on mass reproduction and the division of labour between experts and workers gives way to a more fragmented or networked system of small-scale production and niche markets, involving high levels of knowledge input and customer feedback. In these new economies, culture defined in terms of highly educated workers able to 'process knowledge and manipulate symbols' (Castells 1989) increasingly comes to include culture in the more 'artistic' sense of symbolic or aesthetic meaning creation. These claims in turn relate to the increasing importance of the non-functional expressive, symbolic, aesthetic or cultural aspects of consumer goods and services (Scott 2001, 2004, 2006). It is the consumption of these expressive goods and services more than anything that has driven the growth of the creative industries (Work Foundation 2007). This notion suggests in turn a wider transformation of culture and society towards greater individualization and the need to construct identity and meaning through such expressive consumption. It is in this context that Mike Featherstone (1996) talked of the 'aesthetization of everyday life', and Scott Lash and John Urry (1994) described the 'culturalization of the economy'.

From this perspective, design as a creative industry is defined in terms of its combination of symbolic, expressive, or aesthetic elements with functional goods and services. This goes beyond traditional crafts, or the applied and decorative arts first, because such expressive meanings are now applicable to an ever-expanding range of previously functional goods and services (the latter being transformed into experiences (Pine and Gilmore 1999)), and second, they are now deemed to be central to individual identity in unprecedented ways, such that some commentators argue that contemporary (DIY) citizenship is inseparable from consumption (Hartley 1999; 2005). As such, the citizen-consumer lies at the heart of a consumer market whose limits are infinite; as a creative industry, therefore, the designer produces novelty and social distinction/identity for a commercial market. Thus, the term 'designer goods' has come to stand for a certain kind of high-end and aspirational consumption in which aesthetics, personal identity and profit are barely distinguishable. This is what we might call aesthetics as allure (Thrift 2008).

The identification of design with allure in the creative industries obviously brings with it some ethical and political issues around the promotion of consumption – to which I return at the end. But it also raises issues about the relationship of function and aesthetics in design, both of which are implicated in any relationship to ethics. In order to address these issues we need to look more closely at that separation of function and aesthetics represented by the binary of art and craft. We shall do so through a combination of historical and conceptual analysis with reflections of contemporary practitioners.

II

In 2009, research commissioned by the Australia Council for the Arts, and led by myself, involved in-depth interviews with eighteen high-achieving individuals working across the whole spectrum of the arts, cultural and creative industries. The core issue concerned the perceived relationship between the arts and the creative industries. In response, one visual artist said:

> I feel that [the visual arts] are quite different [from creative industries]. That's because we don't have someone coming to us with a set of parameters and job to complete that needs to go in one way. I don't mean to say a designer is compromised by the client on every job but limited by client's requests and budgets and even the [required] form of the outcome. Designers are very creative, clever people but always have to answer to a brief that they don't set. Even with a good brief – like Greenpeace asking for inspirational work – their work is still mediated by that brief. In my work, I'm interested in the environment but don't produce one-sided work, sometimes it has a darkness to it even though it talks about ideas of living in a better world. It often pushes you away, does not draw you in like advertising and advocacy material which are things that don't have the potential to be poetic, cannot go beyond the way that we see things now.
>
> (Anonymous 2009)

In contrast, three designers working in different fields had this to say:

> Graphic designers are usually working for a client; money for service. This is different for artist and patron, or the commercialization of their art. The caveat on this is you could have a designer that approaches the condition of art in some way – treated now as piece of art rather than graphic art – so things can transmute from one to other. The artist's motivation is to transcend the relationship around creativity . . . to go beyond the designer who is looking at working creativity into a particular transaction – the artist does something over and above that, not the traditional mode of something being bought or sold even though there is some commercialization aspect, but distant from the creation. . . . Design is intensely commercialized at one end of the spectrum, and approaches art at the other.
>
> (Anonymous 2009)

> Designers usually work within constraints from market, client, with the product needing to be right. The artist does not necessarily have this – like pure research versus applied research, pure science versus applied science.
>
> (Anonymous 2009)

> When somebody comes to me for a job I ask them, are you a designer or an artist?
>
> (Anonymous 2009)

The forms of distinction at play in these quotes are complex, with important implications for an ethics of design. The immediate distinction is one between the autonomy of art and the heteronomy of design. This can be traced back to the Renaissance where the notion of the 'artist' came to be distinguished from that of mere craft – techne – and artisanship. This distinction concerned the different status of artistic and manual labour – where one was transcendent, freely creating, and the other dominated by the necessity of work. The notion of 'autonomous' or 'aesthetic' art as it emerged in the mid-eighteenth century and given form by Kant was in part related to this. In Bourdieu's influential work of 1974 (published in English in 1984), the Kantian separation of the higher disinterested faculties from those lower faculties seen to be driven by passions and needs enabled new forms of social distinction to be established between bourgeoisie and proletariat at the end of the eighteenth century. It is clearly this elitist and hypocritical distinction, leading to notions of art transcending everyday life, which is targeted by those who assert the economic basis of all cultural production and thus refuse some pure art standing against a debased commercial cultural industry.

However, autonomous art did not just assert itself against 'industry' or 'manual work' as some grubby everyday life; aesthetics after Kant evoked a space of free play separate from the domination of economic and administrative rationality (Rancière 2009). That is, it did not so much separate itself from everyday life – passions, necessity, labour, money – as from the degraded, conventionalized, and indeed, outmoded forms of culture that modern bureaucracy, industry and commerce brought with it. Aesthetic art also contained a promise to transform everyday life through a renewal of culture. If certain conceptions of art continued to assert autonomy above all (versions of nineteenth-century Romanticism or twentieth-century Modernism, for example) and to position applied, craft-based or decorative art as inevitably compromised or lesser, then there were also powerful counter-currents that both valued the craft in art and the social-ethical responsibilities of art to connect with and transform everyday life.

Thus the constant tussle between art and craft (nicely outlined by Howard Becker (1984) in *Art Worlds*) was often about the status of artistic vision versus mere technique. However, this conflict was offset by a continuing shared sense among artists and artisans of being true to the material and the tools at hand, of a certain fitness-for-purpose embodied within the material world, which Heidegger (1993 [1954]) evoked in his critique of technology as domination of nature. Richard Sennett's recent book *The Craftsman* (2008) develops this notion of craft and extends it to the physical work of the hand and the eye involved in surgery, in design drawing and in software development. Indeed, a commitment to the 'objective' requirements of the aesthetic material, ones that demand a certain 'craft', can be seen in the aesthetic theories of Adorno and in Greenberg's Formalism.

Alongside these concerns with the craft and materiality of art have been strong (related) tendencies that have stressed the social-ethical responsibilities of art and design. That is, it was there to respond to, enhance or help shape the emergent life of modern society. From William Morris (or, before him, William Blake) and the Arts and Crafts Movement, through Art Nouveau, Bauhaus, Art Deco, Constructivism and to the International Style in architecture – craft skills became part of a future-oriented conception of design for living in which the 'aesthetic' found its purpose in a transformed everyday life. Modernism, often castigated for being a Formalist version of art for art's sake, also had strong tendencies towards the new socio-political functionality of art for reinventing modernity. These tendencies indicate that the notion of pure art set against designers working to (someone else's) brief is historically rather precarious.

III

> A designer is . . . limited by client's requests and budgets and even the [required] form of the outcome. Designers are very creative, clever people but always have to answer to a brief that they don't set.
>
> (Anonymous 2009)

From a designer's perspective this is not always a problem; or rather, this is the problem to which their skills and vision are to be applied. 'The designer . . . is looking at working creativity into a particular transaction.' Designers pride themselves on dealing with solutions to functional problems. Some of these are set tight – a logo, for example – and some set more widely – a new public space or an integrated communications strategy. It's the willingness to engage with these problems within the constraints of 'requests, budgets and . . . outcome' that for one respondent marks off the job-seeking artist from the designer.

Most artists, however, also find themselves working for a client; they might have more 'wriggle room' than designers but they mostly have to conform to a brief. Film music, copywriting, public art, photography and illustration, for example, all have set parameters. This is even more the case when it comes to music for toys, adverts and games, or voice-overs, acting theme-park characters, or filming inserts for commercial websites, and so on. Very few artists work outside constraints – and many thrive on them!

On the other hand, certain graphic designers (Peter Saville), or celebrity fashion or product designers (Philippe Starck), and so on, have much more autonomy than many artists. Hence the caveat above: '[that] you could have a designer that approaches the condition of art in some way – treated now as piece of art rather than graphic art – so things can transmute from one to other'. The key distinction remains between 'problem solving' and free exploration; but it is, in fact, a spectrum, a zone of differential tensions, rather than a binary or hierarchy. Nor is the constraint of the brief quite the same thing as saying 'designers are usually working for a client; money for service'. The functionality of design is not necessarily the same as its commerciality. Of course, budgets are a key material constraint that has to be acknowledged (by most performing and visual artists as well); this is not the same as doing it just for the money. The need to make a living is certainly a constraint, but this too is part of the artist's life. There are jobs you would rather remained anonymous, to get the money. 'Some have projects they put their names to, and others they do not put names on' (Anonymous 2009) – and there are ones where you put in more of yourself than simply cost-benefit.

The problem lies not in the fact of an external brief – which is what the designer is about – but in the client's limited vision or the allotted resources not being sufficient to the full demands of the job in hand. And, of course, artists too chafe under similar conditions. These are a source of many ethical choices that professionals make, a complex balance of the need for money, the nurturing of current and future reputation ('Don't put your name on that one!'), and wider ethical-political beliefs (not working for a certain organization or industry). Designers navigate the spaces in which they must make a living just like artists do; both would sometimes prefer to do a job anonymously. But like those artists working within a commercial setting, there is great scope for quality work. Business clients are not to be characterized in terms of some uniform bottom line; the permeation of design within product, branding, marketing, office interiors, logistics, and so on, is extremely sophisticated. Businesses are also judged by consumers, other businesses and design professionals in ways that have direct impact on their image. The different 'design worlds' have the constraints and ethics of many more artistic communities of practice. Equally, designers work for public agencies with wider remits than the shareholders and are set within other kinds of constraints. In this sense there are strong homologies and interconnections between the ethical contexts within which artists and designers work, although there are areas that clearly mark them off (cf. Banks *et al.* 2000; Banks 2007; Gu 2010).

It is also clear that these tensions between 'problem solving' and free exploration that the binary design and art frequently articulates is not the same as that between function and style to which this is often reduced. The rejection of designer-as-stylist role does not just concern the frequent abuse of function that this entails ('It looks nice but can you sit on it?'), but also for the reduction of art to what we have called allure.

> Design thinking . . . is using a skill set of design not to just supply gloss at the end of the development of a product, but to define what the product or service can be right from the start and use design as a framework. It could be put as stylists versus designers. Any kid with Photoshop could be a stylist.
>
> (Anonymous 2009)

The reduction of design thinking to style can thus be a part of that tension between the possibilities inherent in the brief, in the problem to be solved (a new house, a new city, an internet application, a game narrative) and the constraints external to that problem solving. That is, style as surface solution at the expense of the real solution. It is indicative of a radical impulse within design – as in part transformative of the very social realities to which designers sought to respond. Some design traditions – Modernist architecture, city planning, Constructivist signage, social network platforms – could be radically utopian, seeing only a future society as capable of acting on its ideas. Here again design comes close to the aesthetic tradition that stresses the uselessness of art in the face of an instrumentalized and inhuman society.

IV

This brief discussion indicates some of the problems with the reduction of design in creative industries discourse to the aesthetization of everyday life or culturalization of the economy – that is, as directly related to the rise in cultural consumption. This equation of aesthetics with the allure of individual expressive consumption is highly problematic, and flattens out much of what aesthetic art has attempted to articulate. The *utilitas* of aesthetics cannot be reduced to its allure for consumption; but the response is not (or not only) the evocation of art's absolute transcendence of such utility but a recognition that such utility is deeply compromised by its reduction to expressive consumption. The social function of melody, rhythm, movement, line, shape, mass, symbol and image, and their role within the everyday meaning and social interaction, were elements never entirely abandoned by aesthetic art. Indeed, many of the concerns of aesthetic art – to find a space of play, or exploration in a space separate from that of domination – have now become central to popular culture.

The culturalization of the economy registers this in part, but in the creative industries discourse it is reduced to the economic dimension at the expense of any emancipatory element (unless consumption is emancipation). The problem is less that of the industrialization of the arts but the industrialization of everyday culture; the increased reach of goods and services saturated with highly designed symbolic meanings into the interstices of everyday life. This does not end the art-industry problem but transposes it to a new register.

Design's current resurgence as a central contemporary discipline, distinct from both art and allure, is a response to this situation, its activities planted squarely within ethics and politics.

> The broadening of ambitions for design . . . could also include the shape that government takes and citizen's engagement with those things. That's why design has a huge role to play, to rethink what government and citizens are. Culture in Raymond Williams's sense [ordinary, everyday] rather than cultural production. There is something in design (which could be tested in music) that is different from the production of art because it is concerned with cogs, wheels, oil. Whether it's lived culture or industrial process. Art is not like that except for commenting on it, its not same motivation from a creative point of view.
>
> (Anonymous 2009)

Design involves planning and craft; it also involves the aesthetic quality of how it looks, feels and sounds. Famously, the Roman architect Vitruvius suggested three aspects of design – *firmitas, utilitas, venustas*. The first concerns structure – the province of the engineer; the second is the programme – the province of the planner; the third, form or beauty – the province of the artist. How these three aspects are put together involves engineering and craft skills (some cutting edge, some often long acquired, locally embedded and tacit), planning skills ('What is this thing trying to achieve and with what means?' can be a visionary or mundane question) and artistic or creative skills. These are not strictly separated.

In this conception, aesthetic – pertaining to the senses, to perception – can easily become the look, the allure and the surface. However, the aesthetic as I have discussed it – the tradition of modern art since the eighteenth century – is not confined to beauty in this way. It has aspirations to articulate and transform experience, giving it an ethical and political charge that formed the intent of William Morris, Bauhaus, Le Corbusier and Buckminster-Fuller – maybe even Steve Jobs. Thus the aesthetics of design has rarely been simply decorative allure (*venustas*), but always an intrinsic part of the social, cultural and political vision of *firmitas* and *utilitas* – as in the Acropolis or Pantheon, for example.

V

Design has now a higher prestige than at any time in the last 200 years. Designers increasingly distrust aesthetics as allure and look to its wider social and cultural function. Many designers have become increasingly reflective about their practice, its core mission, skills and ethics. In doing so they often claim not to be artists.

> I get annoyed when architects think of themselves as part of an arts rather than a design faculty. It's demeaning to the rest of design. Industrial design

> is profoundly more affecting than architecture. Only 5–7 per cent of buildings are built by architects, whereas industrial design changes the way that cars, Ipods, computers, buses, etc. work. The intellectual reach for the higher ground from architects is, I think, largely unfounded; or rather, other design disciplines have the same intellectual reach, but are not as powerful a part of the profession.
>
> (Anonymous 2009)

This is true to a degree. At the same time, such impulses to wider social responsibilities are by no means alien to the art tradition, as I have outlined. Indeed, the ethical turn in design, where its association with the aesthetic allure of the commodity is giving way to its application to social structures and process, is also to be seen across the creative industries as a whole. There is a widespread shift towards sustainability – not just to green production, but to local markets and livelihoods, and to the cultures that intersect with these. In these processes, older artistic values – of craft, time, patience, the determination by the object rather than self-expression, ethical-aesthetic communities – have re-emerged. No longer just in North America, Europe and Australia but globally, the social and ethical dimensions of culture have been asserted against the purely economic, and the uncoupling of cultural workers from the agenda of the creative industries has gone on apace, if unevenly. Designers and artists are closer together than they ever were, but the banner of creative industries is giving way to something yet to be named.

References

Banks, M. (2007) *The Politics of Cultural Work*, London: Palgrave Macmillan.

Banks, M. and O'Connor, J. (2009) 'Introduction: Creative industries ten years after', *International Journal of Cultural Policy*, 15(4): 365–373.

Banks, M., Lovatt, A., O'Connor, J. and Raffo, C. (2000) 'Risk and trust in the cultural industries', *Geoforum*, 31(4): 453–464.

Becker, H. S. (1984) *Art Worlds*, Berkeley, CA and London: University of California Press.

Bourdieu, P. (1984) *Distinction: A social critique of the judgement of taste*, London: Routledge.

Castells, M. (1989) *The Informational City: Information technology, economic restructuring and the urban-regional process*, Oxford: Blackwell.

Cunningham, S. (2006) *What Price a Creative Economy?,* Strawberry Hills, New South Wales: Currency House.

Department of Communications and the Arts (1994) *Creative Nation: Commonwealth Cultural Policy*, Canberra: AGPS.

Department of Culture, Media and Sport (DCMS) (1998) *Creative Industries Mapping Document*, London: Department of Culture, Media and Sport.

Featherstone, M. (1996) *Consumer Culture and Postmodernism*, London: Sage.

Garnham, N. (2005) 'From cultural to creative industries: an analysis of the implications of the creative industries' approach to arts and media policy making in the United Kingdom', *International Journal of Cultural Policy*, 11(1): 15–29.

Gu, X. (2010) 'Social networks and aesthetic reflexivity in the creative industries', *Journal of International Communications*, 16(2): 55–66.

Hartley, J. (1999) *Uses of Television*, London: Routledge.

Hartley, J. (2005) 'Creative Industries' in J. Hartley (ed.) *Creative Industries*, Oxford: Blackwell.
Hartley, J. (2008) 'From the consciousness industry to creative industries: consumer-created content, social network markets and the growth of knowledge' in J. Holt and A. Perren (eds) *Media Industries: History, theory and methods*, Oxford: Blackwell.
Heidegger, M. (1993 [1954]) 'The question concerning technology' in D. Krell (ed.) *Basic Writings*, New York: HarperCollins.
Hesmondalgh, D. (2007) *The Cultural Industries*, London: Sage.
Howkins, J. (2001) *The Creative Economy: How people make money from ideas*, London: Allen Lane.
Lash, S. and Urry, J. (1994) *Economies of Signs and Space*, London: Sage.
Miller, T. (2009) 'From creative to cultural industries', *Cultural Studies*, 23(1): 88–99.
O'Connor, J. (2010) *Creative Industries: A critical bibliography*, London: Arts Council.
O'Connor, J. (2011) *Arts and Creative Industries*, Sydney: Australia Council for the Arts.
Pine, J. and Gilmore, J. (1999) *The Experience Economy: Work is theatre and every business a stage*, Boston, MA: Harvard Business School Press.
Pratt, A. (2005) 'Cultural industries and public policy: an oxymoron?' *International Journal of Cultural Policy*, 11(1): 31–44.
Rancière, J. (2009) *Aesthetics and Its Discontents*, London: Polity.
Scott, A. J. (2001) 'Capitalism, cities and the production of symbolic forms', *Transactions of the Institute of British Geographers*, 26: 11–23.
Scott, A. J. (2004) 'Cultural products industries and urban economic development: prospects for growth and market contestation in global context', *Urban Affairs Review*, 39(4): 461–490.
Scott, A. J. (2006) 'Entrepreneurship, innovation and industrial development: geography and the creative field revisited', *Small Business Economics*, 26(1): 1–24.
Sennett, R. (2008) *The Craftsman*, London: Allen Lane.
Thrift, N. (2008) 'The material practices of glamour', *Journal of Cultural Economy*, 1(1): 9–23.
Work Foundation (2007) *Staying Ahead: The economic performance of the UK's creative industries*, London: The Work Foundation.

PART II

Communication design

5

HYBRIDITY, HEGEMONY AND DESIGN IN A GLOBALIZED ECONOMY

Karen Fiss[1]

One of the dominating themes in the field of design and ethics for a better part of the last decade has been the inherent power of design to change the world for the better. Numerous initiatives, blogs and conferences have celebrated the unique role that design and 'design thinking' have in solving critical problems facing humanity and the planet. Fundamental questions loom over such 'socially responsible' projects for me: first, I wonder if we can take at face value the distance between market-based and socially oriented design initiatives; or if too much of 'design for social change' is about rebranding, providing new marketing platforms for designers, companies and institutions needing to find new sources of revenue. Second, I question what areas of expertise design brings to these projects: is it siphoning resources away from the non-profit organisations willing to do the not-so-glamorous work required in many cases, or is design consultancy bringing well-informed and well-researched alternatives to the table? Third – and the focus of my contribution to this volume – is how design negotiates or exploits cultural differences.

How do designers establish relationships with collectives and populations it seeks to help or collaborate with – populations that are more often than not disadvantaged and culturally Other? The volatility of this issue was evident in the vociferous online debate during the summer of 2010 between Bruce Nussbaum and Emily Pilloton, as well as others who engaged in the controversy, which raised fundamental questions about whether the new wave of humanitarian design projects was in some way a form of neo-imperialism. The purpose of this chapter is not to discount attempts to engage design in critical social, political or environmental issues; rather, I am concerned about the manner in which critical academic practices and theoretical concepts, intended to be transgressive or transformative, are actually being instrumentalized by the field of design to suit its own market- or brand-driven purposes. Indeed, there remains a gap between talk and action as the profession's global engagement continues to focus largely on facilitating the flow of images and consumer goods across continents, without consideration of the larger political and social effects. Design's altruistic potential is short-circuited, channelled mainly into practices of social entrepreneurship – which target lower income and/or underserved populations – or into practices of 'localization', whereby designers and corporations expand their audience base by marketing messages to specific regional or ethnic groups. I cannot address this broad field within the context of this chapter; rather, the editors of this volume have requested that I expand on an earlier essay I penned on the concept of hybridity as it plays out in some examples of design discourse and production (Fiss 2006: 56–61).

Over the past several years, numerous books and brand experience seminars have been developed to aid designers in communicating with groups outside their routine scope of experience. There are also highly simplistic resource books that have been produced, such as Ronnie Lipton's *Design across Cultures: How to create effective graphics for diverse ethnic groups*, which promises in a less-than-subtle manner to help designers 'connect with every market!' (Lipton 2002). The collection is illustrated predominantly with work commissioned by large companies including McDonald's, Tylenol and Volkswagen, and its pithy subsections cover such topics as 'driving the diversity theme', 'hot art & Afr-icons' and 'more than juste kente'. The author assures the (presumably Anglo-) reader that 'it *is* safe to assume Hispanics love music' (Lipton 2002: 23), among other stereotyped platitudes.

Katherine McCoy, who runs brand experience seminars through a programme called 'High Ground', offers a more sophisticated approach to what she describes as audience-centred design for cultural sustainability. In the mid 1990s, McCoy began arguing that for print communication to survive, its practitioners had to adapt by moving 'toward specialized audiences, focussed messages, and eccentric design languages tailored to each audience's unique characteristics and culture' (McCoy 1995: 146). A decade later, McCoy began to celebrate these localization techniques as a means of protecting the cultural resources of under-represented minorities and indigenous cultures, and as a means of resisting cultural imperialism and consumer monoculture. In 'Hybridity happens', published in *Émigré*, McCoy remarks that she has 'come to value diverse cultures of visual and verbal languages' and adds, 'The globalization of contemporary corporate design is a dull contrast to the vernacular vigor of indigenous, local, and special interest subcultures' (McCoy 2004: 239).

What is troubling about McCoy's highly acclaimed brand-experience strategy is that she cloaks it in the language of political activism, linking it to the legacy of the civil rights movement and the notion of ethnic 'pride' (2004: 42). Her rhetoric appropriates the key concept of 'hybridity', an idea drawn from the academic fields of postcolonial and diasporic cultural studies, yet distorts its original – and highly politicized – meaning. McCoy argues that cultural hybridity should function as a model for design, and she encourages designers to 'let their audiences point them to new hybrid sources of graphic expression' (2004: 39). While she explains that 'hybridity is the result when subcultures rub up against each other' and also when 'a subculture resists the dominant culture' (McCoy 2004: 44), her 'new design vision' does not concern cultural production by subcultures, but rather what is targeted at them. Audience-specific design, then, aims to productively incorporate or harness the 'authentic energy' (2004: 43) of different cultures without considering the political or economic implications of such 'collaboration'.

As the seminal writer Homi K. Bhabha explains in *The Location of Culture*, the authoring of cultural hybridities emerges from those existing on the periphery of the dominant culture and completely rejects any notion of authenticity. The representation of difference and hybridity are not reflections of 'pre-given ethnic or cultural traits set in the fixed tablet of tradition' (Bhabha 1994: 3). Rather,

> The social articulation of difference, from the minority perspective, is a complex, on-going negotiation that seeks to authorize cultural hybridities that emerge in moments of historical transformation. The 'right' to signify from the periphery of authorized power and privilege does not depend on the persistence of tradition; it is resourced by the power of tradition to be reinscribed through the conditions of contingency and contradictoriness that attend upon the lives of those who are 'in the minority'.
>
> (Bhabha 1994: 3)

Bhabha's concept of hybridity is intended to displace the societal model of multiculturalism and diversity (which is based on an exotic understanding of cultural difference), in favour of a more complex and unruly one based on what he terms the 'in-between spaces' of culture – the places and moments of contact between communities – where cultural meaning and identity are continuously negotiated and contested, but never resolved (Bhabha 1994: 54–56). With the understanding that the terms of cultural engagement are always produced performatively, Bhabha's 'third space', opened up by the non-synchronicity of global and national cultures, is a space of potential opportunities where the negotiation of incommensurable temporalities and cultural differences can be consensual and conflicted. By engaging difference without assumed hierarchies, cultural hybridity can confound 'definitions of tradition, and modernity; realign the customary boundaries between the private and public, high and low; and challenge normative expectations of development and progress' (Bhabha 1994: 3). This third space of cultural encounter is by nature ambivalent, antagonistic and potentially subversive. Hybridity, then, cannot be used to describe a mere mixing of cultural codes, but rather denotes a complex strategy that seeks to interrupt, interrogate and destabilize dominant culture along with the underlying narratives and myths used to maintain its power base.

This 'cutting edge of translation and negotiation', this 'split-space' of enunciation, cannot be appropriated or disconnected from its colonial and postcolonial provenance (Bhabha 1994: 56). When hybridity, in the context of design practice, does not emerge from the political complexities and subjectivities of a particular subculture, it can be nothing more than pastiche in the service of brand – and certainly not cultural – sustainability. As Michael Schmidt eloquently observes in an essay published in Steven Heller's *The Education of the Typographer*, 'Localization will not sustain culture, individuality, or custom in the face of expanding capital, service, media, and trade conglomerates. Localization is, in fact, a *tool* of exploitative globalization in the hands of free and unchecked markets' (Schmidt 2004: 58).

A number of graphic artists have thoughtfully employed hybrid communication strategies, not to infiltrate another culture, but to address important questions of location and politics within the context of internationalism. Chaz Maviyane-Davies, a designer from Zimbabwe, created a series of posters in the 1990s based on the United Nations' Universal Declaration of Human Rights as 'seen from an African perspective'. Maviyane-Davies explains that the series

> grew out of the indignation I have always felt in the way that Africans are constantly portrayed. For many, 'Africa' conjures up images of a continent torn apart by hatred and brutality, corpses and corruption. Ignore these images and the continent has no other identity.
>
> (Maviyane-Davies 1996)

To counter this perception, Maviyane-Davies used imagery drawn from a distinctly pan-African iconography to convey the declaration's message that every individual has a right to freedom, free speech, education, just political representation and cultural expression. In the posters, African subjects are employed to represent the Everyman, the international citizen, not simply to enact a 'reversal' of the dominant white paradigm, but to call into question the very notion that a universal subject exists.

In 2006, the young Zimbabwean designer Panganayi Rupango created an abstracted yet vivid portrayal of Zimbabwean youth, loosely using the palette of his country's flag to address the crisis of identity and political disengagement among the younger generation – a situation not limited to his own country (Figure 5.1). Reacting to the fact that 'young people are growing up in an ever-changing world, a "plural" world where they identify more with MTV than their own indigenous culture', Rupango's poster encourages the development of a politicized identity rooted in the younger generation's complex cross-cultural experiences (Mafundikwa 2006).

More recently, graphic designer and illustrator Lydia Ortiz created *Imigrante* (Figure 5.2), a book based on her experiences as a Filipino immigrant and 'soon to be American' (Ortiz 2011). The book's text and images resist following any seamless narrative or chronological biography, instead taking as its organizing device an alphabetical glossary inspired by the 'Welcome to America' packet presented to her by the Citizenship and Immigration Services when she first arrived in the United States. The book offers fragments of memories, reflections and stories that all 'wrestle with cultural, social, political, and religious differences', and reveal how the protagonist's identity is constantly changing and being cast anew (Ortiz 2011). The performative nature of identity comes through clearly in the evocative juxtaposition of her illustrations, which follow a personified eye through numerous

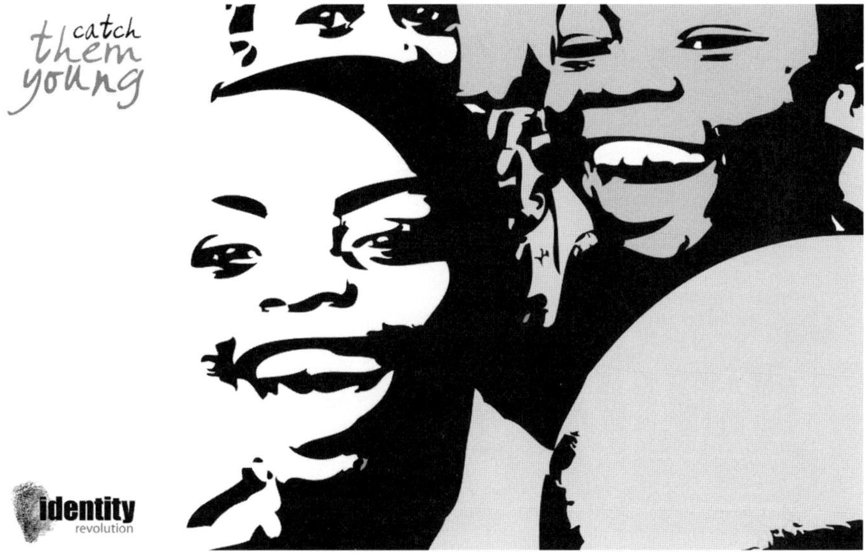

FIGURE 5.1 'Identity Revolution' (Panganayi Rupango 2006).

mutations as it takes on the character of child, nun, Russian doll, hydra and burlesque dancer; all interwoven with photographs, documents and extraordinary decorated letters, which lend the project the quality of a postmodern illuminated manuscript.

The work of Ortiz, Rupango and Maviyane-Davies demonstrates how hybrid design practices can help shape political and cultural identities by undermining static notions of tradition or authenticity, while remaining dynamic and continuously negotiating accepted notions of nationalism, postcolonialism, regionalism and globalism. The necessity of such work is made abundantly clear in the light of exploitative marketing strategies that currently permeate both high- and low-end consumer culture. An extreme example of what can be termed 'cultural cannibalism' was apparent in design work created for Jean Paul Gaultier's Spring–Summer 2005 fashion line. Gaultier presented the collection with the opening title 'Venus Hottentot', evoking the name under which a South African woman, Saartjie Baartman, was exhibited as an exotic sexual curiosity in Europe from 1810 to 1815. After her death at 25, Baartman's body was dissected and her genitals preserved in a jar 'for science' at the Musée de l'Homme in Paris. Baartman's figure fuelled racialized stereotypes of black sexuality, and Gaultier's reference does nothing more than to resuscitate colonial fantasies of Africa in order to endow his haute couture with a primitivist eroticism. The well-known writer and cultural critic bell hooks describes this appropriation of foreign cultures as 'eating the other,' whereby the 'primitive' is stripped of its negative connotations and becomes a desirable quality (hooks 1992: 9–20). Ethnicity and racial difference within commodity culture 'becomes spice, seasoning that can liven up the dull dish that is mainstream white culture' (hooks 1992: 21). Commodifying and consuming difference, however,

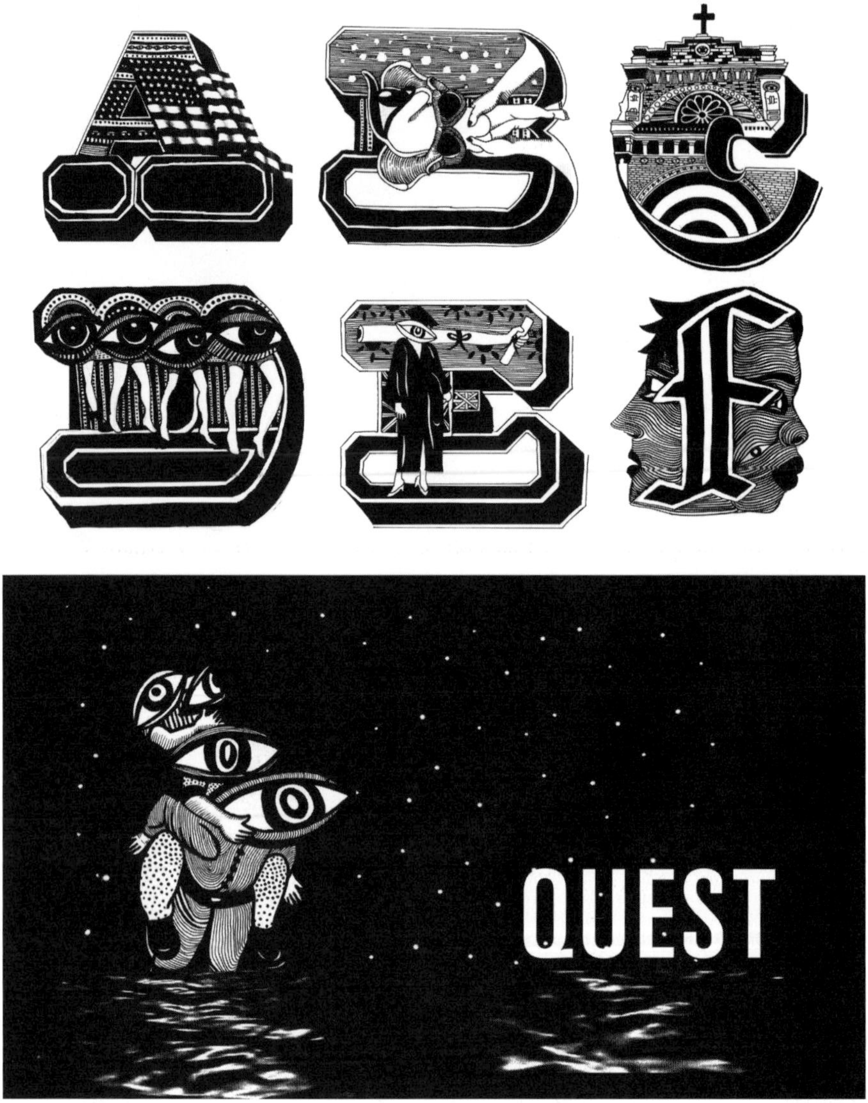

FIGURE 5.2 Spreads from *Imigrante* (Lydia Ortiz 2011).

does not require one to relinquish one's mainstream position or power. And the act of being targeted as a consumer – or chosen as a cultural identity to be consumed – does not result in increased political visibility or empowerment.

Another arena in which cultural cannibalism predominates is in the global travel industry, which routinely packages the exotic for Western consumption. In the poster series *Interclone Hotel*, the architectural team of Elizabeth Diller and Ricardo Scofidio mock the travelling businessperson's or tourist's desire for contained and filtered experiences of foreign cultures. Created for an installation at the Ataturk Airport for the 1997 Istanbul Biennial, the series of illuminated cibachromes served as an ad campaign for a fictional hotel chain with locations in emerging economies. Each 'ad' depicts a generic hotel room customized with visual motifs that correspond to a one-dimensional understanding of the referenced culture. Regardless of the location, guests are assured of the comforting omnipresence of CNN and standardized amenities, 'balancing the comfort of familiarity with exotic cultural inflections' (Diller and Scofidio 1997).

Dinh Q. Lê, a Vietnamese artist, in another set of posters, also responds to the political dimensions of an expanded global tourist industry. While Diller and Scofidio give visual representation to the neocolonial perspective of the Western traveller, Lê interrupts this seamless scopic pleasure with the anonymous voices of the visited. Highlighting the unsymmetrical nature of these cultural encounters, Lê parodies Vietnam's tourism marketing, which has consistently used the natural beauty of the country as well as the history of the Vietnam War to promote sites such as China Beach and the Demilitarized Zone (DMZ). Each of Lê's ersatz travel posters is branded with a logo that combines the silhouette of Vietnam with the title of his 2005 series, *Vietnam: Destination for the New Millennium* – a theme adapted from the slogan used by Vietnam's tourism office. One of Lê's posters implores tourists to visit My Lai for the beauty of its beaches, thus encouraging a convenient

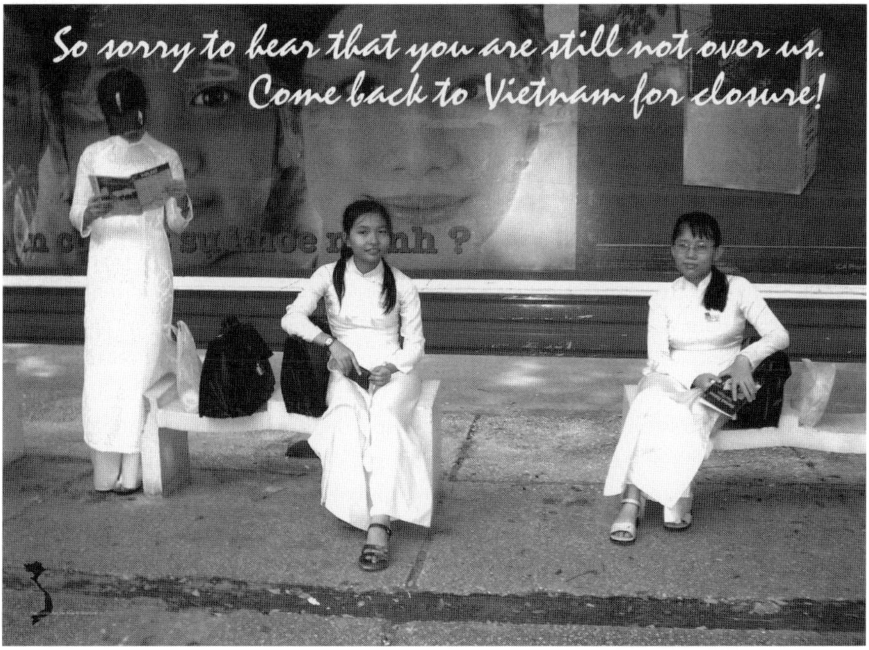

FIGURE 5.3 *Vietnam: Destination for the New Millennium* (Dinh Q. Lê 2005).

historical amnesia about a site where one of the most horrifying massacres of the Vietnam War took place. In another poster, Lê combines a photograph he took – of three young high school students waiting at a bus stop – with an appeal to 'Come back to Vietnam for closure!' (Figure 5.3). By combining the formulaic layout of the generic travel poster with unexpected and ironic slogans, Lê's project critiques efforts by nations like Vietnam to subjugate their own political history and trauma in order to brand their own form of 'exoticism', myth or local appeal for the sake of economic development.

The hybrid nature of the Lê and Diller and Scofidio posters allows for unsettling and repressed histories – and the accompanying emotions – to emerge; histories that in effect resist the closure promised to the foreign tourist. The posters also evoke the sentiment that, while globalization may lead to new cultural encounters and forms of hybridity, the existing economic and political imbalances determine that developing nations generally have to conform to the desires and lingua franca of Western capitalist societies.

Another way designers can repurpose their branding skills within a globalized marketplace is by collaborating with local communities to sustain their own brands as a means of countering the ill-effects of national or transnational corporate ones. For example, the Danish art and design collective Superflex began partnering, in 2003, with a group of farmers from Maués in the Brazilian Amazon to produce a soft drink called Guaranà Power. The farmers had organized themselves in response to a cartel formed by the multinational corporations Ambev and PepsiCo. The companies were using their monopoly purchase power to force the price paid to the farmers for guaranà seeds, which are rich in caffeine, down from US$25 per kilo to US$4, while simultaneously raising the price for consumers of their guaranà-based products. The sharp drop in price for guaranà crops ruined the livelihoods of the farmers and, by extension, the entire economy of Maués.

During a series of workshops with Superflex, the farmers' cooperative (COAIMA) conceived their own soft drink product, packaging and ad campaign slogan: 'Guaranà Power: For Energy and Empowerment' (Superflex 2004). The graphics they created for the bottle are a *trompe-l'oeil* of sorts with the bold black-and-white Guaranà Power label appearing as if it has been placed on top of the red-and-white oval logo for 'Antarctica', the popular guaranà drink produced by AmBev (which is sold in Europe by Pepsi as well) (Figure 5.4). The backdrop for this battle of brands on the label is a photograph depicting several members of the Maués community and a short text introducing COAIMA. The design of Guaranà Power thus literalizes Superflex's belief that global brands can be used as the 'raw material for a counter-economic position' as a 'new kind of intellectual property activism' (Chander 2004). In addition to earning a fair price for their guaranà seed, the farmers also benefit from The Power Foundation, a newly established organization funded with a percentage of the profit from Guaranà Power sales. Superflex and the farmers collectively decide how to use the funds to further develop the project.

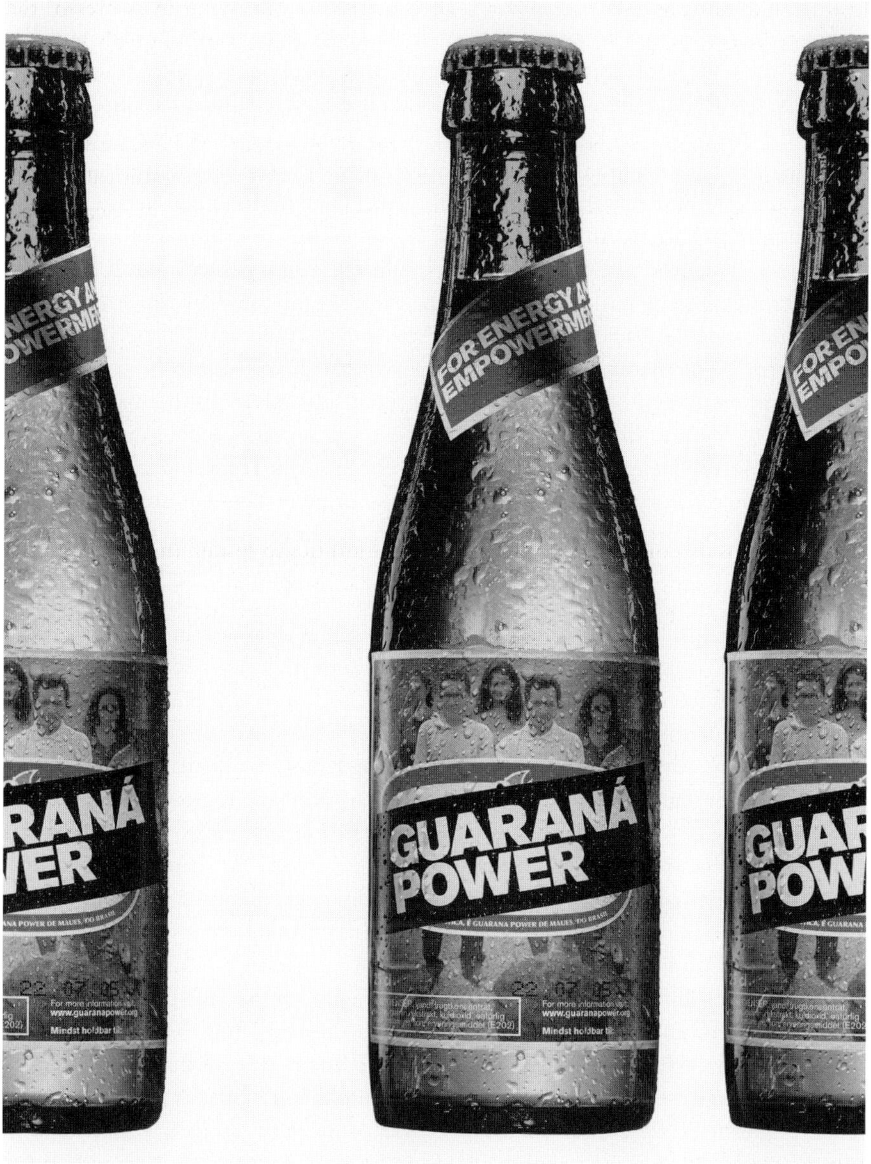

FIGURE 5.4 Maués Farmers and Superflex, Guaraná Power bottle design 2003 (photo: Jeppe Gudmundsen-Holmgreen).

The logo for Guaranà Power became a liability for the group as AmBev threatened legal action to protect its trademark. In response, Superflex and the farmers first undertook a strategy of self-censorship, slapping a band of black colour across their label, and then began to modify their design, eventually using the black censorship band as a background for the white Guaranà Power text. In addition to the legal matters around the logo, there also arose the issue of whether the historic and cultural use of the guaranà berry by the local Guarani tribe had been exploited by corporations such as AmBev. Guaranà Power is thus an example of a collective striving to retain the rights to control its cultural identity (DeMello 2005). The collaborative project has now gained the support of the state government of Amazonas as well as backing from Extra Arte in São Paulo and Vogue Brazil, and the farmers' collective is pursuing plans for worldwide distribution.

The importance of hybridity in the process of subjectivity in the making, or in responses to identity under the pressure of extinction, takes a different form in a series of case studies examined by historian Hazel Clark regarding contemporary design in the territory of Hong Kong. In a recent essay, she explores fashion and home furnishings production in Hong Kong, a city historically positioned as a site of exchange between Asia and the Occident (Clark 2009). The agreement to transfer Hong Kong's sovereignty to China in 1997 provoked a crisis of identity for the territory – what Ackbar Abbas has termed 'a culture of disappearance' (Clark 2009: 13). With the looming uncertainty about its future, the city needed a hybrid or 'hyphenated' subjectivity that could negotiate the future complexities of globalization, while acknowledging its mixed legacies of colonialism, nationalism and capitalism. The 'authentic inauthenticity of Hong Kong, its unsituated situatedness' – its state of constant becoming – in fact helped to define the region's unique design opportunity (Clark 2009: 27). The visual practices examined by Clark allow for such experimentation with hybridity, thus potentially giving shape and substance to a subjectivity that remains in formation. The designers discussed by Clark engage a wide range of strategies, some deliberately exploiting the codes of Orientalism, exoticism and nostalgia through self-parody and quotation.

Clark traces shifts within design that deliberately attempt to speak to multiple audiences from 'East' and 'West'. Beginning in the late 1960s, with attempts by designers such as Henry Steiner to create 'cross-cultural' designs that literally juxtaposed icons (or stereotypes) of Eastern and Western culture (Steiner and Haas 1995), Clark segues to more contemporary instances of hybridity in design that respond more complexly to the liminality of Hong Kong's transitional state and, more generally, to a globalized condition increasingly characterized as disjunctive, diasporic and deterritorialized. While Steiner claims to transform Eastern culture such that 'the influence has been assimilated and the once foreign becomes personal and natural,' Clark argues that his work 'did not result in hybridity': rather, his work resulted in a flat biculturalism, both cultures represented through well-worn tropes, where 'western forms and images equal global, and traditional and stereotyped signifiers equal local' (Clark 2009: 15). Hong Kong culture was thus relegated to stay in the realm of 'tradition' and 'China'.

In contrast, more recent design groups in Hong Kong, interested in expanding their markets in China as well as in the West, have employed a combination of retro-chic and nostalgia, 'tinged with contemporary cynicism and detachment' (Clark 2009: 19). While Steiner believed erroneously that cultures could be seamlessly reconciled and 'naturalized', the hybridity employed by these new companies is productively self-conscious, multivalent and temporally disjunctive. The brand image of Shanghai Tang, for example, draws upon a visual vocabulary from 1930s Shanghai – a 'nostalgic other' for Hong Kong – combined with references from the Maoist period, contemporary Chinese pop art, as well as the Qing dynasty (Clark 2009: 19–20). Their product line has included wristwatches depicting Mao and other Chinese cultural icons, and utilitarian Chinese clothing made unexpectedly in exuberant colours and expensive fabrics. The merchandise labels announce with obvious irony that the products were 'Made in Chinese'. Clark compares Shanghai Tang with other successful brands, such as G.O.D (Goods of Desire), an interior and lifestyle products company, which, rather than parodying traditional cultural forms, offers alternative approaches to designing for a hip Asian identity by making local and vernacular cultural forms and practices relevant to a larger global consumer context (Clark 2009: 22–25).

While financial success may be achieved through the production of certain kinds of visual 'hybridity', by customizing localized or vernacular forms to cross over into foreign markets, this kind of strategic branding will not necessarily undermine cultural stereotypes or lead to shifts in political and social hierarchies. Yet, when hybrid design practice emerges critically from spaces of postcoloniality – from within Bhabha's third space – it can work to destabilize notions of authenticity that necessarily privilege one culture's access to modernity over another's, and can allow multiple centres and peripheries the 'right' to signify in the ongoing negotiations and transformations of cultures. Clearly, in creating work within a global context, it is vital for designers to be aware of the immense gap of understanding that exists between the top-down exploitative practices of transnational corporations – whether in the stealth language of localization or the overtly exoticizing practice of eating the Other – and the potentially subversive strategies associated with hybridity.

Note

1 Parts of this essay were published in Fiss, K. (2006) 'Eating the other', *Print Magazine*, LX (I): 56–61.

References

Bhabha, H. K. (1994) *The Location of Culture*, New York: Routledge.

Chander, A. (2004) 'Illegal art? The artists' group Superflex co-opts global trademarks', FindLaw.com, 13 May. Available at: http://writ.news.findlaw.com/commentary/20040513_chander.html (accessed 5 August 2011).

Clark, H. (2009) 'Back to the future, or forward? Hong Kong design, image, and branding', *Design Issues*, 25(3): 11–29.

DeMello, I. (2005) 'Guarana: geographic indicator', *TED Case Studies*, 780. Available at: www1.american.edu/ted/guarana.htm (accessed 5 August 2011).

Diller, E. and Scofidio, R. (1997) 'Interclone' Available at: www.dsrny.com (accessed 8 August 2011).

Fiss, K. (2006) 'Eating the other', *Print Magazine*, LX (I): 56–61.

Guaranapower.org. (2003) 'Guaranà Power'. Available at: http://superflex.net/tools/guarana_power/search (accessed 5 August 2011).

hooks, b. (1992) 'Eating the other', *Black Looks*, Boston, MA: South End Press.

Lipton, R. (2002) *Designing Across Cultures*, New York: HOW Design Books.

McCoy, K. (1995) 'Graphic design in a multicultural world', *How Magazine*, April: 146–151.

McCoy, K. (2004) 'Hybridity happens', *Émigré*, 67: 38–47.

Mafundikwa, S. (2006) Personal communication (email, 26 March).

Maviyane-Davies, C. (1996) 'Creative Defiance: The graphic design of Chaz Maviyane-Davies'. Available at: www.maviyane.com (accessed 7 March 2011).

Nussbaum, B. (2010) 'Is humanitarian design the new imperialism?' Available at: www.fastcodesign.com/1661859/is-humanitarian-design-the-new-imperialism (accessed 11 July 2011).

Ortiz, L. (2011) *Imigrante*. Available at: http://lydiaortiz.net/Imigrante.html (accessed 11 July 2011).

Pilloton, E. (2010) 'Are humanitarian designers imperialists? Project H responds'. Available at: www.fastcodesign.com/1661885/are-humanitarian-designers-imperialists-project-h-responds (accessed 11 July 2011).

Schmidt, M. (2004) 'Concerns for education in today's typographic universe', in S. Heller (ed.) *The Education of the Typographer*, New York: Allworth Press.

Steiner, H. and Haas, K. (1995) *Cross-cultural Design: Communicating in the global marketplace*, London: Thames & Hudson.

Superflex (2004) Personal correspondence (email, October–November).

6

VALUES AND PRAGMATIC ACTION

The challenges of engagement with technical communities in support of value-conscious design[1]

Noëmi Manders-Huits and Michael Zimmer

Introduction

While concern over the moral and ethical consequences of our modern technological era has existed for some time (see, for example, Moor 1985; Johnson and Nissenbaum 1995; Friedman 1997; Shrader-Frechette and Westra 1997; Nissenbaum 2001), recent focus has been placed on how to develop pragmatic frameworks that ensure particular attention to moral and ethical values becomes an integral part of the conception, design and development of emerging information systems (Camp n.d.; Friedman 1999; Friedman *et al.* 2002b; Flanagan *et al.* 2005, 2008). Each of these frameworks – which we will refer to collectively as Values in Design (VID) – seek to broaden the criteria for judging the quality of technological systems to include the advancement of moral and human values, and to proactively influence the design of technologies to account for such values during the conception and design process.

We, the authors, have been involved in two separate attempts to engage with technical design communities in Values in Design. Unfortunately, the results were discouraging. Drawing from our interventions, this chapter will identify three key challenges of pragmatic engagement with technical design communities: (1) the justification of a value framework; (2) identifying the role of the values advocate; and (3) confronting competing values. Addressing these challenges must become a priority if one is to be successful in pragmatically engaging with real-world design contexts to support the value-conscious design of emerging information technologies. To help illuminate how these challenges might play out in real-world design scenarios, we will contextualize them in relation to a possible future application of Values in Design to address the privacy implications of web search engine query data retention.

The move towards Values in Design

In *Technopoly*, Neil Postman remarked how 'we are surrounded by the wondrous effects of machines and are encouraged to ignore the ideas embedded in them. Which means we become blind to the ideological meaning of our technologies' (Postman 1992: 94). It has been the goal of many humanists, social and philosophical scholars of technology to remove these blinders and critically explore the ideologies embedded in technical systems and artefacts (see, for example, Mumford 1964; Winner 1980; MacKenzie and Wajcman 1985; Latour 1992; Berg 1998). These scholars argue that technologies have social and political biases; they tend to promote certain ideologies, while obscuring others. The concern that technologies have ideologies has been extended into questions of how information technologies specifically have *ethical* and *value* biases (see, for example, Moor 1985; Johnson and Nissenbaum 1995; Shrader-Frechette and Westra 1997; Friedman 1997; Nissenbaum 2001; Tavani 2004; Mitcham 2005). Such scholarship sees information technologies as crucial sites for asserting not only social or political ideologies, but foremost human values of moral import, such as freedom from bias, trust, autonomy, privacy and justice. This research seeks to identify, understand and address the value-laden concerns that arise from the rapid design and deployment of information technologies into society.

Arising from these concerns, various technical design communities have attempted to incorporate values into the design stages of technological systems. For example, the Human–Computer Interaction community has maintained a strong commitment to user-centred design towards the goal of increased usability of technical artefacts (Norman 1990; Nielsen 1993; Raskin 2000). Similar scholarship has emerged from Participatory Design communities (Sclove 1995), where democratic design processes are used to create not only efficient and effective technologies, but also ones that maintain the safety and well-being of users. While commendable for their long-standing commitment to incorporating values into the design of technologies, these frameworks tend to focus their efforts on functional and instrumental values, such as user-friendliness and worker safety, falling short of directly addressing values of *moral* import, such as privacy or autonomy.[2] To fill this void, new pragmatic frameworks have recently emerged to ensure that particular attention to moral values becomes an integral part of the conception, design and development of technological artefacts and systems. These include Design for Values (Camp n.d.), Values at Play (Flanagan *et al.* 2005, 2008), and Value Sensitive Design (Friedman 1999; Friedman *et al.* 2002b). Each of these frameworks – which we will refer to collectively as 'Values In Design' – seek to broaden the criteria for judging the quality of technological systems to include the advancement of moral and human values, and to proactively influence the design of technologies to account for such values during the conception and design process.

Implementing Values in Design: successes and disappointments

The various collaborators who have developed the Values in Design frameworks have enjoyed success in designing technologies. For example, Batya Friedman, Edward Felten and their colleagues relied on the Value Sensitive Design methodology to develop web browser cookie management tools in support of the values of informed consent and user privacy (Friedman *et al.* 2002a). Similarly, L. Jean Camp and her colleagues engaged in Values in Design by embedding the value of trust in web browser tools to protect internet users from consumer fraud and identity theft (Camp 2006; Camp *et al.* n.d.). Mary Flanagan and her colleagues are actively employing VID principles with the RAPUNSEL project, a computer game environment designed for teaching middle-school girls programming skills to help counter gender inequity in maths and computer science while also embodying values such as cooperation, creativity, privacy and independence (Flanagan *et al.* 2005, 2008). And Helen Howe and Daniel Nissenbaum's (2006) TrackMeNot web browser extension was designed to help obfuscate one's web search history records to prevent profiling by search engine providers, fostering the values of privacy and user autonomy. These examples reveal the promise of influencing the design of new information and communication technologies in order to account for moral and human values. Encouraged by these successful implementations of VID frameworks, we, the authors, were optimistic as we attempted to engage pragmatically with the technical design communities of two emerging technological systems, hoping to influence their design in ethical and value-conscious ways.

Vehicle safety communication technologies

Recent advances in wireless technologies have led to the development of intelligent, in-vehicle safety applications designed to share information about the actions of nearby vehicles, potential road hazards, and ultimately predict dangerous scenarios or imminent collisions. These vehicle safety communication (VSC) technologies rely on the creation of autonomous, self-organizing, wireless communication networks connecting vehicles with roadside infrastructure and with each other. In these networks, both vehicles and infrastructure collect local data from their immediate surroundings, process this information and exchange it with other networked vehicles to provide real-time safety information.[3]

Coupled with the predicted safety benefits of VSC applications, however, is a potential rise in the ability to surveil a driver engaging in their everyday activities on the roads and highways. VSC technologies potentially enable the collection of information on where drivers go, when they made their trips and what routes they used. They represent a shift from drivers sharing only general and visually observable information to the widespread and constant broadcasting of precise, digital information about their daily activities. The potential integration of VSC technologies into our daily activities on the public roads threatens to foster a scenario where we might be 'driving into the panopticon' (Reiman 1995) of widespread surveillance, and the erosion of the values of privacy and autonomy as we drive along the roads.[4]

Since VSC technologies and their related technical protocols and communication standards were still in the developmental stage, Michael Zimmer, with support from the PORTIA project, attempted to apply a VID approach to influence the design of VSC technologies so that the value of privacy would become a constitutive part of the design process.[5] Zimmer interacted with VSC project managers and engineers, was given access to technical white papers, and distributed his findings regarding the potential privacy and surveillance threats of VSC technologies. Unfortunately, the results of his engagement with the VSC design community were discouraging. Zimmer's efforts were met with scepticism: some designers viewed the security gained through data encryption as a sufficient means of protecting user privacy, while others disregarded the threat to privacy altogether. Some potential privacy-protecting encryption solutions (see, for example, Boneh *et al.* 2004) were rejected, reportedly owing to concerns over efficiency and costs outweighing the privacy protections gained. Opportunities to engage further with the design community to address user privacy were hindered, as scheduled 'privacy workshops' were cancelled by working groups, while changing personnel and legal concerns stymied sustained collaboration with more sympathetic designers.

While some increased awareness of the privacy concerns of VSC technologies emerged as a result of Zimmer's efforts, full and direct engagement with this design community to achieve the value-conscious design of these emerging technologies remained limited.

User profiling infrastructures

Online organizations are increasingly collecting data on users' browsing and purchasing habits in order to create detailed user profiles, providing the tools to predict user behaviour and provide personalized products and services. For example, online bookstores track and collect information about users' browsing and purchase history on their sites, resulting in the creation of detailed user profiles that allow the site to provide personalized purchase recommendations. Alongside this growing reliance on user profiles is the desire to be able to build, share and transfer profiles across various systems and platforms – the creation of a widespread User Profiling Infrastructure. For example, the user profile created on the online bookstore could also be shared with a different organization, such as a movie rental company, to help predict what kind of movies the customer might want to watch. Similarly, a third party might be able to use a User Profiling Infrastructure to collect information on users' actions across various systems, such as a law enforcement agency monitoring purchasing habits across various websites in order to predict illegal activity.

While potentially useful, the cross-domain user profiling enabled by a User Profiling Infrastructure is fraught with value and ethical considerations, such as trust, informed consent, privacy and control over the flow of one's personal information. Recognizing the importance of addressing these value and ethical concerns, researchers from several Dutch universities and disciplines were invited to join the technical design team to help inform the development of such an architecture. Noëmi Manders-Huits was part of a team of academics specializing in ethics of information technology who participated in the project. Manders-Huits and her colleagues participated in design meetings and discussions, undertook research in relevant ethical literature, and identified critical points for intervention to ensure that the User Profiling Infrastructures under consideration protected user privacy and other ethical concerns.[6] Overall, there was a concerted effort to engage in the value-conscious design of this technology.

This effort turned out to be more challenging than expected. While the technical designers were confronted with the challenges of the novel research field of ethics and technology, the ethicists found it equally challenging to apply ethical principles to the novelty and uncertainty of a still-emerging technical infrastructure. It was especially difficult to properly explicate and translate ethical considerations to workable requirements and specifications for the other project participants actually building the system. In other words, it proved difficult to operationalize the values so they could be put into the technical design.

More discouraging, however, was the insertion of a new project management team who failed to share the commitment to Values in Design or an appreciation for the demands such efforts bring to the design process. When it came time to speed up the progress of the overall project, eliminating (what were perceived as) the complex and time-consuming ethical concerns seemed the easiest route to get the project back on schedule. As a result, the value and ethical considerations of these profiling architectures were set aside.

Summary of implementations

While some of the original framers of the Values in Design frameworks have enjoyed success in designing technologies that sustain moral and ethical values, the attempts by Zimmer and Manders-Huits were disappointing and failed to achieve the desired results. The key difference between the successful implementations by the original framers of VID and the less successful efforts by the authors is the site of engagement.

The successful applications of VID principles noted above share a common characteristic of being situated in the relatively non-hostile design environment of the academic laboratory. Each project's design team was, by and large, comprised entirely of academics committed to the goal of achieving Values in Design, creating a design context quite welcoming of each project's goals. For example, one should expect little resistance against designing technologies that support human values when the design team is housed in Washington University's aptly named 'Value

Sensitive Design Research Lab'. While the existence of such research centres is crucial for the continued development and refinement of VID methodologies, implementations that exist solely within their walls run the risk of being sheltered from the uncertainty of technical design projects and environments outside the walls of academia.

In contrast, Zimmer and Manders-Huits attempted to take the principles of Values in Design outside the laboratory and engage directly with designers of emerging technical systems in their native environments. Rather than benefiting from working within a sphere of designers already committed to designing for values, these imperfect engagements in real-world design contexts illuminate the challenges of moving VID from the academic lab to the industrial planning room.

Key Challenges of Values in Design

Our unsatisfactory attempts to engage in Values in Design illuminate three key challenges that must be addressed before these pragmatic frameworks can be fully and successfully deployed in design contexts outside the academic laboratory: (1) the justification of a value framework; (2) identifying the role of a values advocate; and (3) confronting competing values. These three challenges are interrelated and not necessarily iterative, nor are they mutually exclusive, but we treat them as separate points for clarification and ease of discussion.

Web search query data retention

Web search engines, like most websites, maintain detailed server logs tracking activity on their properties (Google 2005; IAC Search & Media 2005; Yahoo! 2006). Google, for example, records the originating IP (Internet Provider) address, cookie ID, date and time, search terms, results clicked for each of the over one hundred million search requests processed daily (Google 2005). Logging this array of data enhances a search engine's ability to reconstruct a particular user's search activities. For example, by cross-referencing the IP address each request sent to the server along with the particular page being requested and other server log data, it is possible to find out which pages, and in which sequence, a particular IP address has visited. When asked, 'Given a list of search terms, can Google produce a list of people who searched for that term, identified by IP address and/or Google cookie value?' and 'Given an IP address or Google cookie value, can Google produce a list of the terms searched by the user of that IP address or cookie value?', Google responded in the affirmative to both questions, confirming its ability to track a particular user's (or, at least, a particular browser or IP address) activity through such logs (Battelle 2006a, 2006b).

The motivation behind retaining search query data is frequently justified in terms of improving search engine products and, by extension, user satisfaction. Google, for example, states, 'We use this information to improve the quality of our services and for other business purposes' (Google 2005), while the search engine Ask.com explains, 'We collect . . . anonymous information to improve the overall quality of the online experience, including product monitoring, product improvement, targeted advertising, and monetizing commercially oriented search keywords' (IAC Search & Media 2005). Such explanations describe the ongoing quest for the 'perfect search engine', one that would deliver personalized results based on a user's past searches and general browsing history (Pitkow *et al.* 2002; Teevan *et al.* 2005), and deliver advertisements that are deemed useful or desirable for that particular user (Hansell 2005). Given a search for the phrase 'Paris Hilton' for example, the previous query data retained by a search engine can help it determine whether to deliver results about the blonde heiress or a place to spend the night in the French capital, and whether to provide advertisements for celebrity gossip sites or Parisian bistros.

Despite these argued benefits, the practice of collecting and retaining search query data has not escaped controversy. Recent cases of the US Department of Justice requesting search logs from the major search providers (Hafner and Richtel 2006; Mintz 2006) and the release of user search histories by AOL without sufficient anonymization (Hansell 2006) have brought search query retention practices into a more public light, creating anxiety among many searchers about the presence of such systematic monitoring of their online information-seeking activities (Barbaro and Zeller Jr 2006; Hansell 2006; McCullagh 2006), and leading news organizations to investigate and report on the information search engines routinely collect from their users (Glasner 2005; Ackerman 2006). In turn, various advocacy groups have criticized the extent to which web search engines are able to track and collect search queries, often with little knowledge by the users themselves (see, for example, Electronic Frontier Foundation 2007; Privacy International 2007), while both European and US government regulators have started to investigate search engine query retention practices and policies (Associated Press 2007; Lohr 2007).

In summary, while search engine providers claim users will benefit from the personalization of services retaining query data enables, privacy advocates worry about the potential harms of having users' online information-seeking activities routinely recorded and aggregated. Thus, we are faced with a kind of Faustian bargain: while personalized search services might be beneficial to users, they come with particular moral implications. Web search query retention, then, is an ideal site for pragmatic engagement using a VID approach. By engaging in VID, we can work towards the design of web search engines that meet the needs of all stakeholders: provide personalized results for users who desire them and allow search engine providers to sell targeted advertising, while protecting user privacy. Outlining specific design principles to accomplish this is beyond the scope of this chapter, but by envisioning a hypothetical intervention with the search engine industry, we can provide a more concrete description of the pragmatic challenges that emerge in such interventions.

In the remainder of this chapter, we will discuss three pragmatic challenges for implementing moral values in design: (1) the justification of a value framework;

(2) identifying the need for a values advocate; and (3) confronting competing values.[7] These descriptions will be augmented by a rendering of how each challenge might materialize in a hypothetical engagement with search engine designers to address the problem of search query data retention. Illuminating how these challenges might play out in a future real-world design scenario will help guide us to not only a richer understanding of each challenge, but also possible paths to their resolution.

Justification of a value framework

It is important to identify whose value framework we are considering in each particular design setting. The challenge is to identify the extent or limits of the design community: is it composed only of the actual technology designers, for example, the engineers, or does it include contractors, managers, companies, potential customers? In other words, *whose* moral framework are we to study? After the identification of the design community and their values – as far as these are tangible – an important step can be taken with respect to value choices in the design process.

According to us, the aim of a particular VID project needs to be framed in terms of a desirable or preferred normative stance. This is how a technology becomes *conscious* of values. An organic, emergent, moral framework might be favoured to justify the value choices to be encountered, or a particular (pre-)determined moral framework associated with a specific normative outlook. Either way, the starting point for the moral evaluation of a technology needs to be made explicit so that the value commitments of the technology are clear. By implication, the structure of the actual design process of this technology can be attuned to several points of intervention where value choices are made.

Friedman and her collaborators (Friedman *et al.* 2002b) argue, with respect to universal and particular values, that a value-sensitive design should be flexible with respect to local values. The RAPUNSEL project (Flanagan *et al.* 2005) provides a practical illustration: in this computer gaming design, players are tempted to take on part of the design of the game by choosing any particular set of preferences before entering into the game. A potential participant finds herself forced to choose between certain physical attributes, gender, race, etc. before entering the game. Users may not be comfortable with regard to any of these predesigned categories; the designers allow significant flexibility to add nuances to the character. This flexible design feature, however, is easily provided from the safe settings of the academic gaming environment and we wonder if this flexibility is equally manageable outside of these settings. For example, economic interests might constrain the number of options made available in a commercial gaming environment, and any such limitations present artificially simplify the complexity of moral life.

In the case of search query data retention, the design of typical search engine interfaces prioritize simplicity and usability, featuring only a text box for entering keywords, and a search button to initiate the search. Users are, for example, not presented with options to determine if they want the search logged by the provider in order to help personalize future results or advertising. Perhaps some of them would choose to forego those benefits to protect their privacy, while others would not. However, current search engine design does not allow for this decision at the user level, predetermining the ability (or inability) for users to make their own value-driven choices.

The justification of value choices during design demands elucidation of the moral framework being used with respect to values such as freedom from bias, autonomy, privacy and equity. Moreover, it calls for a different way of doing ethics. Where traditionally ethics is a field where past events are discussed and evaluated in order to develop a comprehensive account of all moral phenomena, what is required for a successful implementation of moral theory and values into design is the 'frontloading of ethics' (Van den Hoven 2005), also referred to as the changing of a retroactive to a proactive application of ethics. This is a challenging enterprise. Since technology design cases are fundamentally uncertain and with complex future outcomes, providing an operationable account for ethically evaluating and guiding value choices is difficult. It calls for the (re-)consideration of traditional ethical accounts in the light of the complexity of technological design. This, however, goes beyond the scope of this chapter. More practically, a first step in the 'frontloading of ethics' is establishing the role of a values advocate on technical design teams. However, as the next section will detail, this is often a complicated and contentious task.

Role of the values advocate

The various methodologies for implementing moral values in design suggest that design teams are to be complemented with scientists from disciplines other than engineering, from social sciences or humanities, for example, with the purpose of attending to the value commitments of the designers as well as the design at stake. While, as suggested above, the design teams within research centres dedicated to Values in Design typically include such scholars by default, realizing this goal in real-world design contexts remains a challenge. When approaching a technical design team outside the laboratory, it remains unclear who exactly is envisaged for assuming the role of the 'values advocate', and how one would formulate the criteria for this individual. Choosing either a social scientist or a philosopher to complement the design team may lead to different outcomes; where social scientists have stronger training in empirical research and would therefore be better suited for keeping the empirical ball in play, philosophers and ethicists are generally better trained in analytical skills and may therefore be inclined to pay more intention to the conceptual ball, for example, the clarification and normative determination of values.

The ideal scenario would be to have both types of advocates on the design team, but real-world practicalities often make this difficult. It would not be unusual for designers and engineers to be wary, if not openly hostile, to having someone whose purpose is to advocate for human values thrust on to their design teams. Attempting to add *two* such outsiders could likely spark more than double the resistance. Much, of course, depends on the particular design context the values advocate is trying to enter. With web search engines, there is hope that their origins in academia might make them more amenable to accepting multiple social scientists or ethicists among their ranks.[8]

A further consideration is the extent to which the values advocate must possess relevant engineering knowledge and expertise with regard to the aims and practical possibilities of the technology under consideration. The successful operationalization of values within a particular design context requires specific knowledge of a technology's design scope and limitations. Possessing the relevant technical expertise is also often necessary for acceptance as a member of a technical design team outside the walls of the academic laboratory. However, economic constraints of real-world design contexts might preclude the possibility of 'on-the-job' training for the values advocate, leaving a significant challenge for social scientists or philosophers in the role of the values advocate to obtain the requisite technical knowledge prior to engagement with the design community. Gaining the necessary technical expertise in order to engage with web search engine designers is particularly difficult given that little is known of exactly how search algorithms and related processes operate. While some of the foundational academic research is published (see, for example, Brin and Page 1998; Page *et al.* 1998), more recent glimpses into the inner workings of search engines are rarely provided, limiting the ability for outside advocates to gain in-depth technical proficiency.[9]

If these challenges can be overcome, we envision an array of roles that the values advocate can take within a particular design context: the authoritarian role, the supporting role and the leadership role.[10] In the first role, the values advocate is regarded as authoritative in the ethical and value considerations at hand, implementing value-conscious decisions using a top-down strategy. Such a role is often confrontational, where pressure is exerted (both internally and externally) to ensure proper attention to values. In addition, in this scenario (attention to) values is warranted solely by the expertise of the acquired values advocate; this seems a heavy responsibility. A second role, the supporting role, is a fairly passive accompaniment of the design process, raising awareness at moments where value choices are being made and pointing to possible alternatives without advocating one or the other. An advocate in this role is often merely advisory and might have little more than token input on design decisions. Finally, the leadership role enables the values advocate to be both supporting but also directing when it comes to value choices. By providing insight to the complexity and delicacy of value choices basing on theoretical knowledge as well as acquired practical expertise, the values advocate in their role as leader is able to educate the other members of the design team (and possibly other stakeholders) and to strongly promote certain choices over others where necessary. We argue the leadership role to be the preferred positioning of the values advocate within a design team, taking into account shared responsibility for value choices (whereas the first example of an authoritative role might be too heavy-handed) and a proactive stance of the values advocate (whereas the example of a supporting role might be too passive).

Recent efforts by advocacy groups concerned about web search privacy help illustrate the strengths and weaknesses of these various roles. Privacy International, for example, took an authoritarian approach with its report 'A Race to the Bottom' (2007), strongly criticizing the privacy practices of major internet companies, especially Google.[11] Alternatively, the Center for Democracy and Technology (CDT) (2007) recently issued a report detailing how the largest internet search companies have begun to aggressively compete with one another to offer stronger privacy protections to their customers. This study was written off, however, by those who criticized the CDT for being financially supported by some of the very search engines in the report (Singel 2007). CDT's supporting role with the search engine companies essentially diluted the effectiveness of their advocacy. We argue that a middle-ground between these two approaches would place value advocates in a strong leadership role to work with web search engine providers. From a strong leadership position, the values advocate would be empowered, for example, to take the initiative to convene the leading search engine companies in a non-hostile environment to discuss and decide how to move forward to design future web search products in value-conscious ways.

In any of the three possible roles, it is the challenge for the values advocate to support all value choices with the necessary normative justification. The acceptance of a values advocate in the design team as holder of particular expertise is dependent on the perception that the value choices and positions held by the advocate are rationally and theoretically justified. We think any choice in the design process might potentially have moral import. It is the task of the values advocate to make these as explicit as possible. In some cases the values advocate may also need to justify their own presence in the design team, and why designers, or anyone for that matter, should be concerned with values of moral import in the first place.

Confronting competing values

Perhaps the most apparent challenge of applying Values in Design principles outside the academic laboratory is the inevitability of confronting competing values within varied design contexts. Rather than benefiting from working within the academic sphere committed to the primacy of designing for moral values, design contexts outside academia often include stakeholders whose goals might come into conflict with the protection of these values. [12]

For example, Howe and Nissenbaum's TrackMeNot web browser extension was developed using Mozilla's open-source browser application framework and posted to a website for download by the user and development community. As an academic project, little concern was necessary for production or distribution costs, advertising, profits or other factors typically in play in commercial software development contexts. In contrast, the attempts at pragmatic engagement in design contexts outside academia by Zimmer and Manders-Huits exposed how the pressures of the marketplace – with its focus on instrumental values of efficiency, productivity and profitability – might result in hostility to the privileging of moral values in the design process. As Philip Agre and Christine Harbs warn, standard-setting processes often 'embed a wide variety of political agendas' and the process of developing those standards will be 'contested along a variety of fronts by various parties' (Agre and Harbs 1994: 84). The same can be said for technical design overall; engaging in Values in Design within real-world design contexts will require the ability to negotiate such instances of conflicting values.

We claim that, for a fully engaged and pragmatic application of Values in Design to be successful, it must ensure that values are not only discovered and clarified, but also consciously and deliberately built into design, even if such embedding of values conflicts with other design objectives.[13] This questions the supremacy of some values over others (hierarchy of values) and the way value choices in design are dealt with in the light of supporting value systems or political and ethical views. While some embrace a more cultural constructivist approach, where values are taken as perceived by the majority of the people, we take a more normative position. Here, ethics provides grounds for identifying values and arguing for the enclosure or the supremacy of certain values over others, possibly against the (uncritical) majority opinion. We argue that, for morality to be designed into technical systems and institutions, value choices should be based on well-considered ethical judgements, coherent with our attitude towards how we think the world is best served and structured from a moral perspective. This involves a critical attitude towards certain aims of research and design that are often taken for granted, such as maximum efficiency, maximum profitability, and so on.

When dealing with a commercially operated web search engine, for example, profitability and shareholder value will often come into conflict with attempts to design to support moral values. Specific to the collection of search query data, the search providers claim that they need such information to make their systems more efficient, and also to improve the usability and relevance of their results. The pursuit of these values come into direct conflict of ensuring user privacy, or a user's ability to search and use information free from surveillance or oversight. Applying ethical theory to overcome this value conflict provides different views. From a deontological perspective, for instance, we can hold companies such as Google to their pledge – 'Don't be evil' – and build the case that they have a moral obligation to protect user privacy to its fullest extent. However, there is also the option of a more consequentialist attempt to resolve this value conflict, where Google frequently argues that users will benefit from the personalization of results and advertising, and any potential privacy threats are, on the whole, outweighed by these benefits.

This illustrates the complexity inherent in value conflicts and the variety of arguments that can be crafted to try to resolve them to benefit one position over another. Our challenge, then, is to craft a strategy for pragmatic engagement to push their resolution in favour of value-conscious design of search engines to protect user privacy. We need to work towards confirming the first proposition (that search engines have a moral obligation to protect user privacy), while also confronting the second proposition (that users will not necessarily benefit from personalization, and any benefits do not automatically outweigh the potential harms).

Conclusion

We have identified three key challenges that must be addressed if scholars committed to Values in Design are to be successful in pragmatically engaging within technical design communities in support of the advancement of human and moral values. First, we confront the broad philosophical challenge of providing sufficient justification of the value and moral framework we embrace when engaging in VID. Second, the role of the values advocate must be both clearly defined and justified to fulfil its role as an essential component of technical design teams. Finally, we must find strategies to successfully resolve the inevitable value conflicts when engaging with design communities outside of academia. By viewing these challenges in the context of web search query retention, we have brought to light some of the unique problems that emerge when engaging with real-world technical design communities.

Our goal with this chapter is not to discredit the accomplishments of the existing Values in Design efforts, but merely to show that pragmatic challenges remain. Moreover, like many academic probes, this chapter presents more questions than answers. By bringing focus to these challenges, however, we hope to spark new critical reflection within the Values in Design community (among which we include ourselves) of how to best engage with real-world design communities to proactively influence the design of emerging technologies to take account of ethical and human values and help refine the Values in Design methodologies to increase the chances for success of future pragmatic engagements with design communities.

Notes

1 Portions of this chapter appeared in Manders-Huits and Zimmer (2009), 'Values and pragmatic action: the challenges of introducing ethical intelligence in technical design communities, *International Review of Information Ethics*, 10: 37–44.
2 This is not to say that attention to functional values cannot have a moral or ethical impact. For example, building a user-friendly technology might increase a user's sense of autonomy. The distinction we are making here is a matter of focus: whether attention to moral and ethical values is the primary goal of the design process, or simply a by-product.
3 For more information, see US Department of Transportation, and Vehicle Safety Communications Consortium.
4 For more information, see Zimmer (2005).
5 The PORTIA project is a five-year, multi-institutional, multidisciplinary, multi-modal investigation funded by the National Science Foundation in the Information Technology Research (ITR) program. For more information, see http://crypto.stanford.edu/portia.
6 For more information, see https://doc.telin.nl/dscgi/ds.py/Get/File-52040/TUD_sotas.pdf.
7 See also Manders-Huits and Zimmer (2009); Manders-Huits (2010).
8 Many of the first web search engines, including Google and Yahoo!, originated as research projects at university computer or information science departments.
9 A recent *New York Times* article was notable for its supposed 'inside access' to Google's inner workings, but ultimately provided few details (Hansell 2007).
10 These roles are by no means exhaustive or mutually exclusive, but they are three archetypes that are useful for conceptualizing the varied role of the values advocate.

11 Industry experts criticized the aggressive stance of the report as poorly researched, non-comprehensive and biased (Sullivan 2007).

12 To their credit, Flanagan and her colleagues make it clear in their discussion of the RAPUNSEL project that such projects, when pursued purely within academic contexts, fail to 'address all factors that, for example, a commercial project would be obliged to address' (Flanagan *et al.* 2008). Of course, Camp, Friedman, Flanagan and their collaborators likely acknowledge the privileged position of designing their products in the relatively non-hostile environment of the academic laboratory. Our intent is not to discredit their accomplishments, but merely to show that attention must be paid to the value conflicts that inevitably occur when engaged in value-conscious design in traditional design contexts.

13 This is why we prefer to speak of value-conscious design as a normative interpretation of the VID framework. See also Manders-Huits and Zimmer (2009); Manders-Huits (2010).

References

Ackerman, E. (2006) 'What do Google, Yahoo, AOL and Microsoft's MSN know about you?', *San Jose Mercury News*, 19 August.

Agre, P. and Harbs, C. (1994) 'Social choice about privacy: intelligent vehicle-highway systems in the United States', *Information Technology and People*, 7(4): 63–90.

Associated Press (2007) 'EU data privacy officers launch investigation into Google's internet search engine', *International Herald Tribune*. Available at: http://www.privacydigest.com/2007/05/25/eu%20data%20privacy%20officers%20launch%20investigation%20googles%20internet%20search%20engine%20internationa (accessed 16 January 2012).

Barbaro, M. and Zeller Jr, T. (2006) 'A face is exposed for AOL searcher No. 4417749', *The New York Times*, 9 August: A1.

Battelle, J. (2006a) 'More on what Google (and probably a lot of others) know', Searchblog. Available at: http://battellemedia.com/archives/002283.php (accessed 16 May 2006).

Battelle, J. (2006b) 'What info does Google keep?', Searchblog. Available at: http://battellemedia.com/archives/002272.php (accessed 16 May 2006).

Berg, M. (1998) 'The politics of technology: on bringing social theory into technological design', *Science, Technology, and Human Values*, 23(4): 456–490.

Boneh, D., Boyen, X. and Shacham, H. (2004) 'Short group signatures', *Proceedings of Crypto*, 4: 41–55.

Brin, S. and Page, L. (1998) 'The anatomy of a large-scale hypertextual web search engine', *WWW7/Computer Networks*, 30(1–7): 107–117.

Camp, L. J. (2006) *Reliable, Usable Signaling to Defeat Masquerade Attacks*. Available at: www.ljean.com/files/NetTrustEcon.pdf (accessed 23 September 2006).

Camp, L. J. (n.d.) *Design for Values, Design for Trust*. Available at: www.ljean.com/design.html (accessed 20 September 2006).

Camp, L. J., Friedman, A. and Genkina, A. (n.d.) *Embedding Trust via Social Context in Virtual Spaces*. Available at: www.ljean.com/files/NetTrust.pdf (accessed 23 September 2006).

Center for Democracy and Technology (CDT) (2007) *Search Privacy Practices: a work in progress*. Available at: www.cdt.org/privacy/20070808searchprivacy.pdf (accessed 8 August 2007).

Colmina, B. (1996) 'Battle lines: E 1027', in Hughes, F. (ed.) *The Architect Reconstructing her Practice*, Cambridge, MA: MIT Press.

Cook, J. (1991) 'Global indigenous architecture', in Kodama, Y., Smart, J. and Yannas, S. (eds) *Passive and Low Energy Architecture*, Tokyo: Process Architecture Publishing.

Electronic Frontier Foundation (2007) *Privacy and Search Engines*. Available at: www.eff.org/Privacy/search/ (accessed 28 July 2007).

Ferguson, J. (1975) *Utopias of the Classical World*, London: Thames & Hudson.

Flanagan, M., Howe, D. and Nissenbaum, H. (2005) 'Values at play: design tradeoffs in socially-oriented game design', *Proceedings of the Conference on Human Factors in Computing Systems*.

Flanagan, M., Howe, D. and Nissenbaum, H. (2008) 'Values in design: theory and practice', in J. van den Hoven and J. Weckert (eds) *Information Technology and Moral Philosophy*, New York: Cambridge University Press.

Friedman, B. (1997) *Human Values and the Design of Computer Technology* (CSLI lecture notes no. 72). New York: Cambridge University Press.

Friedman, B. (1999) 'Value-sensitive design: a research agenda for information technology', *National Science Foundation (Contract No: SBR-9729633)*.

Friedman, B., Howe, D. and Felten, E. (2002a) 'Informed consent in the Mozilla browser: implementing value-sensitive design', *Proceedings of the 35th Annual Hawaii International Conference on System Sciences*.

Friedman, B., Kahn, P. and Borning, A. (2002b) 'Value sensitive design: theory and methods', *(Technical Report 02–12–01)*.

Glasner, J. (2005) 'What search sites know about you', *Wired News*. Available at: www.wired.com/news/privacy/0,1848,67062,00.html (accessed 2 August 2006).

Google (2005) *Google Privacy Policy*. Available at: www.google.com/privacypolicy.html (accessed 3 May 2006).

Hafner, K. and Richtel, M. (2006) 'Google resists U.S. subpoena of search data', *The New York Times*, 20 January: A1, C4.

Hansell, S. (2005) 'Microsoft plans to sell search ads of its own', *The New York Times*, 26 September: C1, C8.

Hansell, S. (2006) 'AOL removes search data on vast group of web users', *The New York Times*, 8 August: C4.

Hansell, S. (2007) 'Google keeps tweaking its search engine', *The New York Times*. Available at: www.nytimes.com/2007/06/03/business/yourmoney/03google.html (accessed 28 July 2007).

Howe, D. and Nissenbaum, H. (2006) 'TrackMeNot'. Available at: http://mrl.nyu.edu/~dhowe/TrackMeNot (accessed 27 August 2006).

IAC Search & Media (2005) *Ask.com Privacy Policy*. Available at: http://sp.ask.com/en/docs/about/privacy.shtml (accessed 6 January 2007).

Johnson, D. and Nissenbaum, H. (eds) (1995) *Computers, Ethics and Social Values*, Englewood Cliffs, NJ: Prentice Hall.

Latour, B. (1992) 'Where are the missing masses? The sociology of a few mundane artifacts', in W. Bijker and J. Law (eds) *Shaping Technology/Building Society: Studies in sociotechnical change*, Cambridge, MA: MIT Press.

Lohr, S. (2007) 'Google deal said to bring US scrutiny', *The New York Times*. Available at: www.nytimes.com/2007/05/29/technology/29antitrust.html (accessed 27 July 2007).

McCullagh, D. (2006) 'AOL's disturbing glimpse into users' lives', CNET News.com. Available at: http://news.cnet.com/AOLs-disturbing-glimpse-into-users-lives/2100-1030_3-6103098.html?tag=st.num (accessed 3 December 2006).

MacKenzie, D. A. and Wajcman, J. (eds) (1985) *The Social Shaping of Technology: How the refrigerator got its hum*, Philadelphia, PA: Open University Press.

Manders-Huits, N. (2010) 'What values in design?', *Journal of Science and Engineering Ethics*, 17(2): 271–287.

Manders-Huits, N. and Zimmer, M. (2009) 'Values and pragmatic action: the challenges of introducing ethical intelligence in technical design communities', *International Review of Information Ethics*, 10: 37–44.

Mintz, H. (2006) 'Feds after Google data: records sought in US quest to revive porn law', *San Jose Mercury News*. Available at: http://seclists.org/funsec/2006/q1/1021 (accessed 19 January 2006).

Mitcham, C. (ed.) (2005) *Encyclopedia of Science, Technology, and Ethics*, Detroit, MI: Macmillan Reference.

Moor, J. (1985) 'What is computer ethics?' *Metaphilosophy*, 16: 266–275.

Mumford, L. (1964) 'Authoritarian and democratic technics', *Technology and Culture*, 5(1): 1–8.

Nielsen, J. (1993) *Usability Engineering*, Boston, MA: Academic Press.

Nissenbaum, H. (2001) 'How computer systems embody values', *IEEE Computer*, 34(3): 118–120.

Norman, D. A. (1990) *The Design of Everyday Things*, New York: Doubleday.

Page, L., Brin, S., Motwani, R. and Winograd, T. (1998) *The Pagerank Citation Ranking: Bringing order to the web*. Available at: http://ilpubs.stanford.edu:8090/422/ (accessed 12 January 2007)

Pitkow, J., Schütze, H., Cass, T., Turnbull, D., Edmonds, A. and Adar, E. (2002) 'Personalized search', *Communications of the ACM*, 45(9): 50–55.

Postman, N. (1992) *Technopoly: The surrender of culture to technology*, New York: Vintage Books.

Privacy International (2007) *A Race to the Bottom: Privacy ranking of internet service companies*. Available at: https://www.privacyinternational.org/article/race-bottom-privacy-ranking-internet-service-companies (accessed 10 July 2007).

Raskin, J. (2000) *The Humane Interface: New directions for designing interactive systems*, Reading, MA: Addison-Wesley.

Reiman, J. (1995) 'Driving to the panopticon: a philosophical exploration of the risks to privacy posed by the highway technology of the future', *Santa Clara Computer and High Technology Law Journal*, 11(1): 27–44.

Sclove, R. (1995) *Democracy and Technology*, New York: Guilford Press.

Shrader-Frechette, K. and Westra, L. (eds) (1997) *Technology and Values*, Lanham, MD: Rowman & Littlefield.

Singel, R. (2007) 'Industry-funded group and a compliant Threat Level working to derail Google-doubleclick probe, privacy group charges', Threat Level. Available at: http://blog.wired.com/27bstroke6/2007/08/industry-funded.html (accessed 10 August 2007).

Sullivan, D. (2007) 'Google bad on privacy? Maybe it's Privacy International's report that sucks', Search Engine Land. Available at: http://searchengineland.com/google-bad-on-privacy-maybe-its-privacy-internationals-report-that-sucks-11428 (accessed 29 July 2007).

Tavani, H. T. (2004) *Ethics and Technology: Ethical issues in an age of information and communication technology*, Hoboken, NJ: Wiley.

Teevan, J., Dumais, S. T. and Horvitz, E. (2005) 'Personalizing search via automated analysis of interests and activities', *Proceedings of the 28th Annual International ACM SIGIRCconference on Research and Development in Information Retrieval*: 449–456.

Van den Hoven, M. J. (2005) 'Design for values and values for design', *Information Age, August/September*: 4–7.

Winner, L. (1980) 'Do artifacts have politics', *Daedalus*, 109(1): 121–136.

Yahoo! (2006) *Yahoo! Privacy Policy*. Available at: http://info.yahoo.com/privacy/us/yahoo/details.html (accessed 6 January 2007).

Zimmer, M. (2005) 'Surveillance, privacy and the ethics of vehicle safety communication technologies', in *Ethics and Information Technology*, 7(4): 201–210.

7

DESIGNING WELL

Sustain-able Interaction Design and vegetarianism

Gavin Sade

Introduction

> The question is no longer one of knowing if it is 'good' to eat the other or if the other is 'good' to eat, nor knowing which other. One eats him regardless and lets oneself be eaten by him . . . The moral question is thus not, nor has it ever been: should one eat or not eat, eat this or not that . . . man or animal, but since *one must* eat in any case and since it is and tastes good to eat, and since there is no definition of the good [*du bien*], *how* for goodness' sake should one *eat well?* And what does this imply? What is eating?
>
> (Derrida and Nancy 1991: 114)

From abattoirs to our homes, information and communications technologies (ICT) have become pervasive with microprocessors, televisual displays, and communications networks penetrating almost every aspect of our life world. This world of ubiquitous computing did not occur by accident. Instead, it is the result of large-scale designing that has been the focus of researchers and designers for at least the last three to four decades. The mission statement of the *MIT Oxygen Project* captures the logics of this design focus as bringing 'abundant computation and communication, as pervasive and free as air, naturally into people's lives' (MIT 2004). As a result, a design field has emerged that directly focuses on 'designing interaction with (and habitation within) computer-based systems' (Winograd 1997). This field has become known as Interaction Design. More recent definitions of Interaction Design have shifted from considering design in the context of computer-based systems to designing information and communications technology into the 'ambient social complexities of the physical world' (McCullough 2004).

The phenomenological characteristic of technologies to recede into the background, combined with a design agenda to create transparent technologies, underpins Interaction Design. This not only conceals a ground of unsustainable technologies and practices, but also changes the way we encounter the Other. This ground is rarely questioned as ubiquitous technologies become 'as pervasive and free as air' and readily considered as constituting aspects of our thinking and being. However, the trajectory of this design agenda is far from natural and has not been without its critics. Genevieve Bell and Paul Dourish (2007) have argued that the ubiquitous computing future Marc Weiser (1991, 1993, 1994) envisaged has arrived, but that it is very different from his original visions. They suggest that the original view of seamless interoperability and homogeneity is in reality a messy lashing together of technologies, which designers attempt to render invisible in use, and by doing so, turn it into an assumed natural part of our everyday lives that goes unquestioned in use. Agustin Araya critiques the future vision of ubiquitous computing, arguing that the ubiquitous computing agenda is 'an attempt to obliterate the otherness of certain aspects of the world in such a way that we are no longer aware of the obliteration' (Araya 1995: 235). Langdon Winner reminds us that artefacts, technologies and our designs have political and ethical dimensions and that we are 'willing to make drastic changes in the way [we] live to accommodate technological innovation yet [we] resist similar kinds of changes justified on political grounds' (Winner 1986). Such critiques unsettle the certainty of claims 'that pervasive computing naturally lends itself to many of environmental sustainability's core challenges' (Woodruff and Mankoff 2009).

In order to investigate these differing claims regarding ubiquitous computing, and to address what Tony Fry (1999) describes as steady-state models of sustainability – which do little more than sustain the status quo of unsustainable modes of dwelling – I will take a somewhat unconventional step: to consider Interaction Design through the lens of vegetarianism. Before we begin it is important, I think, to declare that I am a vegetarian. However, my choice of a vegetarian analogy is not an attempt at conversion. This chapter is not an argument for the benefits of a vegetarian diet, and does not present an ethical case for vegetarianism. Instead, vegetarianism is a powerful analogy for rethinking design and consumption, particularly when our being is fundamentally linked to the killing and eating of animals. This process of thinking about eating provides an analogy for thinking about design and sustainability, and an appreciation for the types of changes that need to be made in order to secure our future. The need to create awareness and shift thinking has recently emerged as a concern within the field of Interaction Design. An example of this is the interest in designing home electricity usage meters – smart meters – that promote awareness of energy consumption and environmental impacts. A selection of home electricity meter designs will be reviewed through the vegetarian analogy before going on to consider the different approaches that researchers, artists and critical designers employ to address a similar problem.

From sustainability to sustain-able

Before we continue, it is important to develop an understanding of the term 'sustainability', and its re-formation as 'sustain hyphen ability'. Sustainability cannot be simplistically considered as a property of a product, building or design, as it is often presented. In the literature it is defined more broadly as addressing 'questions of how societies can shape their modes of change in such a way so as to ensure the preconditions of development for future generations' (Becker *et al.* 1999: 4). From this perspective, sustainability is an ongoing process: a concern and care for the quality of the relationships between society and the environment that support our continued life across time. It is this aspect of sustainability that Tony Fry (1999) sets out to reclaim when he adds a hyphen to the word, invoking the full meaning of both to *sustain* and *ability*. Such reframing of sustainability, as sustain-ability, is required to counter how the term has become misused within advertising and politics, and the way discourses of sustainability implicitly privilege existing economic models. This rhetoric is so pervasive that Fry suggests 'that many sustainable products are implicated in sustaining the unsustainable' (Fry 2003). Thus eating well, and designing well, demands a commitment to a continued process aimed at reshaping the relationship between consumption, designing and the environments that make our being possible.

While sustainability is commonly associated with the environmental movement and viewed as being primarily concerned with addressing current ecological crises – climate change, for example – its roots, Guattari suggests, 'can be traced to a more general crisis of the social, political and existential' (Guattari 1995: 119). As we are called to change our daily behaviour – for example, to reduce our carbon emissions or water use – sustain-ability and the ecological crisis become directly connected to our lifestyles. No longer is the problem something external to the self, but instead it is directly related to our way of living and hence our worldviews, morals, ethics and politics. So much so that Guattari refers to it as a crisis of subjectivity, and Fry (1999) cites our unavoidable anthropocentrism as part of the problem.

Considering the pervasive presence of the ecological crisis, it is no surprise to see that in the Interaction Design literature there has been a growing interest in sustainability – designing well. This 'burgeoning interest' (Nathan *et al.* 2008) is cited as stemming from 'a collective higher calling – an ethical responsibility to acknowledge, address, and improve our own health, the health of our environment, and promote more sustainable lifestyles' (Paulos *et al.* 2008). Yet despite this interest, Eli Blevis (2007) notes that sustainability has not yet become a central ideal of Interaction Design; it might be more meaningful to say that the field has yet to see sustain-ability as a central design ideal. To date, Interaction Design has typically approached sustainability as an instrumental design problem that can be addressed by applying existing methods. Many projects continue to operate within existing paradigms of Interaction Design, addressing the problem by designing new pervasive technological solutions. While many projects focus on raising awareness or changing behaviour, there is often a productivist underpinning – the projects result in new products or services that require new products for access. That said, there is an increasing interest in projects that involve 're-visioning consumption or enabling citizen science' (Goodman 2009), for example Natalie Jeremijenko's seminal 'Feral Robotic Dogs' (2005). Run as workshops and classes in an educational context, this project transforms existing toys – robot dogs – into a platform for 'sniffing out' toxic chemicals, which are then released on local industrial sites.

When we think about sustainability it can be difficult to really understand what is actually at stake. Is sustainability simply the latest design trend, the latest 'difference'? Why should Interaction Designers be concerned about sustain-ability? What is the price of inaction? What is the urgency? These are not easy questions to consider, especially from the air-conditioned comfort of our homes and offices in developed nations. In many instances the phenomena cited as indicators of unsustainable human activity are not experienced directly. Instead, this knowledge is presented by way of information and communication technology. So, despite the critiques of ICT, this same technology has been integral in allowing us to understand the dimensions of the ecological crisis. What we see by way of this technologically augmented vision is that human society is capable of large-scale transformations of our planet, and is capable of destroying whole environments, ecosystems and species, and even the human race. For example, Ransom Myers and Boris Worm (2003) reported that the 'global ocean has lost more than 90 per cent of large predatory fish', including the ones we like to eat and are still eating, such as tuna, marlin, cod and flounder. If we are capable of such profound destructive transformations, it follows that we are also capable of achieving the shift in thought and lifestyle required by sustain-able design.

On becoming, and being, a vegetarian

> Our understanding of animals these days, for example, is in part embodied in our skill in buying pieces of them, taking off their plastic wrapping, and cooking them in microwave ovens. In general we deal with things as resources to be used and then disposed of when no longer needed.
>
> (Dreyfus 1993: 295)

The central defining characteristic of vegetarianism is the conscious choice not to eat animals, or, if rephrased, the removal of one food source from a diet. The choice is made notwithstanding our omnivorous nature and in spite of the fact that animals are a socially acceptable source of food. Thus, from a design perspective, vegetarianism can be considered a redesigning of eating; it is an ethics that is posited in action, which problematizes eating and hence being. The problem is not that animals taste good, as I am continually informed, or that of agriculture, which can be equally unsustainable; it is an ethical dilemma that we face once we acknowledge that life on the planet has value irrespective of its value to us. On the one hand, there is the slaughter and butchery committed to sustain our existence, and on the other, a desire to avoid erasing the difference between humans and animals – especially the difference between killing an animal and murdering a human – for fear of the atrocities such a position leads to.

> This question is not 'Can they reason?', nor 'Can they talk?' but 'Can they suffer?'
>
> (Bentham 1789)

As a redesigning of eating, becoming vegetarian (or vegan or localvore) can be thought of as a redirective practice and can be considered as analogous to Fry's concept of elimination design (Fry 2009). The question of 'what can I eliminate' is both political and ethical, and inevitably involves value judgements (Fry 2009: 80). In the context of vegetarianism, there is a range of political and ethical values that lead one to eliminate animals from one's diet, including, but not limited to, concerns about the environment, about the treatment of animals, social justice, personal health and religious beliefs. The elimination of animals from a diet is not a 'be less bad' approach or some form of sacrifice in the name of sustain-ability. This view ignores the culinary diversity of, and the ethical rationale, for a vegetarian diet. In this context, vegetarianism can also be considered as analogous to Fry's (2009) second redirective practice – recoding – where the way one sees animals is transformed. From a vegetarian perspective, animals are recoded, as they are no longer called food. Irrespective of personal views on the statement that animals do not equal food, the thought necessarily requires the consideration of the ethics of eating as well as food production and consumption.

Becoming vegetarian transforms one's relationship with food as well as the act of eating. Every act of eating now involves a question regarding the ingredients and source of the food to be consumed. In order to sustain a vegetarian diet and remain healthy, a vegetarian needs to ensure their diet contains enough vitamin B12, essential amino acids, long-chain n3 fatty acids, iron and other minerals commonly obtained from meat: a task that is entirely possible, and which requires one to learn about non-meat food sources and their qualities. However, this change from a meat-centric diet to a vegetarian diet involves more than the substitution of meat; it involves learning how to cook a whole range of new vegetarian meals that are created from a vegetarian perspective. Like Peter Singer (1975), many vegetarians find interest in cooking only after they become vegetarian. As a vegetarian, I've been introduced to a range of foods that I would have never considered previously: a vegetarian lifestyle requires both a process of learning and discovery, a change in values and shift in the frame of reference.

The supermarket is full of foods that contain animal by-products, which requires a vegetarian to read the ingredient labels on processed food. For example, the production of many beers involves finings made from animals, likewise gelatine is found in many products. This not only makes becoming vegetarian fraught with possible compromises, as friends are more than willing to point out, but also raises a multitude of questions about food consumption and production. This process of learning may expose other related ethical choices, such as organically grown foods,

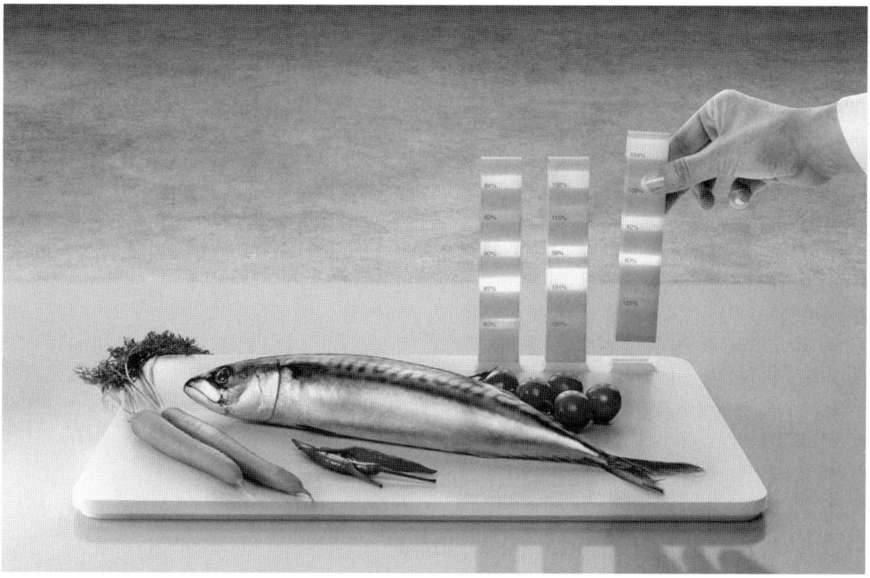

FIGURE 7.1 The Nutrient Probe by Philips Design. This speculative design was presented at the *Sustainable Futures Exhibition* at the Design Museum in London in 2010 and could easily be a proposal for a future commercial product. While providing information about nutritional value of food 'scanned' by a 'user', the design could be considered as reducing human decision making through encoding the logics of health and nutrition into an automatic process. However, as the image above shows, the ethics of eating are not directly addressed. Instead, the design presents a functionalist approach to sustain-able eating revolving around a speculative technology capable of efficiently determining how 'swallowable' a food may be in respect to human nutritional requirements (Philips Design, 2010). The question of should I eat animals is not explored through design, but left to human choice (Image copyright Philips Design – Food Probe Project 2010).

locally grown food and even growing one's own food. Such choices may lead to visiting smaller community-based stores or connecting with social communities concerned with food production and consumption. Of course, being vegetarian does not mean one will follow all of these paths, or ask such questions about eating. Likewise, many non-vegetarians become equally concerned about their food and follow these paths. In the context of our analogy, the important point is that to ensure vegetarianism is a sustainable way of life, a vegetarian must think consciously about consumption, and that this conscious thought opens up opportunities for learning, growing and improving. The characteristics of the vegetarian analogy suggest that our designs should provide similar opportunities and possibilities, an important consideration for Interaction Design.

Simply removing meat from a diet does not make one more sustainable. The fruit and vegetable sections of modern supermarkets easily conceal the problems of food production. Thus it is worth considering a comparable ethical eating practice known as localvorism, where a concern for how far food has been transported (often known as food miles) is primary. While localvorism involves a similar mindfulness as vegetarianism, it does not remove something that is assumed to be as central to our being as eating meat. However, localvorism is significant in the way it connects eating to locality in the face of globalized food production and distribution. In a time of ecological crisis, localvorism may become a far more precarious practice than vegetarianism. Without even considering the way climate change might influence food production, thinking about localvorism reveals that survival without eating meat may be near impossible in many parts of the world. In the context of Interaction Design, localvorism is a far more challenging analogy in the light of the great distances the materials and products travel and which form the ground of Interaction Design.

Another aspect of vegetarianism that is important in the context of ethics and design is that the choice to be vegetarian leads to changes in social relationships. Singer, in *Animal Liberation* (1975), described how he and his wife were worried that by becoming vegetarian they would be cutting themselves off from their non-vegetarian friends. In many countries and cultures, social occasions revolve around eating meat – in Australia it is the barbecue (BBQ). Becoming vegetarian leads to encounters at social gatherings involving food, where someone will inevitably take umbrage at a vegetarian's decision, trying to convince them of their mistake. This often becomes the catalyst for conversations about eating while dining with friends and family. In the context of Interaction Design, this becomes a question about how a design might necessitate conversations about sustain-ability within everyday social activities, analogous to the conversations about vegetarianism while eating.

As opposed to brand loyalty, or the choice of one consumer product or service over another, being vegetarian is a strong and often lifelong commitment that plays an important part in how one defines oneself. 'I am a vegetarian' is a statement that requires daily consideration. Beyond simply thinking about what to eat, there are issues such as concern over how to respond socially when confronted at a family BBQ about being a vegetarian, or dilemmas involved in purchasing other products such as feather down pillows or leather shoes made from animal products. The point of this short discussion about vegetarianism is to show how it is possible to reframe thought about eating – and by analogy about designing – by questioning something that is taken for granted as a fundamental aspect of our being human. This exposes the ethics of consumption and asks us to consider how we value 'others' beyond anthropocentric worldviews. This question is vital if we are to act to sustain the complex web of life on Earth that supports our dwelling. If we are to secure our future, design cannot simply continue as it has to date. Instead, design must engage with the difficult and fundamental issues related to our unsustainable modes of being – our choices, values and lifestyles.

Reframing electricity and energy use

Extending the eating metaphor developed so far, I will now focus on designing in the context of a different form of consumable energy – electricity. The continual presence of electrical energy has become an integral part of life in developed nations, so much so that it is almost impossible to imagine how a society could

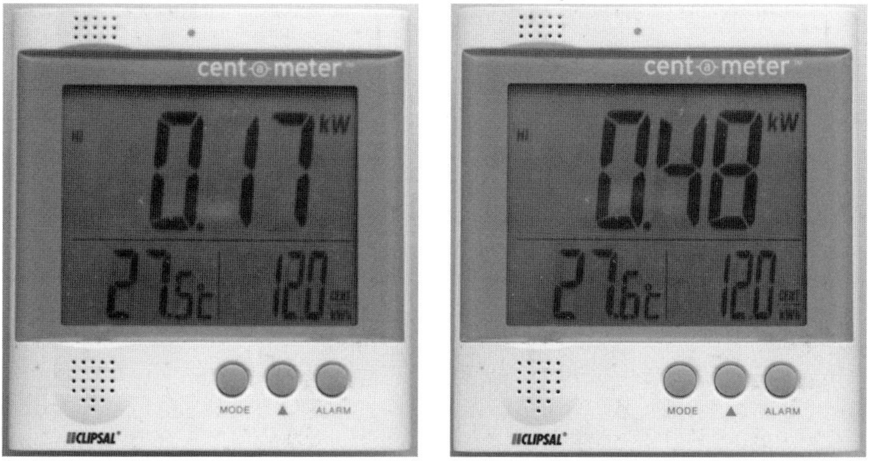

FIGURE 7.2 These two images of a Cent-a-Meter taken before and after turning on a home desktop computer. The computer consumes approximately 0.3kW per hour, which, based on the emissions factors for Queensland electricity production, produces roughly 0.3174kg of CO_2 emissions per hour (Australian Government 2004). This particular smart meter provides only momentary measurements and does not log energy use or display usage patterns over time (photographs by Gavin Sade 2009).

sustain itself without electricity. However, like food, once electricity becomes the focus of our attention we see that the production, distribution and consumption of electricity are fraught with political, economic and ethical problems. Recently, there has been significant interest in the design of smart meters and associated systems that display home electricity consumption and the resulting carbon emissions. It has been argued that these products increase awareness of home electricity consumption and can be designed to persuade and motivate changes in behaviour (Darby 2006; Lu 2008; Paulos *et al.* 2008; Roth and Brodrick 2008; Kimura and Nakajima 2009; Zapico *et al.* 2009). Such meters are currently being distributed through the Queensland State Government ClimateSmart home energy survey service.[1] The faith placed in this design solution for the problem of electricity consumption necessitates a review of the virtues of such designs.

Commercial products

There are an increasing number of commercially available electricity meters that can be retrofitted to existing dwellings. These range from the most basic meters that display electricity use, cost and carbon emissions for the whole dwelling, like the Cent-a-Meter pictured in Figure 7.2, to single device meters like the Kill-A-Watt.[2] The first generation of meters on the market typically only display the current usage and have limited ability to display temporal usage patterns. These designs make it difficult to gain an insight into electricity use patterns over days, weeks, months, seasons and years. In contrast to these first-generation meters, designs such

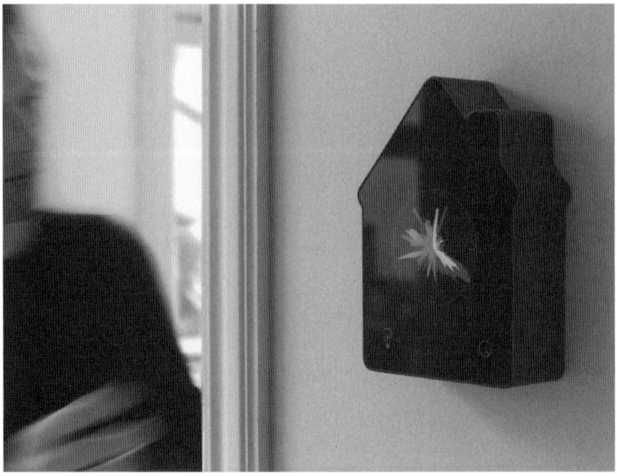

FIGURE 7.3
The Energy AWARE Clock shows energy consumption over time (image copyright Interactive Institute, Sweden).

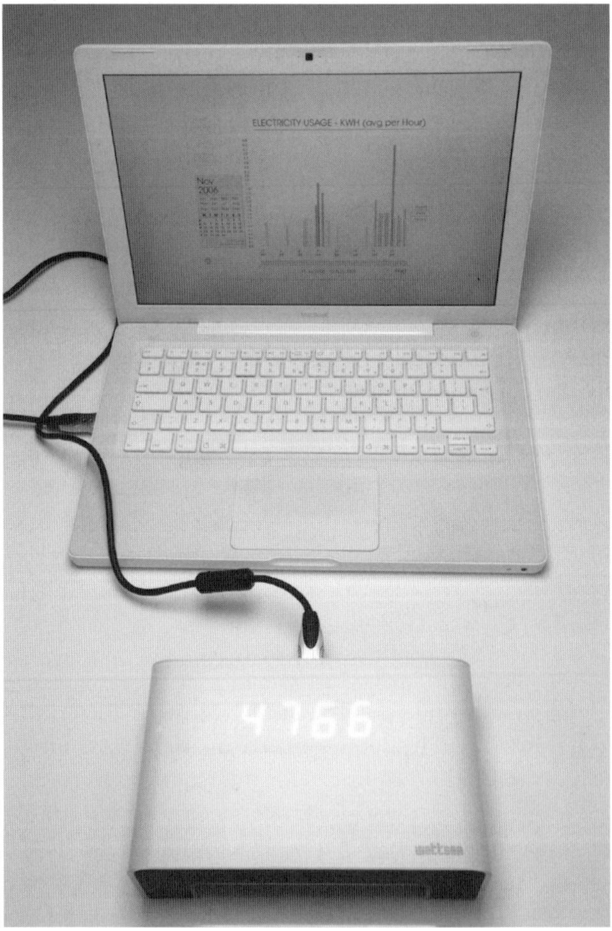

FIGURE 7.4
DIY Kyoto's Wattson meter connected to a laptop showing the Holmes software (image copyright DIY Kyoto Ltd).

as the Energy AWARE Clock, which uses the visual metaphor of a clock to display energy usage patterns across a 48-hour period, present temporal use patterns. Later generation meters, such as the Wattson meter and Holmes software made by DIY Kyoto or the TED 5000, which connects to Google PowerMeter, provide more functionality, including the ability to log and visualize data, and connect to network services.[3]

While studies have indicated that the use of these types of electricity meters can provide energy savings of between 5 and 15 per cent (Darby 2006), there is no evidence that these changes are sustained over the long term (Parker *et al.* 2006). Nor do any studies seriously consider what happens when batteries in battery-powered meters, such as the Cent-a-Meter, inevitably go flat. Thus, there is a clear need for longitudinal studies in order to substantiate claims of behaviour change. To address such concerns, researchers and designers are working on smarter technologies that 'give consumers and businesses better tools to save energy, save money, and reduce their carbon footprint' (Google 2009). Beyond the passive meters, future design scenarios see the electricity grid as a network where 'every node will be awake, responsive, adaptive, price-smart, eco-sensitive, real-time, flexible, humming – and interconnected with everything else' (Silberman 2001). Such scenarios echo the original ubiquitous computing scenarios presented by Weiser. As a result, these scenarios can be subjected to similar critiques as Araya (1995), Bell and Dourish (2007) or Winner (1986), as mentioned above.

It may be argued that the design of many smart meters does not address questions of electricity production, distribution, consumption, health and the environment. Following the vegetarian eating analogy, the question is not 'How do these designs improve electricity use?', but rather 'How do these designs conceal or reveal the ethical and political aspects of electricity consumption and production?' Many of the electricity usage meters reviewed – such as the Cent-a-Meter and the meters provided by the Queensland Government ClimateSmart programme – ostensibly normalize forms of electricity production by displaying only kilowatt-hours (kWh), cost and carbon emissions resulting from individual electricity consumption.[4] While showing carbon emissions might be viewed as informative in terms of environmental impact, the fact remains that these devices render all sources the same – coal or nuclear power stations, wind farms, biomass or local roof-mounted solar products. The focus on a single numerical indicator of performance, combined with an emphasis on reducing energy use, appears to reinforce an economics of scarcity. This is a logic that implicitly assumes that electricity can only be produced from non-renewable sources, such as fossil fuels, as opposed to abundant renewable energy available from the sun, wind, tides, etc. From the perspective of eating, vegetarianism or localvorism, the choice of energy source is an important aspect of electricity consumption, possibly more so than simply reducing energy usage. The analogy shows that the design and use of these meters does not engage with the complex issues such as renewable versus non-renewable sources, centralized large-scale production versus decentralized and micro-production.

The design of electricity meters, and the associated advertising, is underpinned by the notion of eco-efficiency and follows a 'million small steps' approach to securing a sustainable future. This is problematic because, as William McDonough and Michael Braungart suggest, the notion 'eco-efficiency' is essentially a 'be less bad' approach that casts humans as bad and fails to address larger problems of destructive systems. To accept the 'be less bad' solutions is 'to believe that poorly designed, dishonourable, destructive systems are the *best* humans can do' (McDonough and Braungart 2002: 67). From this point of view, electricity meters are no more than a patch used to conceal the politics, ethics and economics of electricity. So it is easy to overlook the simple fact that nothing has actually been eliminated – the cycle of creation and destruction has been preserved. In fact, the designs are grounded in a productivist paradigm; in the US alone there are calls for 40 million meters to be produced and installed to reduce carbon emissions (White House Press Release 2009). This design also reveals a technological approach to problem solving, where a new technological gadget/product/service is required to help consumers reduce their energy consumption. One is left to ponder whether the possible savings (which are yet to be substantially proven in the research) will outweigh the embedded energy costs associated with the production, distribution and installation of 40 million meters.

The design of existing meters places responsibility for energy consumption and reduction with the end user, a practice that nevertheless remains clearly framed within the established economic and political status quo. The need for a new mass-produced gadget, and its propensity to conceal more fundamental issues, illustrates how design can work to sustain the unsustainable. With this meter design nothing of the existing system has been redirected, eliminated or recoded. From a sustain-able Interaction Design perspective, we can conclude that these designs do not place an ethical value on the source of our energy, thus do not remove unsustainable sources of energy from our diet or transform the meaning of energy. While these gadgets do not demand ongoing and mindful attention to consumption, their use does offer the potential for learning and at least some degree of awareness, which might lead to the reconsideration of our relationship to electricity. However, the eco-efficiency argument removes much of the delight and self-satisfaction that may be gained from embracing renewable and local sources of energy.

DIY approaches

The currently limited uptake of sustain-able Interaction Design approaches means that, like the experience of becoming a vegetarian, it is very much like a do-it-yourself (DIY) project. I will now briefly consider some of the DIY approaches to home energy meters. DIY projects can be considered in the vein of 'citizen science' – which has been a recent focus within Interaction Design (Paulos *et al.* 2008; Goodman 2009). However, there has been limited discussion of DIY approaches in respect to energy meters within Interaction Design as most of the research has focused on designer-led projects that result in commercial products.

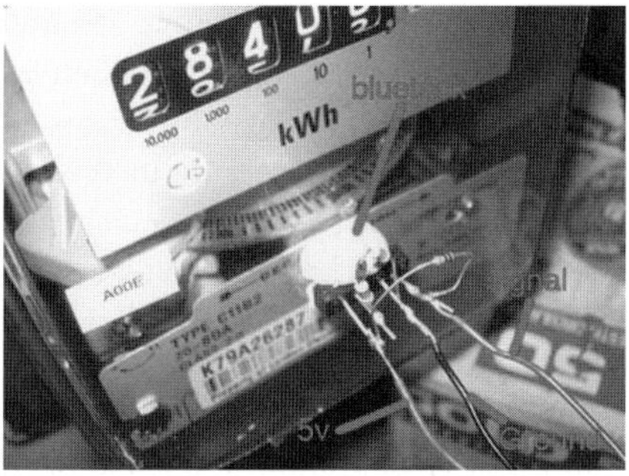

FIGURE 7.5 Image from the Pachube DIY tutorial on connecting a typical mains meter to the internet (Haque 2009, image copyright Pachube).

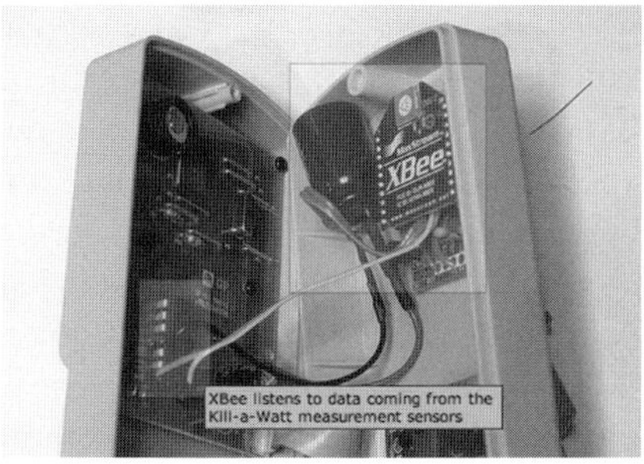

FIGURE 7.6 Tweet-a-Watt: image of a Kill-A-Watt that has been augmented with an XBee module so it can 'tweet' energy use (Fried 2009a, image copyright Adafruit Industries).

Figures 7.5 and 7.6 show two examples of DIY projects related to home electricity monitoring. Figure 7.5 is an image from a Pachube tutorial (Haque 2008) that illustrates how to connect a typical mains electricity meter to the internet. This DIY project does not involve opening up the mains electricity meter, but instead it shows how to connect electronics to the front panel to read the speed at which the 'wheel' inside is spinning. It is a 'parasitic' hack that allows hobbyists to build their own electricity meters, and requires only a basic understanding of electronics and programming. Of specific interest is that this DIY project can be created with open-source hardware and software, as opposed to closed commercial models. Pachube, which predates Google PowerMeter, provides online data-logging facilities and acts as a gateway that allows users to pass electricity-use data to other applications for any purposes one can imagine. Figure 7.6, Tweet-a-Watt, produced by Lady Ada (Limor Fried), is another example of a parasitic hack. This project involves adding a wireless networking card to a commercial product – the Kill-A-Watt. By adding a network connection to this commercial device, a hobbyist is able to parse their electricity-use data to Twitter or any other internet service (Fried 2009a). By modifying multiple Kill-A-Watts, it is easy to create a network of electricity monitors that can be easily reconfigured and used in a more forensic manner than meters that provide one value for total home usage. The Lady Ada website also has instructions on creating visualizations of the resulting data sets (Fried 2009b), which offers a meaningful way of learning about energy use patterns and has potential for DIYers to create visualizations readable on a human scale.[5]

The Open Energy Monitor is a project aimed at creating open-source 'energy monitoring, control and analysis tools for energy efficiency and distributed renewable microgeneration' (Lea *et al.* n.d.).[6] It is mentioned in this section on DIY as the designs for the hardware and software are published so end users can build their own versions of the system. Thus, this project does not aim to simply create a closed commercial product, but instead, by publishing designs as open source, it allows people to rework, modify and adapt the design to their own specific situation and needs. It is also worth noting that the design is directly concerned with monitoring multiple sources of energy and in a manner that can be expanded upon – something that is not seen in many of the commercial energy meters on the market, including those reviewed earlier in this chapter.

If it is assumed that computation and communications technologies already are, or will become, ubiquitous, then it is possible to consider that knowledge of how these technologies work may be equally as important as knowing about how to grow or obtain food. By hacking commercial products, DIY projects such as the two discussed above, point to an alternate approach to engaging with the worlds of ubiquitous computing, where the end users are not simply configured as consumers or software users. Likewise, the process and practice of making DIY energy meters reveals the 'messiness' (Bell and Dourish 2007) of otherwise invisible technological infrastructures that are considered ubiquitous. From this perspective we see that the seamless view of ubiquitous technology renders users within the political and ethical logics of its design. DIY projects play within the seams, revel in the messiness of technology, provide opportunities for learning about otherwise closed designs, and can subvert the otherwise dominant narratives of designed products and systems.

Art, critical design and research

> Interaction Design can be a test space where designers engage with different technologies (not just electronics) before they enter the market place, exploring their possible impact on everyday life through design proposals – from a variety of perspectives: commercial, aesthetic, functional, critical, even ethical.
>
> (Dunne 2005)

The final examples we will consider are drawn from research, art and critical design. These cases have been drawn together because they share a common characteristic. Each project goes beyond the functional and utilitarian approaches to design to explore its poetic and aesthetic dimensions. The emphasis on aesthetics is significant as it is this combination of ethics and aesthetic experience that allows each of the following examples to reveal and/or estrange an otherwise invisible background technology.

The Power Aware Cord and Energy Curtain are drawn from two research projects run by the Interactive Institute in Sweden, and are also included in the *Visual Voltage* exhibition. One project, 'STATIC!', set out to 'investigate interaction design as a means of increasing our awareness of how energy is used and for stimulating changes in energy behaviour' (STATIC! 2006). The use of pervasive technologies to display ambient data has been a focus of research of Jaap Ham, Cees Midden and Femke Beute (2009), who investigated whether ambient

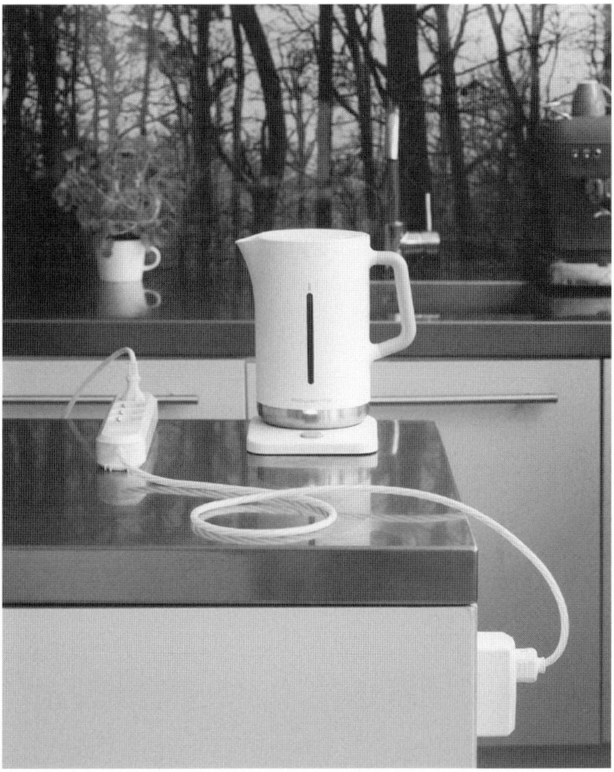

FIGURE 7.7
The Power Aware Cord: an illuminated electrical cable shows the flow of electricity (image copyright Interactive Institute, Sweden; photographer Carl Dahlstedt).

information displays can influence energy consumption patterns within the home. However, what distinguishes the 'STATIC!' project is its use of critical design approaches to explore the design of everyday items such as power cables, curtains and lights, and to reconsider the aesthetics of energy use by making the otherwise invisible flows of energy within the home visible (Backlund *et al.* 2006). As a result, they produced a series of designs that work to make flows of energy visible within the home that go beyond quantitative numerical displays. For example, the Power Aware Cord illuminates to show the flow of electricity and draws attention to its otherwise hidden paths of travel (Gustafsson and Gyllenswärd 2005). The Energy Curtain glows at night and displays a brightness proportional to the amount of light that fell on it during the day. By connecting with local flows of energy, both works offer literal interpretations of Keith Armstrong's principles of ecosophical new media (Armstrong 2002).

The work *Field* by Richard Box (2004) and *The Electric Fields of California* by Larry and Debby Kline (2002) both involve 'planting' fluorescent tubes in the ground beneath high-voltage power transmission lines. The electromagnetic fields created by these transmission lines cause the tubes to glow. These works bring into view both the invisible electromagnetic fields produced by power lines, the core

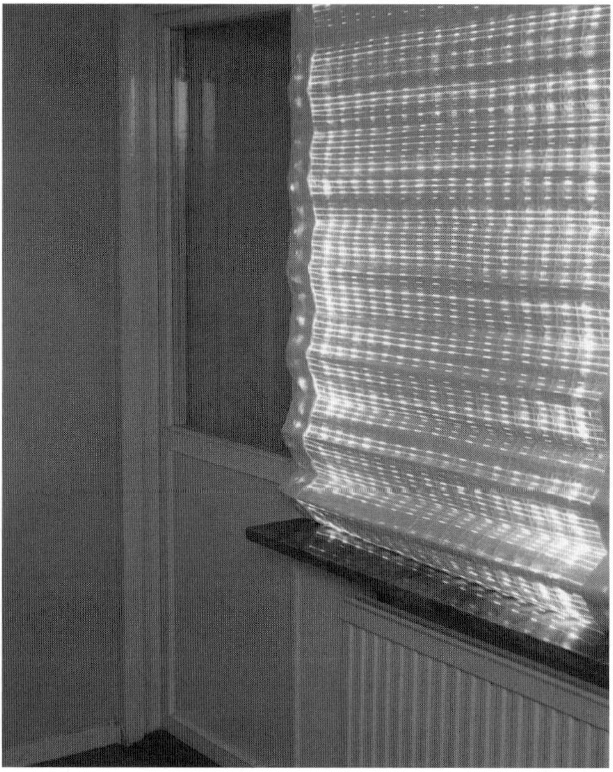

FIGURE 7.8 The Energy Curtain: this curtain glows based on the amount of sunlight it has absorbed in the proceeding day (image copyright Interactive Institute, Sweden; photographer Carl Dahlstedt).

physical feature of today's distribution networks, and imposing towers and tracts of unused land beneath the power lines. These works raise numerous questions, ranging from those related to the impact of the electromagnetic fields and the quantities of energy lost in transmission, through to the ways we use and do not use land.

'Nuage Vert no. 01' by HeHe in Figure 7.9 uses a laser to draw an outline around the smoke produced by power plant chimneys in urban areas (Evans and Hansen 2008a, b). The work won a Golden Nica at the Ars Electronica Prix in the electronic arts category for its exploration of 'the sociopolitical relevance of the interaction as manifested by its innate potential to expand the scope of human action' (Ars Electronica 2007). These two works highlight the otherwise invisible sites of production and very physical networks of distribution, and problematize electricity distribution and production.

'Natural Fuse' by Usman Haque is a functional design that employs plants as both carbon sinks and circuit breakers. Haque (2009) describes 'Natural Fuse' as 'a micro-scale CO_2 monitoring and overload protection framework that works locally and globally'. As opposed to the designs produced in the 'STATIC!' project, 'Natural Fuse' involves a number of individual units that form a much larger whole, a collective carbon sink. Each individual unit can be set to either selfless or selfish

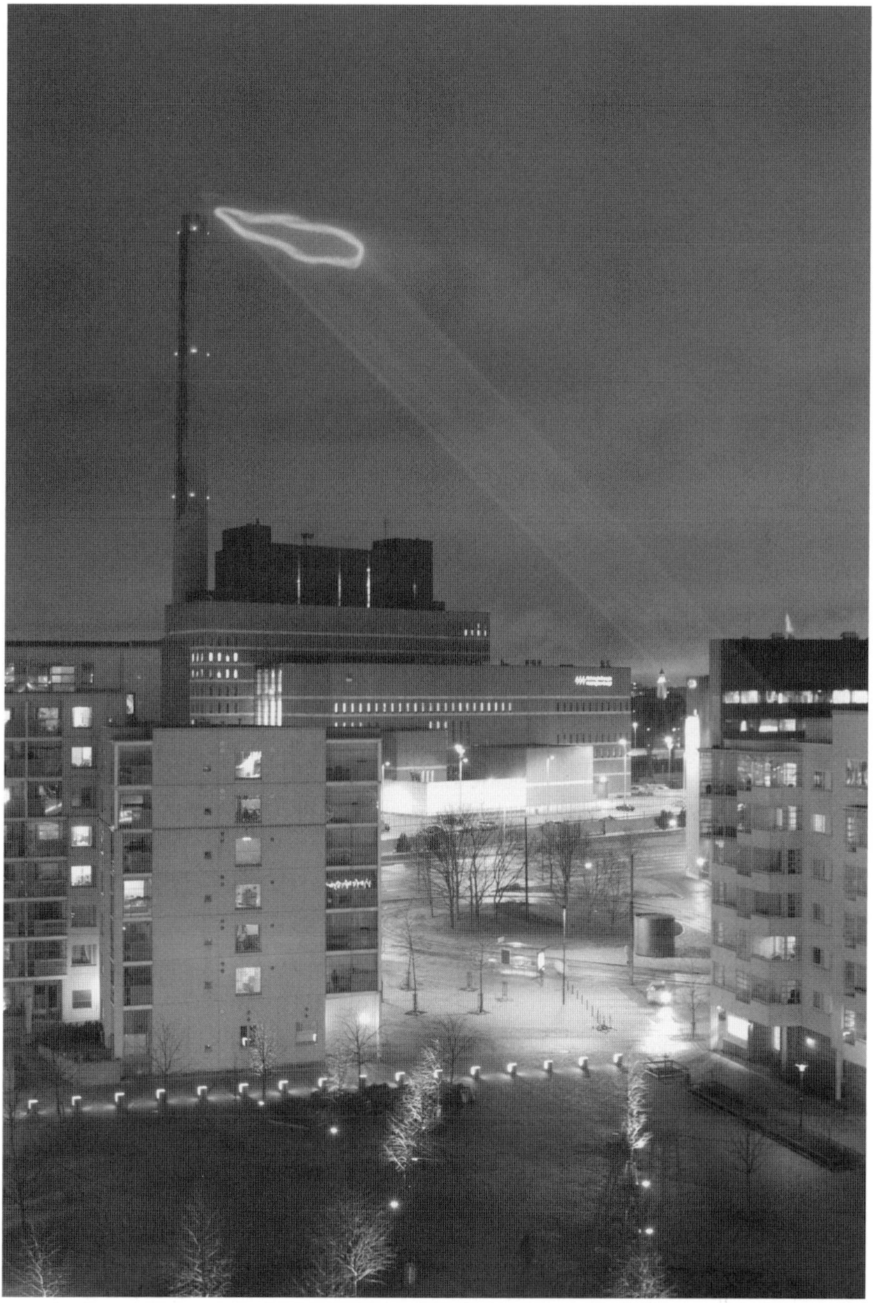

FIGURE 7.9 'Nuage Vert no. 01' (Green Cloud) Helsinki by HeHe: laser outlining smoke produced by a power station in Helsinki (image copyright HeHe 2007).

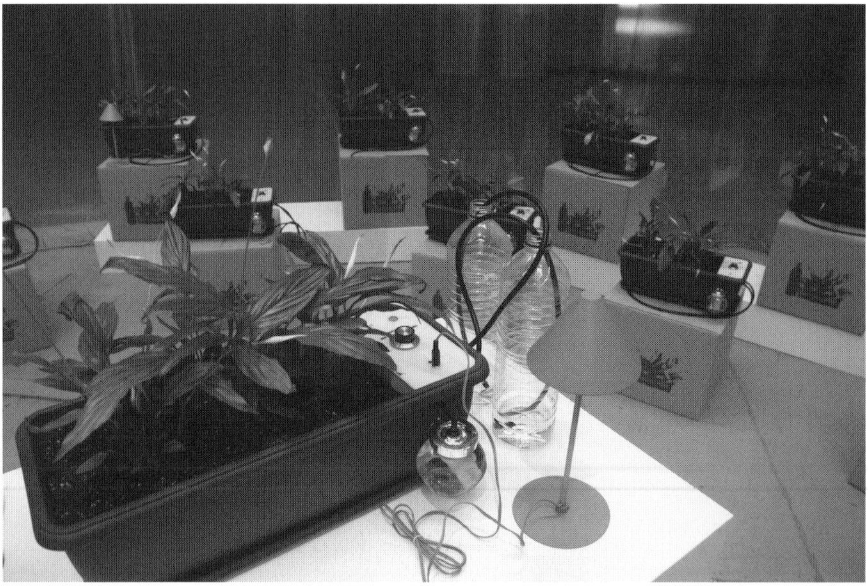

FIGURE 7.10 'Natural Fuse' by Usman Haque (image copyright Usman Haque).

mode; the selfish mode uses more energy than the individual's unit can sink and hence relies on the energy savings of others. If the whole system consumes more energy than it can offset, it begins randomly killing individual plants in the network. This work highlights the very problematic nature of carbon offsetting schemes by reducing the distance between energy consumption and carbon sink, and foregrounding the way that individual decision making regarding energy use affects everyone. As Haque discovered, a single indoor plant is not able to sink very much carbon and any benefits gained are lost once the plant dies. A similar satirical project, 'Cheatneutral' (www.cheatneutral.com), playfully comments on the absurdity of carbon offsetting by posing as a business that will allow one to offset their infidelity by paying another couple to remain faithful. Both works highlight how carbon offsetting is not actually an answer to the problems of energy use, but instead a panacea that allows the continuation of otherwise bad habits.

The final example is Anthony Dunne and Fiona Raby whose work *Is This Your Future?* was exhibited at the Science Museum in London in 2004. These are not functional designs, but are instead a series of speculative designs for a future where energy is produced by 'domestic hydrogen production and child labour; bio-fuel created from human waste; and meat-based microbial fuel cells' (Dunne and Raby 2004). The designs were based on existing technologies and work to unsettle our assumed relationships with energy production by presenting visions of alternate futures. Dunne and Raby mindfully create designs that make energy production strange in a way that at times makes us uncomfortable. Their goal was not to create functional products within an existing system, but to use design to explore alternate

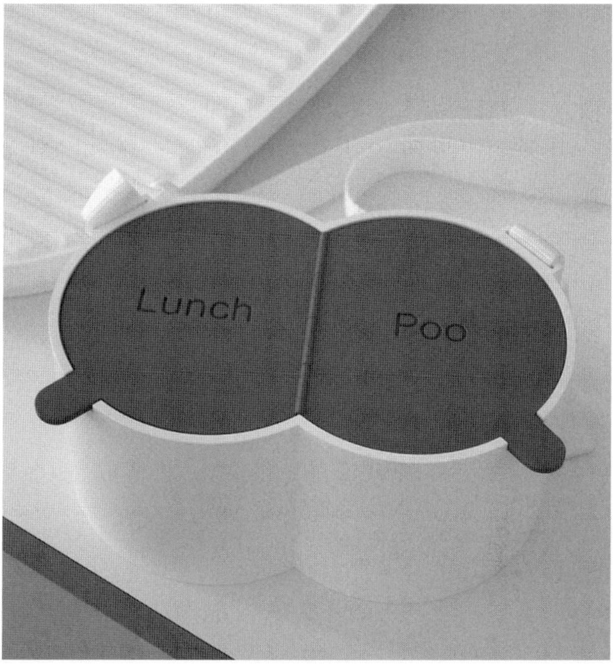

FIGURE 7.11
'Human Poo Energy Future – Poo Lunch Box' (Dunne and Raby 2004; image copyright Dunne & Raby; photographer Jason Evans).

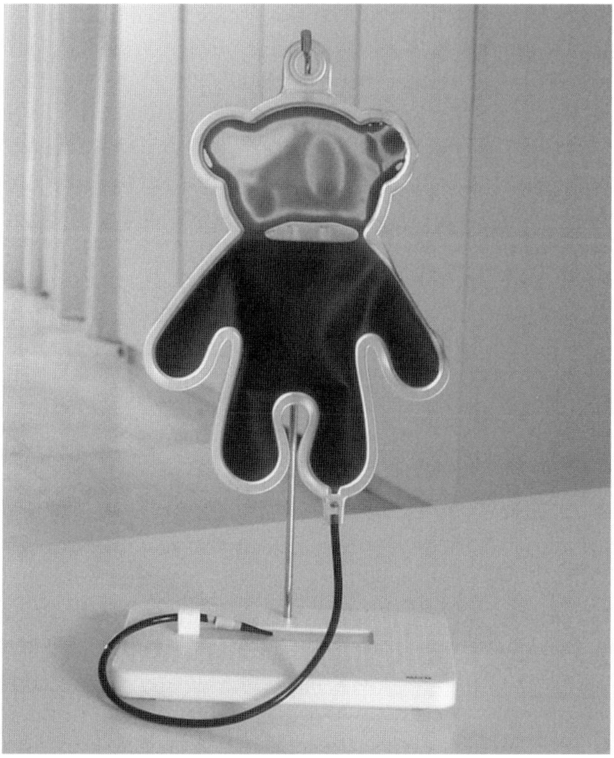

FIGURE 7.12
'Blood/Meat Energy Future – Teddy Bear Blood Bag Radio' (Dunne and Raby 2004; image copyright Dunne & Raby; photographer Jason Evans).

futures with a critical eye, foregrounding ethical, social and political issues. From a vegetarian's perspective, the 'meat microbial fuel cell' is particularly poignant as it presents a future where electricity is produced from animals and meat grown within the home. These designs literally bring the ethical questions related to the use of animals for energy into the home, making it part of everyday life, instead of concealing it in distant factories.

Likewise, designs that use waste, such as human excrement, to produce electricity raise questions regarding not only the sources of our diet, but the literal waste of our biological nutrient cycle – an unharnessed energy source. Such energy production from human waste echoes McDonough and Braungart's (2002) consideration of the cherry tree, which produces 'copious amounts of waste' that falls to become compost and nutrients for the tree, thus presenting a completely alternate model to energy production and consumption than those inscribed in the commercial energy meters that value efficiency and energy reduction. Projects such as *Is This Your Future?* act as triggers for thinking about our future energy habits, opening up possibilities that extend far beyond those privileged by the current design of home energy meters, and achieved not by modifying existing energy behaviour, but by shifting the focus of design from simple problem solving and eco-efficiency to addressing energy in the context of questions of ecology, decomposition, digestion and metabolism.

This survey of approaches to design in the context of energy consumption is only partial, but includes energy meters that are only just functional in terms of transforming our relationship to electricity; networked meters that provide temporal information required to understand patterns of consumption; DIY approaches that involve opening the black boxes of ubiquitous computing; and finally, artistic and critical design approaches that employ poetic and aesthetic methods to raise critical questions about our relationship to electricity. What this initial survey shows is that researchers, artists and critical designers are far more likely – because of the context of their designing – to explore how to make the ubiquitous technology of electricity production unfamiliar. Through this process, they engage in a conversation about the design of these otherwise invisible technologies, which provides an approach for considering the design of other forms of ubiquitous computing.

Conclusion

By thinking about vegetarianism it is possible to reframe thought about eating and, by analogy in the context of this chapter, designing our relationship to food, energy and electricity. The shift in thought and action required by vegetarianism provides a model for thinking about sustain-ability specifically because it demands a questioning of something that is not simply taken for granted but is considered a fundamental aspect of our being human. Vegetarianism exposes the ethics of consumption and asks us to consider how we value Others beyond anthropocentric worldviews. The analogy poses more questions than it answers, but this is essential if we are to discover what designing well means. To secure our future, design cannot simply continue as it has to date. Design must engage with difficult and fundamental issues related to our unsustainable modes of being (lifestyles).

Extending the analogy of eating into the domain of electricity production, distribution and consumption reveals that design can either (unknowingly) mask and reinforce unsustainable practices, or raise critical questions. The most compelling examples are not always commercial designs. The non-commercial designs seen in this chapter do not always solve problems or serve functional purposes, but instead open possibilities for thought. Designs such as Dunne and Raby's 'Is This is Your Future?' allow us to encounter alternative futures, and hence reflect on the present. Such encounters render the world we take for granted in ways that require us to confront questions that many commercial designs seek to conceal, thus providing possible models for rethinking both design and our practices of being, our lifestyles.

While this chapter started by stating that it was not an argument for vegetarianism, it concludes by encouraging Interaction Designers who have a concern for sustain-ability to consider a research exercise that would involve being a vegetarian for a period of time or eating food produced within 240km (150 miles) of where they live. Alternatively, they might like to design their own experiment of removing from their life something else that they assume to be fundamental to their being that inherently challenges notions of sustainability. In other words, apply design research methods to task and investigate how this 'design choice' changes otherwise daily routines. Keep in mind 'that the adventure of such a change of eating habits is, for many people, an exciting and deeply satisfying adventure [and] part of the adventure is the discovery of new sources of culinary delights' (Gruzaldski 1989). In conducting such an experiment, designers may encounter similar adventures within their own practices.

Notes

1 See Queensland Government ClimateSmart program: www.climatesmarthome.com.

2 See product website: http://www.clipsal.com/homeowner/products/energy_efficient_solutions/energy_consumption_monitor. The Kill-a-Watt is sold by Think Geek from: www.thinkgeek.com/gadgets/travelpower/7657.

3 The Wattson electricity meter, by DIY Kyoto is available here: www.diykyoto.com/uk/wattson/about. Holmes is the software product by DIY Kyoto that can be used with the Wattson: www.diykyoto.com/uk/holmes/why-use-holmes. The Energy Detective, one of the more advanced network-connected electricity meters: www.theenergydetective.com/ted-5000. Google PowerMeter is an online service that logs energy usage data and provides a range of visualization capabilities: www.google.org/powermeter.

4 Most meters do allow the user to enter a fixed CO_2 emissions factor, and there are experiments that involve social comparisons of emissions; it is close to impossible to understand what carbon emissions mean in terms of the climate crisis. Are the 3kg of emissions I produce per week good, bad or normal? Will a saving of 15 per cent of 3kg even make a difference – considering the targets scientists indicate as being needed?

5 See details on graphing data from the Tweet-a-Watt here: www.ladyada.net/make/tweetawatt/graph.html.

6 See http://openenergymonitor.org/emon.

References

Araya, A. A. (1995) 'Questioning ubiquitous computing', in C. J. Hwang and B. W. Hwang (eds) *Proceedings of the 1995 ACM 23rd Annual Conference on Computer Science*, Nashville, TN, 28 February–2 March.

Armstrong, K. (2002) *Towards an Ecosophical Praxis of New Media Space Design*, PhD thesis, Faculty of Creative Industries, Queensland University of Technology, Brisbane.

Ars Electronica (2007) 'Ars Electronica prix interactive art category'. Available at: www.aec.at/prix_categories_en.php?cat=Interactive%20Art (accessed 1 November 2009).

Australian Government, Department of Climate Change (2004) *National Greenhouse Accounts (NGA) Factors*. Available at: www.climatechange.gov.au/publications/greenhouse-acctg/national-greenhouse-factors.aspx (accessed 1 November 2009).

Backlund, S., Gustafsson, A., Gyllenswärd, M., Ilstedt-Hjelm, S., Mazé, R. and Redström, J. (2006) 'STATIC! The aesthetics of energy in everyday things', in T. K. Friedman, T. Love and E. Corte-Real (eds) *Proceedings of Design Research Society Wonderground International Conference 2006*, Lisbon, Portugal, 1–4 November.

Becker, E., Jahn, T. and Stiess, I. (1999) 'Exploring uncommon ground: sustainability and the social sciences', in E. Becker and T. Jahn (eds) *Sustainability and the Social Sciences: a cross-disciplinary approach to integrating environmental considerations into theoretical reorientation*, London: Zed Books.

Bell, G. and Dourish, P. (2007) 'Yesterday's tomorrows: notes on ubiquitous computing's dominant vision', *Personal Ubiquitous Computing*, 11(2): 133–143.

Bentham, Jeremy (1789) 'A utilitarian view' in P. Singer and T. Regan (eds) *Animal Rights and Human Obligations* (1989), Englewood Cliffs, NJ: Prentice-Hall.

Blevis, E. (2007) 'Sustainable interaction design: invention and disposal, renewal and reuse', in *Proceedings of the SIGCHI Conference on Human Factors in Computing Systems*, San Jose, CA, 28 April–3 May .

Box, R. (2004) *Field*. Available at: www.richardbox.com/ (accessed 1 November 2009).

Darby, S. (2006) *The Effectiveness of Feedback on Energy Consumption: a review for DEFRA of the literature on metering, billing and direct displays*, Environmental Change Institute, University of Oxford. Available at: www.eci.ox.ac.uk/research/energy/electric-metering.php (accessed 1 November 2009).

Derrida J. and Nancy, J. L. (1991) '"Eating well" or the calculation of the subject: an interview with Jacques Derrida' in E. Cadava, P. Connor and J. L. Nancy (eds) *Who Comes after the Subject?* London: Routledge.

Dreyfus, H. (1993) 'Heidegger on the connection between nihilism, art, technology and politics', in C. B. Guignon (ed.) *The Cambridge Companion to Heidegger*, Cambridge: Cambridge University Press.

Dunne, A. (2005) Royal College of Art press release: 'New head of Design Interactions'. Available at: www.rca.ac.uk/pages/news/tonnydunneappointedas2540.html (accessed 10 January 2006).

Dunne, A. and Raby, F. (2004) 'Is This Your Future?' Available at: www.dunneandraby.co.uk/content/projects/68/0 (accessed 20 October 2009).

Evans, H. and Hansen, H. (2008a) 'Nuage Vert no. 01'. Available at: http://hehe.org.free.fr/hehe/NV08/index.html (accessed 20 October 2009).

Evans, H. and Hansen, H. (2008b) 'Nuage Vert'. Available at: www.pixelache.ac/nuage-blog (accessed 1 February 2010).

Fried, L. (2009a) Tweet-a-Watt. Available at: www.ladyada.net/make/tweetawatt (accessed 20 October 2009).

Fried, L. (2009b) Tweet-a-Watt graphing with Google Visualizer. Available at: www.ladyada.net/make/tweetawatt/graph.html (accessed 20 October 2009).

Fry, T. (1999) *A New Design Philosophy: An introduction to defuturing*. Sydney: University of New South Wales Press.

Fry, T. (2003) 'The voice of sustainment: an other economy', in *Design Philosophy Papers*. Available at: www.desphilosophy.com/dpp/dpp_journal/feature/body.html (accessed 1 July 2009).

Fry, T. (2009) *Design Futuring: Sustainability, ethics and new practice*. Sydney: University of New South Wales Press.

Goodman, E. (2009) 'Three environmental discourses in human–computer interaction' in *Proceedings of the 27th international Conference Extended Abstracts on Human Factors in Computing Systems*, Boston, MA, 4–9 April.

Google (2009) 'Comments of Google Inc. submitted in response to the notice of intent to issue a funding opportunity announcement for the smart grid investment grant program'. Available at: www.google.com/googleorg/docs/GoogleSmartGrid.pdf (accessed 20 October 2009).

Gruzaldski, B. (1989) 'The case against raising and killing animals for food', in T. Regan and P. Singer (eds) *Animal Rights and Human Obligations*, Englewood Cliffs, NJ: Prentice-Hall.

Guattari, F. (1995) *Chaosmosis: Anethico-aestheticparadigm*, trans. Paul Bains and Julian Pefanis, Bloomington, IN: Indiana University Press.

Gustafsson, A. and Gyllenswärd, M. (2005) 'The PowerAware Cord: energy awareness through ambient information display', in *CHI '05 Extended Abstracts on Human Factors in Computing Systems*, Portland, OR, 2–7April.

Ham, J., Midden, C. and Beute, F. (2009) 'Can ambient persuasive technology persuade unconsciously?: using subliminal feedback to influence energy consumption ratings of household appliances', in *Proceedings of the 4th International Conference on Persuasive Technology*, Claremont, CA, 26–29 April.

Haque, U. (2008) 'Connecting your electricity meter to Pachube'. Available at: http://community.pachube.com/node/65 (accessed 1 November 2009).

Haque, U. (2009) 'Natural Fuse'. Available at: www.naturalfuse.org (accessed 1 February 2010).

Jeremijenko, N. (2005) 'Feral Robotic Dogs'. Available at: www.nyu.edu/projects/xdesign/feralrobots (accessed 1 February 2010).

Kimura, H. and Nakajima, T. (2009) 'Applying smart objects for persuading users to change their behavior', *International Journal of Multimedia and Ubiquitous Engineering*, 4(3): 21–36.

Kline, D. and Kline, L. (2002) 'The Electric Fields of California'. Available at: www.jugglingklines.com/electric_fields.htm (accessed 20 October 2009).

Lea, T., Hudson, G. and Tagore, S. (n.d.) 'Open Energy Monitor Project'. Available at: http://openenergymonitor.org (accessed 1 December 2010).

Lu, E. (2008) 'Testimony of Edward Lu Advanced Projects Program Manager, Google, Inc.' *Senate Committee on Energy and Natural Resources Hearing on Smart Grid*. Available at: http://energy.senate.gov/public/_files/GoogleTestimony030309.pdf (accessed 1 December 2010).

McCullough, M. (2004) *Digital Ground: Architecture, pervasive computing, and environmental knowing*, Cambridge, MA: MIT Press.

McDonough, W. and Braungart, M. (2002) *Cradle to cradle: Remaking the way we make things*, New York: North Point Press.

Massachusetts Institute of Technology (MIT) (2004) 'Project Overview' of *MIT Project Oxygen*. Available at: http://oxygen.lcs.mit.edu/Overview.html (accessed 1 July 2005).

Myers, A. and Worm, B. (2003) 'Rapid worldwide depletion of predatory fish communities', *Nature*, 423: 280–283.

Nathan, L., Blevis, E., Friedman, B., Hasbrouck, J. and Sengers, P. (2008) 'Beyond the hype: sustainability and HCI', in *CHI '08 Extended Abstracts on Human Factors in Computing Systems*, Florence, Italy, 5–10 April.

Paulos, E., Foth, M., Satchell, C. and Younghui K. (2008) 'Ubiquitous sustainability: citizen science and activism (workshop)', *Tenth International Conference on Ubiquitous Computing (UbiComp)*, Seoul, South Korea, 21–24 September.

Parker, D., Hoak, D., Meier, A. and Brown, R. (2006) 'How much energy are we using? Potential of residential energy demand feedback devices.' Proceedings of the ACEEE Summer Study on Energy Efficiency in Buildings, Asilomar, California, August. Available at: http://www.fsec.ucf.edu/en/publications/pdf/FSEC-CR-1665-06.pdf (accessed 1 November 2009).

Philips Design (2010) 'Design Probes – Projects – Food'. Available at: http://www.design.philips.com/about/design/designportfolio/design_futures/design_probes/projects/food.page(accessed 10 May 2010).

Roth, K. and Brodrick, J. (2008) 'Emerging technology: home energy displays', *ASHRAE Journal*, 50(7): 136–138.

Silberman, S. (2001) 'The Energy Web', *Wired*, 9(7). Available at: www.wired.com/wired/archive/9.07/juice.html (accessed 12 October 2009).

Singer, P. (1975) *Animal Liberation: A new ethics for our treatment of animals*, New York: New York Review.

STATIC! (2006) 'Design of Increased Energy Awareness'. Available at: www.tii.se/static/research.htm (accessed 1 November 2009).

Weiser, M. (1991) 'The computer for the twenty-first century', *Scientific American* (September): 94–100.

Weiser, M. (1993) 'Some computer science problems in ubiquitous computing' *Communications of the ACM*. New York, Association for Computing Machinery.

Weiser, M. (1994) 'The world is not a desktop', *Interactions*, 1(1): 7–8.

White House Press Release (2009) 'President Obama Announces $3.4 Billion Investment to Spur Transition to Smart Energy Grid'. Available at: www.whitehouse.gov/the-press-office/president-obama-announces-34-billion-investment-spur-transition-smart-energy-grid (accessed 1 November 2009).

Winner, L. (1986) *The Whale and the Reactor: A search for limits in an age of high technology*. Chicago, IL: University Chicago Press.

Winograd, T. (1997) 'From computing machinery to interaction design' in P. J. Denning and R. M. Metcalfe (eds) *Beyond Calculation: The next fifty years of computing*, New York: Springer-Verlag. Available at: http://hci.stanford.edu/winograd/acm97.html (accessed 10 February 2006).

Woodruff, A. and Mankoff, J. (2009) 'Environmental sustainability' *IEEE Pervasive Computing*, 8(1): 18–21.

Zapico, J. L., Turpeinen, M. and Brandt, N. (2009) 'Climate persuasive services: changing behavior towards low-carbon lifestyles', *Proceedings of the 4th International Conference on Persuasive Technology*, Claremont, CA, 26–29 April.

8

DESIGN AND ETHICS IN DIGITAL MENTAL HEALTH PROMOTION

Oksana Zelenko

The role of design in promoting resilience

Following developments in digital technologies, online promotion of mental health and well-being has begun to emerge as a field in its own right. Over the past decade, resilience promotion and education have increasingly become part of the Australian national debate and have entered the state health policy agenda. Numerous initiatives that aim to strengthen individual and community resilience have been developed for primary and secondary school curricula (Stewart *et al.* 2006) and, more recently, for undergraduate tertiary education. The recognition of the importance of resilience has led to a rise in the number of resilience-promoting initiatives and an expansion of communication platforms through which they are deployed. While the digital domain is recognized as having an important role to play, with the internet described as 'a potentially powerful health communication tool' (Stewart *et al.* 2006), the rapid growth of innovation in health communication technologies has prompted an inquiry into the value and potential contribution of visual and Interaction Design to promoting health and well-being. Alongside this upsurge in the production of digital resilience tools, their use in health education has become the subject of much debate, which goes beyond the issues of optimal technical feasibility and integration of new applications into existing infrastructures of mental health services. Questions posed by mental health practitioners interrogate the forms and principles of digital communication at large, with specific questions targeting aesthetic, visual and Interaction Design, which have a potential to influence the comprehension and assimilation of health-related information. This chapter investigates the role of design in promoting resilience online using contemporary Information and Communication Technologies (ICT) and presents a case study of using design-based research methods to develop a set of resilience-promoting tools for children.

The process of determining what role design practice holds in promoting resilience in digital settings is complex. In part, it is contingent on how design as a practice is understood by non-design disciplines, a key understanding that informs its applications in the health domain. Some of the key questions may include: Who is the designer? That is, who makes key decisions? What underpins the choice to use digital technology? What factors shape the design goals and drive the design process? How do these decisions impact on the final outcome? What are the appropriate mechanisms for evaluating the outcomes? Furthermore, is it a question of understanding the relationship between design as a practice and the practice of promoting resilience?

The exploration of these parallels needs to commence with the definition of resilience. 'Resilience' is a term used in physics to refer to a quality of a given material that renders it elastic, malleable and, if compressed, capable of regaining its original shape. In the context of mental health, resilience is a complex notion defined as the capacity of individuals and collectives to cope and thrive despite facing adversity in day-to-day life (Stewart *et al.* 2006). The ease with which the metaphor is transferred often conceals, or at the very least obscures, the duality of the underpinning principle of resilience: that it is at once a distinct capacity or skill and the process of its acquisition. Most existing digital applications take the skills-based approach in which key attributes are explicitly identified and represented for rote learning (Zelenko 2006).

Across the board, the rapid rise in the frequency with which the term 'resilience' is used has led to it becoming a highly charged term, with digital applications limited not as a consequence of non-negotiable specificity of identified attributes, but for its other key constituent – the process – remaining largely unrecognized by designers. Skills-based definitions lack contextual specificity and describe resilience in broad terms, such as having 'coping skills' or as a capacity to 'bounce back'. Such approaches could be described as didactic as they rely on a stock repository of existing attributes in an attempt to accommodate a range of possible individual responses. In this sense, didactic approaches suggest a correct method of acquiring resilience. Where experience of resilience has been encapsulated into specific understandings and presented through digital media, the approach runs the risk of reducing resilience to a generic set of attributes, removed from the original context that gave rise to them.

Online resilience resources escape a concrete definition, leading most often to descriptions that acknowledge diversity, as 'there is no profile of a resilient person' (Gordon Rouse *et al.* 2001), so it can be said that there is no single genre for online initiatives intended to promote it. Instead, as with resilient people, activities that share a set of principles or characteristics relating to resilience behaviour generally fall under the umbrella of resilience promotion. The following five attributes are said to be shared by all resilient people: cognitive superiority (capacity to think strategically about resources available and evaluate strengths); autonomy (independent decision-making skills); androgyny (capacity to transcend gender stereotypes); social skills (acceptance of cultural, ethnic diversity and of mental and physical abilities, skills for forming friendships); internal locus of control (capacity for motivation and initiative in driving change) (Gordon Rouse *et al.* 2001). Resilience promotion includes those resources that, through the interaction experience, aim to develop one or more of these qualities in users.

I suggest that representations of resilience, which might range from broad principles through to highly detailed models of resilience acquisition and development, lay the foundations and the basis for its promotion through other platforms, for example, digital. The implications of the skills-based approach leads to promotional initiatives that are limited by the content of existing resources, rather than offering opportunities for new representations and understandings to be constructed. The distinction between resources that represent predetermined resilience attributes (where resilience is content captured and intended for reuse and replication) and resilience as a way of being or engaging with the world (as a process that is experiential) leads to a closer examination of the foundational approaches used to drive their development, whether off or online. Making a distinction between representations of resilience as content and as experience is crucial because consideration of one and not the other, as this chapter aims to show, leads to different sets of design goals, contribution, outcomes and user experiences.

Online resilience promotion: interative or just 'digital'?

The emerging field of digital mental health promotion does not yet have a well-established set of principles to guide the development of new applications. A review of existing resources shows that the relationship between new media technology, its design and mental health promotion has predominantly occurred at the level of technical implementation, digitization and content transference (Zelenko 2006, 2011). Given this, the emerging concerns of public health domains with digital aesthetics have largely arisen because, in mental health promotion, the term 'digital interactivity' is often used interchangeably with the term 'digitization', where digitizing a resource means to transfer it directly from an offline resource to the digital environment. The direct transference has implications for the study of any digital resilience-promotion initiative as its effectiveness becomes inevitably linked to its offline counterpart. The lack of distinction between the concepts of 'digital' and 'interactive' has, so far at least, restricted the role of new media to that of a 'digital container' for existing content. Consequently, the majority of existing resilience-promoting tools are structurally age-old frameworks taken from familiar and conventional offline formats – for example, jigsaw and word puzzles, spinning wheels, board games, collage-style activities, animations, digitized storybooks and information brochures. More broadly, subscribing to an existing body of design conventions, standards or codes is a characteristic of the broader field of interactive media design and game design.

This chapter does not suggest that there is no value in users engaging with didactic resilience resources, but rather that their value may be limited owing to a lack of opportunities for users to engage more deeply with the enclosed content.

The digitization approach diminishes opportunities for the experience of deeper engagement as it reduces the potential for new interaction to a set of non-negotiable parameters, making the effectiveness and value of the resource in part contingent on how well it has preserved the original representation. In such cases, it could be said the efficacy of a digital resource is measured by its 'verisimilitude to existing technology (paradigms) rather than creative exploration of new and unique potentials that are intrinsic to the technology itself' (Brown 1994: 29).

Designers often use established design conventions to short-circuit the time it takes users to adapt to the new environment. Hence the emphasis on the use of metaphor in Human–Computer Interaction which, if used successfully, guarantees an instant degree of familiarity and, therefore, faster adaptation time (Laurel and Mountford 1990; Dunne 2005; Heim 2007). However, defaulting to existing models of understanding the world comes at a cost of a creative response which, by definition, falls outside any predetermined structure or existing representation. At the level of interface design, such approaches are characterized by the use of iconic – or representational – interface, which by definition is restrictive to emergent responses to help us maintain a 'sense of security in the technology' (Brown 1994: 28-30). Defaulting to design conventions in an attempt to guarantee technology uptake shuts down any unintended uses, resulting also in the negative framing of interaction outside an established structure as erroneous rather than intentional. Based on this vantage point, a single response can be thus viewed as either an error or as an intended design goal; it can either be a measure of success or an indication of failure to fulfil the design brief.

Reductionist approaches to promoting resilience online somewhat parallel standardization approaches in mainstream education systems, where particular applications of ICTs are perceived as instrumental to 'speeding up' learning outcomes of large and diverse student cohorts (Narayanan 2008). One example of this is a relatively recent innovation designed to facilitate student learning on a large scale – the learning object – introduced as a mechanism for accommodating large numbers of students, earning it the title 'weapon of mass instruction' (Butson 2003: 667). Tony Fry refers to a culture of 'naïve enthusiasm' regarding similar uses of new media in education and questions claims to its effectiveness as a form of knowledge transfer in classrooms (Fry 1999: 254). Such views confront the perception that technology is a marker of progressive development, and instead suggests that it may have the potential to produce a form of social regression.

While the notion of design as a practice with potential for shaping learning experience is well established within educational and design research communities, it has not yet found its way into the health services field in the form of well-informed applications. That is, to date there are no online mental-health-promoting resources that recognize that acquisition of resilience skills is processesual and that investigate process-based approaches to promoting it. Instead, the digital platform is predominantly used for presenting existing content, positioning it in a supportive – or even subsidiary – role. Furthermore, the implications of the above mentioned views of ICTs on digital resilience promotion are vast. ICTs have often been granted the same privilege of unquestioned entry into mental health promotion practice on the basis of it 'advancing' what already exists, where advancement is synonymous with having online presence. A shift towards reconceptualizing digital interactivity in resilience promotion is one possible pathway towards transforming the role of ICTs in mental health promotion.

Interface as a site of self-representation

Technologies are culturally invested and saturated – not just at the level of their content, which reflects cultural assumptions, perspectives and biases – but also at the level of the design process. Within a post-structuralist perspective, interfaces (whether designed by individual designers or collaboratively) and the associated design processes remain embodiments of cultural values, practices and beliefs, which represent specific ways of seeing, understanding and being in the world. Where representational approaches to technology design 'privilege particular models of the world and the human subject', foregrounding 'one worldview among many, one possible system of categories among numerous others' (Manovich 2001: 16), the act of privileging a single (decontextualized) viewpoint is at risk of establishing it as a form of 'public pedagogy' (Lumby and Probyn 2003: 2) imbued with authority over any subsequent responses.

For approaches to interactivity and 'user' engagement, interfaces are reflections of attitudes and assumptions of the educators and designers. The notion of new media as a cultural object (Manovich 2001), therefore, provides a useful conceptual framework for considering whose values and voices are represented within emerging designs, and how the underpinning design process has shaped their prominence. When understood as ideologically charged, digital interfaces become important sites of self-representation, while the process of designing them becomes a mechanism for promoting particular worldviews. Understanding design as a process of 'political construction of technology' (Tatum 2004) raises the ethical question of whose conceptions and understandings of resilience ought be reflected in the existing health-promoting resources. Where the interface is a site of promoting a particular understanding of resilience over others, children, as an already marginalized group across both the health-promoting and design fields, are placed at an even greater risk of exclusion. The vulnerability of children's position as an under-represented group in the process of designing and evaluating new digital technologies is commonly acknowledged (Silverstein *et al.* 2007) with specific research methods, such as those developed by the Australian Research Alliance for Children and Youth (2005), designed to 'legitimize' children's participation in the formal process of research.

Resources developed to facilitate children's resilience need to be based not only on children's understanding of what resilience is, but also ensuring that they have the means to ground and contextualize any existing representations of resilience put before them. I suggest that the process of designing digital resilience resources needs to provide ample opportunity for children to promote their own understandings using appropriate methods. One possible way of supporting children in this process would be to consider increasing the degree of their participation in design decision making as a vehicle for enabling them to take part in determining what constitutes resilience according to their individual lived experience.

Currently, there is insufficient opportunity for children to construct their own understanding of, and relationship to, the notion of resilience. Digital tools that present ready-made responses and coping scenarios set up an expectation of users as followers, navigating through predetermined pathways – a perspective that in the design field is judged as an act of resignation or 'unquestioningly submitting to a designer's worldview' (Drucker and Nowviskie 2004). Fry refers to this kind of experience – where decision-making is outsourced – as a 'loss of agency' (Fry 1999: 253). As a way of response, other proponents of meaningful engagement in virtual worlds, like Janet Murray, suggest ways of regaining lost agency in highly interactive settings through 'immersive agency' (1997), as a sense of control resulting from creating meaningful change within a virtual world.

Founded in Scandinavia on principles of cooperation and collaborative engagement (Sanoff 1990), a well-established research methodology that grants a high degree of agency to participants is participatory design (PD) (Muller and Kuhn 1993). Best characterized by its 'grassroots' approach (Muller 1992), PD is based on a basic premise that people affected by design decisions should participate in the making of those decisions (Sanoff 1990). Historically, uses of PD gained momentum as a result of public housing development projects in the 1960s in the US, involving prospective occupants for the proposed district as primary decision makers in the construction process. Since then, applications of PD across a broad range of fields from urban development and planning through to business and health care have been reported (Robertson *et al.* 2010).

However, PD's implementation and potential in the context of resilience promotion is yet to be fully explored. To date, it has not been used to engage children in practice-based research on resilience. Direct participation disrupts traditional dynamics within the design process where the designer is in possession of expert knowledge upon which a product is designed. Here, professional expertise assumes a centralized decision-making role. This process has its roots within the post-industrial system of labour division, in which 'the basic trend in work organization was to separate conception from execution' (Empsak 1993: 16), or the ideas from implementation. Contrasting other existing processes of product quality assurance, PD requires participants to engage across all or most phases of the design process, as opposed to the final phase, which is the case with a user-centred or human-centred design.

Where ethical questions are defined as those involving judgement, and therefore free choice to make such a judgement, PD becomes a framework of design decision making that opens existing definitions and models of resilience up to renegotiation, placing them under scrutiny and subverting their 'epistemic certainty' (Gigliotti 1995: 289). An open structure in a designed object thus reframes interaction as *intervention*. Participation affords children an opportunity to identify support networks, environmental factors and coping mechanisms from the concrete basis of their lived experience. Beyond representing resilience, in a PD framework children have the means to reconstruct these understandings in a formalized setting of a design practice, which seeks to legitimize their contribution. Participation reframes interaction to give precedence to the idea of process over object, shifting understandings of design into temporal and processual dimension.

The rationale for using PD in resilience-learning applications has significant parallels with constructivist views of pedagogy, which hold that knowledge is created by individual learners and that knowledge formation is strongly linked to the surrounding environment and the socio-emotional dynamic corresponding to the learner's experience of that environment. Kolb's experiential learning theory (Kolb 1984), for example, holds that learning occurs when participants have control over the direction of their learning; when they have direct contact with their personal, social and research problems, and when instruments for self-evaluation are readily available.

Reconceptualizing the role of design

By framing new media technologies as processes that offer what Anthony Dunne calls 'behavioural opportunities' (Dunne 2005), resilience learning becomes focused on the experience and not the outcome. This view of resilience promotion presents an ethical question that is twofold: on the one hand, there is the need to employ democratic methods to create new resilience-promoting resources (that is, to design tools using an equitable and participatory process), but which, on the other hand, simultaneously represent – or embody – the democratic essence of participation. In other words, an 'ethical' resilience interface would be one designed using inclusive methods, and one that embodies and perpetuates the values of inclusion and participation into the future, ensuring that the integrity of the participatory process is carried through into future uses.

Designing for resilience is designing for indeterminability

By involving children in designing resilience resources, participation in the design process can provide rich opportunities for their learning. For a number of decades parallels have been drawn between learning experience and designing – framing design as a practice that transforms knowledge and 'produces new constructions and representations of reality' (Cazden *et al.* 1996: 76). Where technology must accommodate multiple representations of reality, indeterminability becomes a key design goal. Jesse Tatum writes that designing for indeterminability ensures that 'technology becomes a realm not of singular solutions to specific challenges, but of almost infinitely variable choice' thus increasing its 'political legitimacy' (2004: 69). PD frames design process as a space of negotiating ethics, voice, authorship and presence. As such, a participatory approach could be argued to constitute an ethical approach precisely because it decreases the 'representative power' of any existing models of resilience, by making it incomplete and open to renegotiation.

Shifting the degree of responsibility for the designed object

In a participatory framework, a designer's responsibility shifts from creating a representation of resilience that users may find meaningful to ensuring adequate means for participants to construct their own meanings. Any existing examples of resilience are reframed as conceptual triggers intended to secure the continuity of interaction, as opposed to serving as exemplars of resilient behaviours or attributes intended for rote learning and replication. This process requires a degree of systematic responsiveness to the contextual specificity of participants' experiences and a corresponding methodology for incorporating these into the design process.

In this regard, and similarly to other characteristically 'responsive' (Gray and Malins 2004: 21) research methodologies – action research (AR), for example – PD is committed to the changes that participants undergo throughout the research process. Further alignment apparent through each methodology's acknowledgement of participants as collaborative researchers, or 'co-investigators' (Hearn and Foth 2004), ensures sustained participation throughout the research process. AR remains a highly recommended methodology for new media projects on the basis of 'its grounding in actual processes of change, the primacy it gives to respondent phenomenology, and its flexible, open and eclectic conceptualizing processes' (Hearn and Foth 2004: 3). Drawing on the 'responsiveness' feature of AR, the PD research process remains open to the nuances of individual and collective participants' responses, but goes further to reframe more fundamentally the traditional roles of designer and user as dialogic.

Case study – designing digital resilience tools

The case study of using PD to design a digital application for promoting children's resilience online forms the foundation of my practice-based PhD research, entitled 'Resilience by Design' in order to highlight its emphasis on children's agency in the design process. I collaborated with nearly fifty children, involved as co-researchers and co-designers, in the process of developing an overarching framework and then the interfaces for a digital resilience-promoting programme. The project was designed in a way that allowed children to systematically engage in the design process, contributing their knowledge and experiences as primary drivers for the phases of design.

Two groups of primary school students aged 10 were involved. The children were from two school sites, with each group containing approximately 20–25 students. Both groups were involved in the project for approximately two years throughout their enrolment in the final years of primary schooling (2007–2008). Their participation was sustained throughout all project phases, including the conceptual design phase, paper prototyping, testing the usability in prototyping stages, and the creation and trials of the final set of digital tools.

Structuring children's participation in the design and research process

Using the PD framework, I introduced the creative workshop as a key method of engaging children in the design process. Creative methods of generating content and collecting data are increasingly used in the research of children's experience (Australian Research Alliance for Children and Youth 2005; Greene and Hogan 2005: 14). In the four modules comprising eight workshops, children explored the notion of resilience both as a set of distinct attributes and as a process of their acquisition. In each workshop, children were encouraged to contextualize and prioritize attributes of resilience based on relevance to their personal, social and community settings. The workshop activities guided a transition between the formal meaning of resilience and the articulation of children's own, situated meanings of resilience, its qualities and how it relates to them. Table 8.1 illustrates how this process unfolded as children identified, manipulated and prioritized aspects of resilience throughout the design phases and in the evaluation stages.

Figure 8.1 illustrates how this participatory process unfolded in actuality, using archival documentation combined with concrete examples of research outcomes. Participant responses from a qualitative evaluation of the creative process reported that the process of designing the tools was of primary benefit, which resulted in the following design brief: that the digital tools needed to be designed to mirror the participatory *process* of creative workshops to allow other children an equal opportunity to situate their understanding of resilience as those involved directly in the design process.

TABLE 8.1 Resilience by Design: applying Participatory Design framework to design of resilience tools (Copyright Zelenko 2011).

	Extent of participation	*Outcome of participation*
Participants as co-researchers and co-designers	define conceptualize represent/visualize	resilience definitions/models
	co-determine	project goals and priorities
	shape	process, interface and interaction
	evaluate and refine	project outcomes

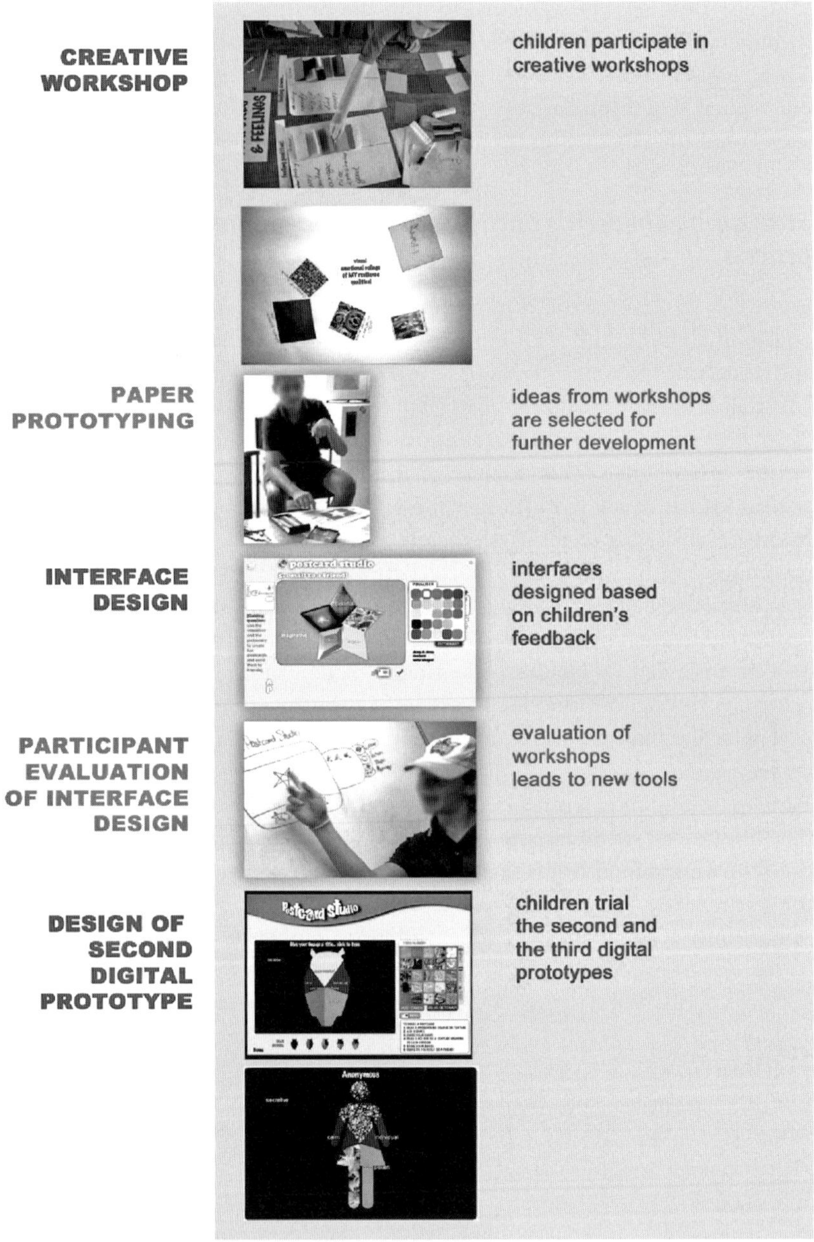

FIGURE 8.1 Resilience by Design: documenting Participatory Design framework using research outcomes (copyright Zelenko 2011).

Participant-generated representations of resilience

In conceptual development and the early prototyping sessions, the participatory process enabled children to create rich context-specific representations of resilience (Figures 8.2–8.4) that are firmly grounded in their socio-emotional realities, prioritizing those attributes of resilience they perceive as significant to their day-to-day coping. The self-portraits children created revealed their capacity to think abstractly and to construct sophisticated visual compositions that communicate the experiential complexity of being resilient.

The underpinning rationale and the ethical basis for applying PD in the context of resilience promotion is its framing of children at the creative core of the project and their lived experiences as valid sources of knowledge. PD takes children's contribution beyond the initial step of acknowledgement of their views to active integration into the social construction of the meaning of resilience. Evaluation

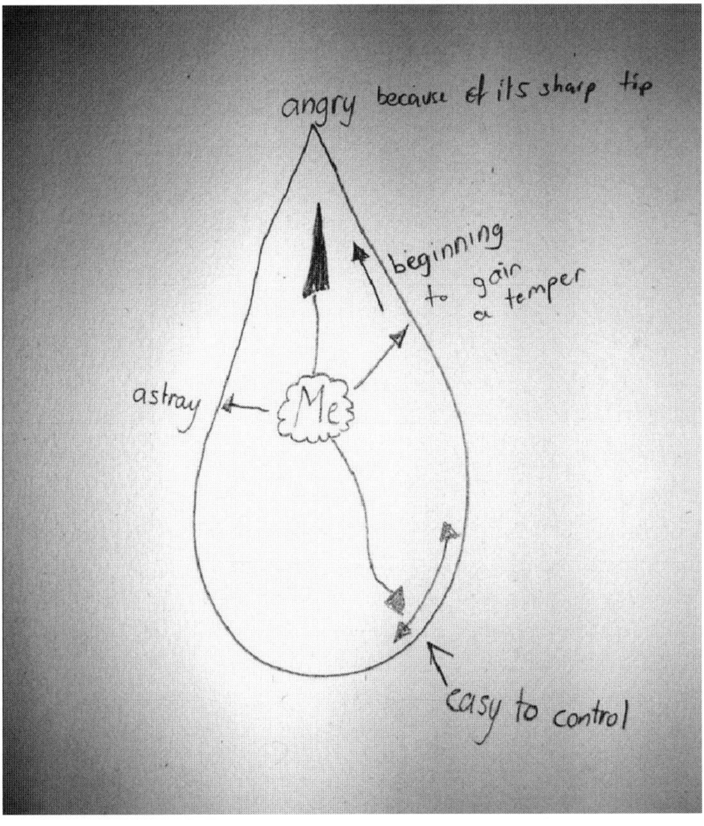

FIGURE 8.2 Creative workshop outcomes: a boy describes his individual qualities through the form of his chosen symbol (copyright Zelenko 2011).

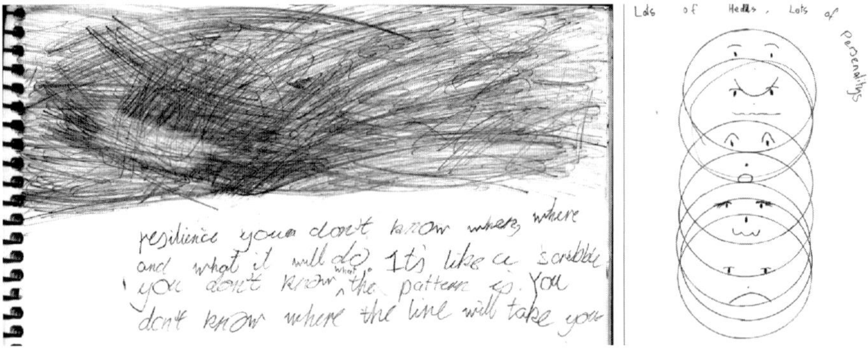

FIGURE 8.3 Resilience journal: two abstract representations, one accompanied by a poem: 'resilience you don't know when, where and what it will do. It's like a scribble. You don't know what the pattern is. You don't know where the line will take you.' (Boy, age 12) (copyright Zelenko 2011).

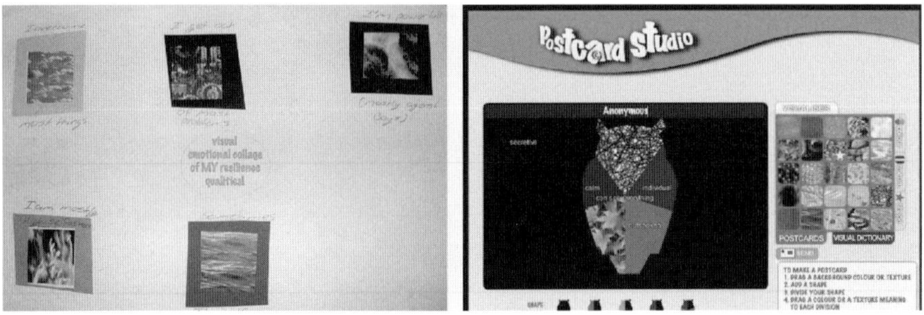

FIGURE 8.4 Module Three: self-portrait created using visual resilience code (copyright Zelenko 2011).

showed that within this collaborative process, children felt empowered in the experience of transforming the meaning of resilience and through the newly developed awareness of their agency and decision-making capacity. The PD process allowed for subjective, and often contradictory, responses to be juxtaposed and documented as equally valued units of knowledge. Consequently, resilience came to be understood as a complex, multifaceted and perpetually evolving concept.

Conclusion

PD facilitates the process of interaction that is dialogic and collaborative and that supports a model of resilience based in lived experience and the richness of its contextual specificity. The 'Resilience by Design' case study presents one possible design solution to the questions concerning the developmental processes and uses of new media technologies in the emerging field of digital resilience promotion. In the context of resilience promotion, participation shifts children and the design process away from a peripheral and marginal position and into the core of creative decision-making. Among the key outcomes of applying the PD model is its contribution to reframing of children not as users but as co-creators, both at the level of designing the technology and also potentially at the level of contributing to the design of resilience-promoting initiatives. Existing resilience tools have restricted, to a large extent, opportunities for interaction, with the parameters of resilience predetermined at the conceptual level by the creators of the programme. In digital programs that deny opportunities to intervene with represented models of resilience, the children are virtually – and therefore literally – invisible. Participation opens new directions for exploring models of resilience promotion that are unique to the digital context, in which the role of the child, the designer and the mental health practitioner are redefined.

References

Australian Research Alliance for Children and Youth (2005) 'Count me in!', *Guidelines on involving children in research*. Available at: www.kids.nsw.gov.au/publications/count_me_in.html (accessed 10 September 2010).

Brown, Paul (1994) 'The ethics and aesthetics of the image interface', *ACM SIGGRAPH Computer Graphics*, 29(1): 28–30.

Butson, R. (2003) 'Learning objects: weapons of mass instruction', *British Journal of Educational Technology*, 34(5): 667–669.

Cazden, C., Cope, B., Fairclough, N., Gee, J., Kalantzis, M., Kress, G., Luke, A., Luke, C., Michaels, S. and Nakata, M. (1996) 'A pedagogy of multiliteracies: designing social futures', *Harvard Educational Review*, 66: 60–92.

Drucker, J. and Nowviskie, B. (2004) 'Speculative computing: aesthetic provocations in humanities computing' in S. Shreibman, R. Siemens, and J. Unsworth (eds), A *Companion to Digital Humanities*, Oxford: Blackwell.

Dunne, A. (2005) *Hertzian Tales: Electronic objects, aesthetic experience and critical design*, Cambridge, MA: MIT Press.

Empsak, F. (1993) 'Workers, unions and new technology', D. Schuler and A. Namioka (eds), *Participatory Design: Principles and practices*, Hillsdale, NJ: Lawrence Erlbaum Associates.

Fry, T. (1999) *A New Design Philosophy: An introduction to defuturing*, Adelaide: University of New South Wales Press.

Gigliotti, C. (1995) 'Aesthetics of a virtual world source', *Leonardo*, 28(4): 289–295.

Gordon Rouse, K.A., Longo, M. and Trickett, M. (2001) 'Fostering resilience in children', *Bulletin*: 875–899, The Ohio State University. Available at: http://ohioline.osu.edu.b875/index.html (accessed 20 October 2010).

Gray, C. and Malins, J. (2004) *Visualizing Research: A guide to the research process in art and design*, Aldershot: Burlington.

Greene, S. and Hogan, D. (2005) 'Preface', in S. Greene and D. Hogan (eds), *Researching Children's Experience*, London: Sage.

Hearn, G. and Foth, G. (2004) 'Action research in the design of new media and ICT systems', *Current Issues in Communications and Media Research*, New York: Nova Science.

Heim, S. (2007) *The Resonant Interface: HCI foundations for interaction design*, Boston, MA: Pearson/Addison Wesley.

Kolb, D. A. (1984) *Experiential Learning Experience as a Source of Learning and Development*, Upper Saddle Valley, NJ: Prentice Hall.

Laurel, B. and Mountford, S. J. (1990) *The Art of Human–Computer Interface Design*, Reading, MA: Addison-Wesley.

Lumby, C. and Probyn, E. (2003) *Remote Control: New media, new ethics*, Cambridge: Cambridge University Press.

Manovich, L. (2001) *The Language of New Media*, Cambridge, MA: MIT Press.

Muller, M. J. and Kuhn, S. (1993) 'Introduction – special issue on participatory design', *Communications of the ACM*, 36(4): 24–28.

Muller, M. J. (1992) 'Retrospective on a year of participatory design using the PICTIVE technique', *Proceedings of the SIGCHI Conference on Human Factors in Computing Systems*, 455–462.

Murray, J. (1997) *Hamlet on the Holodeck: The future of narrative in cyberspace*, Cambridge, MA: MIT Press.

Narayanan, G. (2008) 'Moving beyond the plentitude: an Indian fable', Keynote address at *ED-MEDIA 2008 – World Conference on Educational Multimedia, Hypermedia and Telecommunications*, 30 June–4 July, Austria.

Robertson, T., Bødker, K., Bratteteig, T., and Loi, D. (eds) (2010) Proceedings of the 11th Conference on Participatory Design, PDC 2010, Sydney, Australia, 29 November–3 December.

Sanoff, H. (1990) *Participatory Design: Theory and techniques*, Raleigh, NC: Henry Sanoff.

Silverstein, J., Nissenbaum, H., Flanagan, M. and Freier N. G. (2007) 'Ethics and children's information systems', *Proceedings of the American Society for Information Science and Technology*, 43(1): 1–7.

Stewart, D., Sun, J. and Hardie, M. (2006) *An Ounce of Prevention. . .*, QUT 'Resilient Children and Communities Project', Final Report, Brisbane: Queensland University of Technology.

Tatum, J. S. (2004) 'The challenge of responsible design', *Design Issues*, 20(3): 66–80.

Zelenko, O. (2006) *Promoting Resilience Online: A survey of currently available digital tools designed to promote resilience in primary school children*, Queensland University of Technology, School of Public Health, Centre for Health Research (internal report).

Zelenko, O. (2011) 'Resilience by design: a participatory approach to designing an interactive digital application for promoting children's resilience', (unpublished PhD thesis), Brisbane: Creative Industries Faculty, Queensland University of Technology.

9

INTERACTION DESIGN, MASS COMMUNICATION AND THE CHALLENGE OF DISTRIBUTED EXPERTISE[1]

John Hartley

Introduction

This chapter considers some implications of the rise of design as a master-metaphor of the information age. It compares the terms 'Interaction Design' and 'mass communication', suggesting that both can be seen as a contradiction in terms, inappropriately preserving an industrial-age division between producers and consumers. With the shift from mass media to interactive media, semiotic and political power seems to be shifting too – from media producers to designers. The ethical argument underlying the chapter is that it is important for the new discipline of *Interaction* Design not to fall into habits of thought inherited from the *mass* industrial era. Instead of a top-down, expert-in-charge ethic, where the designer is the causal agent and the consumer or user is the end-point, it will be increasingly important to develop a 'user ethic' where productivity arises precisely from *interaction* between expertise and use; the relationship between designer and user is mutual, dialogic and participatory. Because users bring their own diverse expertise to the encounter, I argue for the significance of 'distributed expertise' – including social network markets (Potts *et al.* 2008), DIY-culture, user-led innovation, consumer co-created content, and the use of Web 2.0 affordances for social, scientific and creative purposes as well as for entertainment (Hartley 2009). I consider the growth of distributed expertise as part of a new paradigm in the growth of knowledge, which has evolved through a number of phases, from *abstraction*, to *representation*, to *productivity*. In the context of technologically mediated popular participation in the growth of knowledge and social relationships, the chapter argues that the design and media-production professions need to cross rather than maintain the gap between experts and everyone else, enabling all the agents in the system to navigate the shift into the paradigm of mass productivity.

Design status

With the rise of computer communication, an entire professional group – I won't go so far as to use the word 'class' (Florida 2002) – has arisen around the interface between computers and humans, and between computers and organizations. These occupations have successfully shaken off the humble designation of the 'technician' (from the IT department) to aspire to higher status under the banner of 'design' (from the art school).

It is in this context that we can observe the rise of 'Interaction Design', an apparently neutral descriptor for an area of specialist expertise. The innovation encapsulated in this name is that it associates human/computer interaction with aesthetic rather than scientific disciplines, shifting the field of study from its background in engineering, computer and cognitive science towards a future in the arts and design. Some insiders see this shift as a rift, causing the discipline of Interaction Design to develop in two different directions at once. Jonas Löwgren explains Interaction Design as a discipline going in two directions: 'One interpretation is to view Interaction Design as an extension of HCI [Human–Computer Interaction]. Another interpretation is to view Interaction Design as a design discipline, with more in common with architecture than with engineering and behavioral sciences' (Löwgren 2011). It is noteworthy that the same journey from the lab or workshop to the studio has been taken by other previously technical professions, including design, both in general and in particular forms such as graphic design, in the contemporary period. Going back in time, the European Renaissance itself was heralded by the transformation of anonymous artisanal craftsmen into named individual artists who remain bankable to this day – from Giotto, Leonardo, Michelangelo (architecture, painting and sculpture) to Tallis, Shakespeare, La Varenne (music, theatre, cuisine). Thus 'Interaction Design' is by no means alone in rebranding *as art* a direction whose pull seems irresistible in any post-medieval society.

Indeed, the status hierarchy of our times puts the designer, as opposed to technicians or even engineers, on a pedestal, on a par with artists. The abstract idea of 'design', once elevated to such a plane, is then available to organize large investments, involving both pecuniary (economic) and symbolic (cultural) values. Perhaps because of its rising or aspirational status, the word 'designer' has escaped the confines of a technical expertise and now applies to myriad occupations distributed throughout the economy. It is the default descriptor of the information age, just as the engineer was the master-metaphor for the mechanical–industrial era. So profoundly has our age invested in the concept of design, in fact, that it is also the latest euphemism for the entity previously known as God. The existence of a deity is claimed to be demonstrated by evidence of '*intelligent design*' in nature (Dawkins 1986). Indeed, while many of us are sceptical about the religious godhead, nevertheless we remain creationists in relation to design. We attribute fabulous powers to designers, including the godlike ability to create.

Division of creative labour

What is at stake in the professionalization of human and cultural values in the service of business? The professionalization of 'Interaction Design' is a problem, not because it is commercial or too variable a field to define, but because its capture by professional experts in the service of firms reproduces an existing and more fundamental divide – that between *producers* and *consumers*. In this model, inherited from the heyday of industrial capitalism going back to the nineteenth century, designers are on the production side; the value they add is to *do something to consumers*.

Here, then, is the nub of the ethical problem I want to identify: 'Interaction Design' *abstracts* both 'design' and 'interaction' from the everyday domain, and relocates them within expert systems from which most humans are excluded. Consumers only appear as the end-point of a production process in which they play no creative or even active role. In this model, 'interaction' describes not relations among humans but how a technological system (created by experts) 'interacts' with 'users'. 'Design' is not seen as a human attribute but as a certificated business practice. It takes what is abundant – 'embedded behaviour in human environments' (Berridge 2007: 90) – and makes it a scarce resource for profit.

Now, of course, such specialization based on ordinary practices is commonplace. The knowledge economy works by taking tacit knowledge (for example, cookery) and making it explicit (the recipe), replicable (published) and entrepreneurial (celebrity chefs) (Leadbeater 2000). Such a process is generally beneficial. A human attribute is improved, and returned to ordinary people as a professional service. The problem arises only when this division of labour between producers (the expert system within business) and consumers (seen as passive, out-of-the-loop and manipulable) is taken to extremes; when the tension between economic values (design as a creative service for sale) and cultural values (interaction as a dialogic mode of communication, practised by everyone) are not reconciled.

In the industrializing economy of the nineteenth century, this tension was not seen as a problem by creative, engineering, scientific or technical specialists – in a mass society there was an incentive for 'workers by brain' to get as far away from the common mass as possible. To be abstracted from the industrial workforce was a proper aspiration, because one's white-collar social and economic status was thereby improved. At the same time, craft-based artisans were absorbed into a working class predominantly made up of unskilled labourers and factory hands, and their status declined. Instead of a gradient along which different degrees of specialization could be plotted among a population that was essentially engaged in the same enterprise – industrious productivity using individual creative talents – there emerged instead an arrow of causation. Producers *caused* transformations (of materials, meanings), of which consumers were the *effects*. It was at this point that consumers came to be understood in terms of *behaviour*, for that was taken to be evidence of the extent to which causation by producers and marketers had taken effect. Thus, producers came to be associated with organizational action, purpose and scientific causation, while consumers came to be associated with individual behaviour, distraction and irrational caprice.

However, such a division is not so easy to justify in the knowledge economy, or in the context of creative innovation. For although trained expertise is clearly vital, equally important is the role of users and consumer co-creators (OECD 2007), many of whom will bring their own expertise to a problem that is solved collaboratively rather than competitively. This is the process of mass creativity that Charles Leadbeater (2008) has dubbed 'we-think', and J. C. Herz calls 'harnessing the hive' (2005). It means that the human dimension of the growth of knowledge, of creativity, of design and of interaction can't be left entirely to the experts. With the emergence of the knowledge economy, neither can innovation itself.

The professionals have been slow to admit the implications of this paradigm shift, not least because it erodes their monopoly over creative supply. The tension between producers and consumers is made more complex by *technologies* that are at once the product of scientific expertise and universally available for just anyone to use. But professional self-preservation seems to dictate that designers continue to stand between users and technologies. Thus we can observe a continuing assumption that *Interaction Design* is the expertise needed to facilitate users' interactions with technology and to see users as synonymous with consumers.

Here, for instance, is how the term itself has been defined on Wikipedia: 'Interaction Design (IxD) is the discipline of defining the behavior of products and systems that a user can interact with' (Wikipedia 2011). Here's another definition, from a website dedicated to the discipline: '"Interaction Design" refers to the shaping of interactive products and services with a specific focus on their use' (Löwgren 2011). And another, closer to my home:

> ACID is the Australasian Cooperative Research Centre for Interaction Design. We find better ways for people to interact with each other using communication technologies. Our expertise lies in helping people participate in the digital world. ACID conducts deep and substantial research in Interaction Design and user experience design.
>
> (ACID 2010)

Seemingly, it is all simple and clear. Interaction Design is a commercial service profession, 'helping people participate' in their interactions with computers, and thence with each other, for a fee.

Contradictions in terms?

When I take a closer look at the two words in the phrase 'Interaction Design', I can't help thinking that they look uncomfortable together. Is this a case of Heisenberg's uncertainty principle: you can have design, or you can have interaction, but you can't have both at once? My uncertainty stems from my own disciplinary background in media studies. The argument I want to make is that design is facing the same challenges now as television has done throughout the broadcast era. Or, to put it another way, here we go again.

In my field of media, communication and cultural studies, the relations between various two-term oppositions have, for many years, been a focus of analysis, and sometimes a bone of contention:

Producer	/	*Consumer*
Supply	/	Demand
Expert	/	Amateur
Provider	/	Client
Corporation	/	Customer
Organization	/	Individual
Causal action	/	Behavioural effect
Television	/	*Audience*

Is this the tacit mental model that generates a new opposition?

Designer	/	*User*

Here is where the ethical alarm bells begin to ring. Does the definition of Interaction Design, which originated in computer science, unwittingly reproduce *mass communication theory*?

This is where the notion of a 'contradiction in terms' comes in. It alludes to one of the founding texts of contemporary communication studies, a paper by the sociologist Philip Elliott (1972) called 'Mass communications – a contradiction in terms?' Elliott was drawing attention to the disparity between *face to face* communication and *mass* media. 'Interaction Design' (the term) similarly reproduces a disparity between experts working in corporate or professional organizations (on the one hand) and consumers, creating content in social networks (on the other). Sometimes this disparity can amount to disparagement, as each side harbours suspicions about the other. A well-known contemporary critic of the 'cult of the amateur', for instance, is Andrew Keen (2007):

> We are teetering on the edge of catastrophe. Blogs, wikis and social networking are, indeed, assaulting our economy, our culture and our values. Web 2.0 is pushing us back into the Dark Ages. That's a big deal. It's a message that needs to be shouted from every available soapbox – even from a loathsome blog like this. It deserves to be broadcast in the most electric of oranges.
>
> (Keen 2006)

Keen is extreme, but he is not alone; his polemic struck a chord among many commentators, often those closely identified with legacy media technologies such as printed newspapers. The more specialized the creative sector of the economy, the more militant the occupations within it seem to be about *maintaining* the distance between themselves and the punters. Thus, technical or craft skills keep large-scale media production crews or product designers in specialist firms isolated from their customers, while human-contact professions, such as marketing and performance, spread more easily into other firms, across the economy (Cunningham 2008). Throughout the broadcast era, these two tribes – producers, served by arcane crafts, and consumers, serviced by 'marcom' (the professionalized science of promotion – see, for example, *Journal of Integrated Marketing Communications*) – saw very little of each other. Experts designed and made things; consumers used them up and threw them away (Whiteley 1997). Very rarely did the twain meet, much less interact, because from the point of view of the experts, interactivity was a design functionality in the product (not the user), while for consumers interactivity was what they did with each other (not the product).

This lack of communication between producers and consumers is what led Elliott to question the *communicative* credentials of *mass* media. How could consuming an industrial product be seen as communication? In the mass era, communication was essentially one-way – *from* powerful and central organizations, *to* a feminized, suburban, domestic family audience. There was clearly a yawning gap between them in terms of ownership of the means of production, power, influence and opinion-formation.

The *research field* of mass communication was captured by this asymmetry – it became the study of how corporate and state ownership and control of mass media resulted in manipulated populations, who were persuaded by commercial and political campaigns to hold opinions, make decisions and perform actions that they would otherwise not have chosen, which were not (according to the critics) in their interests as citizens or in terms of their 'real' class, gender, sexual or ethnic interests.

Abstraction and representation

Semiotic representation is a fundamental driver of language, being the means by which humans make signs (such as words or images) stand for something else (such as meanings or ideas). Meanwhile, the political kind of representation is a means by which we make *someone* (a politician) stand for *someone else* (indeed, lots of someones) – that's the essence of kingship as well as representative democracy.

Semiotic representation – symbolic values (meanings)

Political representation – democratic values (decisions)

When successfully conjoined in relations of mutual cordiality, such representation can, of course, produce spectacular results. On the semiotic side, Shakespeare represented his culture; on the political side, democratizing polities can make decisions that improve the lives of all. These two kinds of representation were industrialized

– massively scaled up and marketized – during the same period, beginning in nineteenth-century Europe, the period we call modernity. In both cases, industrialization accelerated the abstraction and specialization of previously tacit human knowledge (say, from making clothes, food or music to being a fashion designer, chef or composer). The same has happened to the function of representation itself. The extension of markets and franchises produced an ever-widening asymmetry between those whose meanings or choices were represented (the populace) and those who were active agents in making both meanings and decisions.

However, the improvements in scale brought about by the regime of representation were not without cost. Design cannot exist as a domain of specialist expertise without abstraction. Activities, processes and artefacts that are part of everyone's daily life and labour must be abstracted from the domestic context, and also the manual part of fabrication must be abstracted from the mental part. Only then can design emerge as a separate field. This is a long-term historical process with its roots in ancient divisions of labour (for example, by gender and social hierarchy), but it was not until the beginning of modernity that abstraction took on industrial proportions. The factory system scaled up specialization and the division of labour, and required a radical separation of design from manufacture. Perhaps this is why the Design Institute of Australia (the 'representative' industry body) is still insistent that designers are a class apart: 'A designer plans things for manufacture or construction. The difference between a designer and a craftsperson or artist is that designers usually develop things that have requirements set by others and will ultimately be produced by others' (Design Institute of Australia 2011). The fruits of the design-led manufacturing process were so good, and so cheap, and so plentiful, that they supplanted artisanal fabrication among the population at large. It was at this point – the point at which aesthetics (culture) met commerce (economy) in the commodification of design – that design itself became representative. It was undertaken by increasingly high-prestige specialists on behalf of whole populations, whose choices were represented by those of designers (Sudjic 2008). The asymmetry between specialists and everyone else grew to extreme proportions, because as people (now markets) enjoyed the use of ever-more sophisticated designs, so their own skill-set was reduced. As society's creative horizons widened, the scope for self-made creative innovation among the general population narrowed.

Before industrial urbanization and the factory system, ordinary people had produced for themselves many of the necessities for sustaining life, home and culture. Then along came Adam Smith and his pin factory (Smith 1776: 1.1), and a new, abstract understanding of the productivity of the division of labour. The industrial process of abstraction and specialization reached into the household. Production turned to consumption as 'housewives' were encouraged, by price, quality – and design – to abandon DIY and head for the [super]market. Previously productive aspects of domestic life, such as growing food, cooking, sewing and home-making, and also cultural pursuits such as singing and dancing, were replaced by the cash nexus and shifted across to consumption. Thus semiotic productivity was abstracted from people's everyday lives, even as they enjoyed the expansion of its products.

This characteristic of industrial society is shared by popular culture, which also became representative as opposed to artisanal during industrialization. This was when folk culture transformed into pop culture. Storytelling, singing and the like were abstracted from the household and sold back in the form of media. Both design and media massively increased the amount of visual representation in general circulation, from designs on pots to illustrations in media. However, *self-representation* declined, as the population at large produced for themselves fewer and fewer of the meanings and decisions in which they lived. The professionalization of design *converted* the masses into 'passive' consumers and audiences, or so it has seemed for many critics.

Nevertheless, people were not passive. They had to learn new skills. For instance, if you stop making clothes, cooking food and singing songs, and start buying fashion, eating out and listening to recordings, you need to learn how to choose among *symbolic and status-based* alternatives within social network markets (Potts *et al.* 2008), and this is where the popular media came into their own. As cultural subsistence (sing-it-yourself) declined and the cultural market economy grew, the media became the forum in which symbolic values were established and exchanged. Ideas, products and designs competed for popular attention (Lanham 2006). Far from consuming passively, people began to represent their own identities via such choices, including the spectacular subcultures of the 1960s and after (Hebdige 1979), fanship (Hills 2002), and the competitive music-and-movie playlists on contemporary social networking sites such as YouTube (Burgess and Green 2009).

Down the tube?

The modern mass media are based on *representation*, semiotic and political. They abstract individual humans (celebrities and stars), both real and imaginary (in news and drama), from the anonymous throng and make them *stand for* everyone else in society, both symbolically and democratically. Because broadcast television in particular reached an almost universal audience, at least in developed countries, it was easy to believe that everyone was spoken for on TV. *Everyone was represented* – ordinary life and everyday choices were the real subject of mass media – but simultaneously *no one spoke for themselves*. Everything was realist but nothing was real.

On the plus side, television's domestic setting, live immediacy, leisure-time availability, casual continuity, operational simplicity (two knobs on the TV set) and the human scale of a screen that was suited to faces and dialogue, were all appropriate for the context in which it thrived best: private life and family-building in conditions of expanding consumer affluence and the suburban experience. On screen, broadcast television excelled at head-to-head dramatic conflict, both fictional and factual, in drama, comedy, news, sport and kids' shows. While encouraging people to stay at home, it taught neighbourly comportment and experiential and national togetherness, and it continuously brought new information and experience to all sections of the public. It could also coordinate population-wide (sometimes planet-wide) attention to, and emotional investment in, periods of excitement and high uncertainty, as during sporting finals, end-of-season cliffhangers, elections and political crises, and moments of wonder or terror, such as the moon landings, 9/11, the Asian tsunami or the inauguration of President Obama. It was the semiotic bell-wether of change for a population living through change.

This model of democratic inclusion is typical of broadcasting: not to identify separately but to enfold narratively; not to speak *for* but to speak *to* a universal audience. Broadcast TV wants to encompass its audience and entertain them, but it doesn't want them to do very much in return, except watch. And because of this, representative television remains a problem. The high capital cost of production and highly regulated distribution networks resulted in an extreme division of labour between corporate expertise and lay audiences. For their part, because they didn't appear to be doing anything very much and were de-skilled compared with producer occupations, audiences always seemed to be at the mercy of powerful persuaders, commercial marketing, political manipulation, and jackass behaviour. The model was not so much communication as contagion, as Elliot feared.

So network television came to represent the universalization of corporate will, encapsulated in advertising that reduced audiences to consumers, agency to behaviour, and modernity to an endless pipeline of products, carried from manufacturers and retailers to waiting, willing, wanting housewives, whose job it was to buy the things that were advertised, serve them up to the family (slouched on the couch watching TV), then clean up the house and the bodies in it using more TV-advertised products. Broadcast television perfected its role as the purveyor of what was needed to sustain domestic life by reducing it to a flow of consumption – products came into the house, went through the alimentary system and then safely out again, chased by cleansing agents from toothpaste to Toilet Duck. No wonder they called it the Tube.[2]

Towards direct consumer (user) productivity

Broadcast television clearly had its limits as a system of representation. These limits will be experienced by any expert system where a small professional group represents everyone else. The same applies to Interaction Design, if it retains a distinction between designers and users that is modelled on the industrial producer/consumer divide. Without meaning to do any harm, such a model nevertheless continues the industrial tradition of expert control, hanging on to a provider mentality, retaining the distance between producer and consumer, confining agency to the producer, and reducing consumers and audiences to the status of an 'effect' of actions over which they have no control.

Such legacy thinking applies to many areas of professional practice, across the creative disciplines, from architecture and art to media production, software development and writing. This is because social institutions, such as professions, change more slowly than technologies. As a result, new systems and possibilities may already be in full flower while existing institutions continue to do – and do well – what they have been doing all along.

Here, then, is where the wrecking ball of innovation may hit the established edifice of industrial representation. With the widespread accessibility and uptake of Web 2.0, consumption need no longer be seen as *behaviour*, to be manipulated by experts and denounced by critics, but as *action*, a new phase of productivity and DIY creative potential, but now *distributed* across whole populations and not confined to abstracted professionals and experts (Hartley 2008: 28). The process of creative destruction of industrial-era representational systems has indeed been set in train by the internet. It is not felt immediately or evenly by all those who will be affected by it, whether they are the TV industry, political representatives or interaction designers. But the wrecking ball is in full swing. TV screens are transforming into monitors and computer terminals. Television is migrating out of the house, into the street, heading downtown. It is miniaturized and mobile. Television began as 'one-to-many' broadcasting, but is developing into a global network – like a phone system – with many possible content providers and viewing platforms. In other words, it is playing catch-up with the internet. Already it is downloadable. You can customize your viewing schedule and create your own shows. With YouTube and other video-sharing sites you can 'Broadcast Yourself'. So television is falling forward into participatory culture (Jenkins 2006; McCarthy 2009), converging with consumer co-created content and distributed production whether the established players like it or not.

The question for the future is this: can TV combine the 'do-it-yourself' and 'do-it-with-others' (DIY/DIWO) attributes of the internet with the broadcasting pleasures of the couch? Can you *self-represent* and be an informed citizen, a creative consumer and a truly networked communicator – all at once? Can television be created – or designed – directly '*by* the people' rather than by representatives, and still tell compelling stories?

The greatest challenge to broadcast television comes as the regime of representation gives way to a new model of communication – not mass but based on the *direct productivity* and action of the agents previously known as consumers. Here is where both semiotic and political innovation is most intense and most urgent. Existing players are experimenting with new business models, programming formats, advertising strategies, not to mention cost-cutting and downsizing. Meanwhile, independent players – both individuals and enterprises, both non-market consumer-co-creators and ambitious entrepreneurs – are coming up with new uses for television, broadcast and otherwise, based not on expert provision to passive consumers (or even interactive users), but on social networks (Potts *et al.* 2008).

Productivity design

Caught up as it is in the same historical changes, design can no longer be seen as the preserve of designers. Creativity is made up of the activities and productivity of the millions who interact in the social networks that are now dispersed throughout the community. With the growing ubiquity of digital media, consumers (both individually and aggregated) are becoming a source of innovation, often more dynamic than firms. The social network swarm outperforms the IP-protected lab, and at twice the speed (Herz 2005).

If it is true that we are evolving from an era of *representation* to one of *productivity*, from expert provision to 'distributed expertise', what does this mean for Interaction Design? The question goes beyond whether it should invest in a technical or an aesthetic future. Instead, the important question is whether it should switch allegiance from the producer to the consumer, from supply to demand, from expertise to participation. The principal value proposition in the field of Interaction Design is to recognize the shift from representation to productivity, and the value of population-wide agency and participation in digital creative innovation. Research is needed, not so much on how to *provide* services to a consumer, but how to identify ways that community-wide creativity can be propagated, improved, and integrated, via markets as well as public agencies and institutions, with the growth of knowledge.

Web 2.0 applications build on ubiquitous computational power and connectivity in advanced economies to enable user-created content. This poses an increasing challenge to established players, including large corporations. Interaction is more decisive than design, but it is the interaction among people and agencies in complex networks, not the interaction of users (consumers) with technologies (proprietary applications), that we must understand. The internet is a creative community based on productive agents in social networks, some of global scale. But this did not develop directly from expert designers providing consumers with marketized solutions. The rapid growth of the online economy is based on innovations that originated outside of the market economy, from the internet itself (security), to the World Wide Web (academic) to the achievements of 'we-think', such as Wikipedia and Open Source (social networking). Thus, it is important to develop a research programme that is not solely focused on firms, and not dedicated to the proposition that experts provide solutions for clients. The model must be participatory, to assist the development of creative productivity among communities of interest wherever they may be found, for their own purposes. It is from participatory culture itself that the most important changes will emerge. The commercialization of applications and the marketization of internet services are second-stage processes of adoption and retention, where markets are coordinating mechanisms, not the 'generative edge' of creative innovation itself (Zittrain 2008).

The real importance of consumer-created content and participatory culture is that they require new ways of thinking about both creativity and innovation in the growth of knowledge. Neither design nor innovation is any longer the exclusive preserve of specialist experts. The industrial model of an IP-protected expert pipeline, controlling value-adds along a value chain and concentrating expertise inside the firm (the IKEA model of consumer participation, if you like), is also under challenge. Now, both innovation and profitability require a collaborative interface with users, who may be other firms, but who also include 'consumers' (the word no longer makes any sense) in general.

Practical applications

To investigate human values and public good as well as economic benefits, we must include the development of *new models of enterprise* based on *participatory culture* and *consumer productivity*, and new approaches to innovation policy. Such research must encompass human and cultural factors as well as science and technology. To do so, it needs to develop an ethic of dialogic participation, not to erase the distinction between producer and consumer, expert and amateur, but to reduce the asymmetry between them by allowing agency, causation and productivity to both sides, rather than retaining a one-way model. A co-creative model will not eradicate the *difference* between a professional designer and their client, or between the developers of interactive affordances and their users, but it will allow for design to be a stake in the game for both parties, and for the solution to Interaction Design problems to be an achievement or outcome of the relationships among these different agents and agencies, not the property of just one privileged player.

How can Interaction Designers take seriously the challenge of ubiquitous creativity and innovation, and how can they coordinate, adopt, retain and marketize the innovations enabled by consumer-created content, user-led innovation and crowd-sourced knowledge? The research agenda needs to be expanded from the industrial or representative question (what can producers do to consumers?) to the productivity question (how can the creative productivity of users and consumers contribute to the overall growth of knowledge and values, both economic and cultural?). Research is required to identify how this expanded notion of creative productivity in the design field will impact on the theory and practice of professional services in three interlinked contexts: creative professionals, enterprises and managers (practitioners); national and international R&D networks (policy); and business models and processes for new enterprise formation and corporate/community uptake (business strategy).

In each of these three contexts, the development of distributed expertise can be boosted rather than resisted. As many participatory designers already recognize in their own collaborative models of practice, it's not a threat to professional design but a resource, where users are a significant source of innovation. It is in the interest of expertise itself to promote the development of 'entrepreneurial' users and consumers, who then form part of the co-creative community, in just the same way that it is vital for fashion houses to educate, develop and support high-end users or icon consumers who 'get' what they are trying to do, and will take a risk on their behalf by wearing their designs in influential and sometimes unpredicted ways, thereby contributing to the emergence of the new. In the field of Interaction Design, the notion of the entrepreneurial consumer does not have to be confined to the rich (Daphne Guinness) or the famous (Kate Moss, J-Lo); it can be developed much more widely among online users as a population. Looking to the future, there are opportunities for Interaction Design researchers to assist in this developmental process (as well as assessing it) by working to extend creative and digital literacy among users; incorporating consumer co-creation and start-up enterprise formation (in the same way that, in fashion, certain youthful amateur bloggers have been incorporated into the mainstream professional fashion media: see, for example, *Teen Vogue* n.d.).

Interaction designers can be at the forefront of developing a distributed network structure and collaborative work, open to both producers and consumers. While remaining professional (individual) and commercial (organized in firms), Interaction Design can – as many do – commit to open innovation, on the principle that knowledge shared is knowledge gained. This requires a new approach to copyright, intellectual property and digital rights management – for instance, along the lines of the Creative Commons movement, and certainly in the direction of permitting consumers to *share* copyright materials of their own and others' making. Some moves in this direction are already apparent in the policy domain (Hargreaves 2011). Such approaches suggest a new kind of relationship among agents in a system, going far beyond the binary opposition between producers and consumers. Here, the relations are among *agents* and *enterprises* in a complex *networked system* (or interlocking systems). Indeed, it may be necessary to supersede the very idea of 'interaction' design, replacing it with *productivity design.*

Some of the stakeholders in *productivity design* would include:

- *SMEs and sole traders*, including amateurs, fans, subcultures, community organizations, individual consumers and consumers as crowds (creative development);
- *access corporations* (for example, Cisco, Intel and telcos, to explore demand pressures and user-led expansion of population-scale networks);
- *content corporations* (to develop formats for participatory media and community-relations for participatory content, for example, in games);
- *marketing agencies* (human and collaborative aspects of products and services);
- *designers, artists and other creative professionals* (design of collaborative and demand-led services);
- *legal and regulatory agencies* (seeking to modernize IP law, content regulations, privacy and defamation legislation in an era of open complex participatory networks);
- *cultural institutions* (digital communities of users and co-curators – libraries, galleries, museums, archives);
- *educational providers* (propagating digital creativity);
- *property developers* (interface with existing and new communities to develop urban stories as well as structures);
- *health agencies* (patient experience and feedback, user-led therapies; self-help communities, health communication).

Among the challenges for evolving professions with technical, aesthetic and social components will be that expertise itself will no longer be a scarce resource for direct commercial exploitation, but a participatory attribute of popular culture. Expertise is a kind of community 'commons', available for multi-agent networked use both within and beyond commercial institutions like the firm or the market. If the era of semiotic and political representation is indeed giving way to a new paradigm based on mass creativity, consumer productivity and distributed expertise, then the design professions, and those of the mass media, will need to understand the cultural and creative dynamics of user experience. The days of the consumer as an effect of the agency of others are over; and the days of godlike design are over, too. A useful ethic of design is to understand the spontaneous emergence of order in complex systems, not to look for the hand of an external, causal intelligence. Design is part of popular culture, and Interaction Design, like popular media entertainment, will prosper by adapting to its participatory demands.

Notes

1 An earlier version of this chapter was published in Bulgarian as: Hartley, J. (2009) 'Interaction design, mass communication and the challenge of distributed expertise', *Sociological Problems Quarterly* [Социологически проблеми]: 3–4. I thank Orlin Spassov for that opportunity.

2 The wording of the paragraphs above borrows from my chapter in Turner, G. and Tay, J. (eds) (2009) *Television Studies After TV: Understanding television in the post-broadcast era*, London: Routledge. See also Hartley, J. (2012) *Digital Futures for Cultural and Media Studies*, Malden, MA: Wiley-Blackwell, pp. 119–120.

References

ACID (2010) 'About ACID'. Available at: www.acid.net.au/index8420.html?option=com_content&task=view&id=12&Itemid=65 (accessed 26 July 2011).

Berridge, G. (2007) *Events Design and Experience*, Oxford: Butterworth-Heinemann.

Burgess, J. and Green, J. (2009) *YouTube: Online video and participatory culture*, Cambridge: Polity Press.

Cunningham, S. (2008) 'Creative careers: what the census tells us.' Presentation to Queensland Academy of Creative Industries. Available at: https://wiki.cci.edu.au/display/CEMP/Creative+Careers+-+what+the+Census+tells+us (accessed 21 July 2011).

Dawkins, R. (1986) *The Blind Watchmaker: Why the evidence of evolution reveals a universe without design*, London: Penguin Books.

Design Institute of Australia (2011) 'What is a designer?' Available at: www.design.org.au/index.cfm?id=186 (accessed 21 July 2011).

Elliott, P. (1972) 'Mass communications – a contradiction in terms?' in D. McQuail (ed.) *Sociology of Mass Communications*, Harmondsworth: Penguin.

Florida, R. (2002) *The Rise of the Creative Class*, New York: Basic Books.

Hargreaves, I. (2011) *Digital Opportunity: A review of intellectual property and growth*, London: Intellectual Property Office. Available at: www.ipo.gov.uk/ipreview.htm (accessed 21 July 2011).

Hartley, J. (2008) *Television Truths*, Malden, MA: Blackwell-Wiley.

Hartley, J. (2009) *The Uses of Digital Literacy*, St Lucia: University of Queensland Press; New Brunswick, NJ: Transaction Publishers.

Hebdige, D. (1979) *Subculture: The meaning of style*, London: Routledge.

Herz, J. C. (2005) 'Harnessing the hive: how online games drive networked innovation' in J. Hartley (ed.) *Creative Industries*, Malden, MA: Blackwell-Wiley.
Hills, M. (2002) *Fan Cultures*, London: Routledge.
Jenkins, H. (2006) *Convergence Culture*, New York: New York University Press.
Journal of Integrated Marketing Communications (2011) Available at: http://jimc.medill.northwestern.edu/JIMCWebsite/site.htm (accessed 21 July 2011).
Keen, A. (2006) 'The Great Seduction', *The Cult of the Amateur*. Available at: http://andrewkeen.typepad.com/the_great_seduction/2006/10/my_book_now_not.html (accessed 21 July 2011).
Keen, A. (2007) *The Cult of the Amateur: How blogs, wikis, social networking, and the digital world are assaulting our economy, culture and values*, London, New York: Doubleday/Random House.
Lanham R. (2006) *The Economy of Attention*, Chicago, IL: Chicago University Press.
Leadbeater, C. (2000) *Living on Thin Air: The new economy*, London: Penguin.
Leadbeater, C. (2008) *We-Think. Mass innovation, not mass production: The power of mass creativity*, London: Profile Books.
Löwgren, J. (2011) 'Interaction Design', in M. Soegaard and R. F. Dam, (eds) *Encyclopedia of Human–Computer Interaction*. Available at: www.interaction-design.org/encyclopedia/interaction_design.html (accessed 21 July 2011).
McCarthy, R. (2009) 'The rise of the active audience and Stephen Colbert', Flow TV: 9.05. Available at: http://flowtv.org/?p=2292 (accessed 21 July 2011).
OECD (2007) *Participative Web: User-created content*. Available at: www.oecd.org/dataoecd/57/14/38393115.pdf (accessed 21 July 2011).
Potts, J., Cunningham, S., Hartley, J., and Ormerod, P. (2008) 'Social network markets: a new definition of the creative industries', *Journal of Cultural Economics*, 32(3): 167–185.
Robertson, T., Bødker, K., Bratteteig, T., and Loi, D. (eds) (2010) *Proceedings of the 11th Conference on Participatory Design*, PDC 2010, Sydney, Australia, 29 November–3 December.
Smith, A. (1776) *An Inquiry into the Nature and Causes of the Wealth of Nations*. Available at: www.econlib.org/library/Smith/smWN.html (accessed 21 July 2011).
Sudjic, D. (2008) *The Language of Things*, London: Allen Lane.
Teen Vogue. (n.d.) 'Key players'. Available at: www.teenvogue.com/industry/2009/02/teen-fashion-bloggers (accessed 21 July 2011).
Whiteley, Nigel (1997) *Design for Society*, London: Reaktion Books.
Wikipedia (2011) 'Interaction Design'. Available at: http://en.wikipedia.org/wiki/Interaction_Design (accessed 21 July 2011).
Zittrain, J. (2008) *The Future of the Internet – and How to Stop It*. New Haven, CT: Yale University Press. Available at: http:// yupnet.org/zittrain (accessed 21 July 2011).

PART III

Built environment

10

LIVING WITH STRANGERS

Urban space, affect and civility

Emma Felton

> The city can be seen . . . in terms of a kind of psycho-geography: it is the scene of our collective emotional life.
>
> (Robins 1996: 130)

The collective and the Other

The question of how strangers live together in relative harmony as cities increase in scale, density and complexity is a growing concern for urban planners, administrators and scholars of the city. Alongside an unease about the potential for things to go awry is speculation about the capacity for public urban space to enhance civic appreciation of living with difference through encounters with strangers. The majority of the world's population is now living in cities, and random and repetitious encounters with people from all cultures and all walks of life is a central feature of contemporary urban life (Pardy 2011). New and emergent forms of urbanism developing in the twenty-first century require new ways of reconceiving cities. Based on nineteenth-century town planning, the mechanisms of administrative rationality attempt to impose order on everyday life in the city. On some level, strategies are necessarily destined to fail because little account is made of the unruly and unconscious manifestations of citizens' emotional lives (Lefebvre 1991; Pile 1996; Donald 1999). An ethos of 'public good' is frequently predicated on assumptions about how people use and live in cities, and how they *should* live. I suggest that greater attention to people's affective engagement in urban space, through an understanding of the experiential realm of city life, can be useful when reconsidering the role and planning of urban public space in contemporary city. The experience of urban life engages distinct psychological, affective and corporeal modalities (Simmel 1950; Sennett 1970; Lefebvre 1991) and urban living requires a 'creative competence' (Patton 1995) manifest in tolerance, openness and civility to others, which may be reproduced in the public realm.

A focus on the *experience* of public, urban space brings to the fore knowledge about feelings of inclusion or exclusion, belonging and participation. Many factors come into play in the experience of urban space, not least the subjectivity of urban dwellers and the broader geopolitics of place. But the built environment, with its urban amenity and the opportunities it provides for engagement, is a key component in how the city is used and experienced. For Ash Amin, public space at its most optimum, with its amenity and infrastructure, can be seen as a cultural resource that provides the means of 'collective service and security, connectivity and symbolic and affective commonality' (Amin 2010: 2). Less tangibly, the communicative characteristic of the city impacts on perception and experience, sustained and distributed by media commentary and representation, government discourse, and in a wider context, the duties and rights of the stranger and their stances towards the world (Amin 2010: 12). In the nexus between the private world of the citizen moving through the public spaces of the city, urban space also becomes a sphere of intimacy in which feelings towards the self and others, to nation and its outside are experienced and acted out in formative ways (Berlant 2008).

While the contemporary city is frequently celebrated as one of 'difference, diversity and inclusion', it is underscored by a less fêted narrative. Difference – socio-economic, ethnic and cultural – produces tensions and conflict whose basis lies in the emotional dimension of everyday life. The eruptions of youth violence in London and other major British cities in August 2011 attracted commentary that speculated on the causes of violence. Although opinions vary, there is some consensus on the role of economic disadvantage that contributed to a sense of marginalization and payback when gangs of teenagers looted and burned shops and cars. The contemporary city is also a melting pot of religions on a scale not previously witnessed. The reassertion of religion and religious differences is played out in the public domain, as Maree Pardy observes, 'with religious groups and individuals making particular claims on public space both on the basis of their religious identity and in accord with secular society's respect for religious freedom' (Pardy 2011: 7). Tensions around difference are *affective* responses: they inform attitudes and behaviour with tangible consequences. As a central modality in people's relationship to place, *affect* – through its trajectories of desire and fear – is central to the experience of place. The emphasis on emotions and their manifestation in urban public space acknowledges an emerging complexity of the city in which the relationship with the stranger has become more fundamental than ever (Moisi 2009: 20).

In attempting to account for the relationship between subjectivity and place (the city, in this case), psychoanalytic approaches point to the centrality of emotions as the basis for both human and non-human relationships. Although running the risk of oversimplification – this chapter does not allow for a detailed exploration of the complexity of ideas involved – a summary of the role of emotions and their relevance to our engagement with urban life is presented here. Steve Pile's rereading of Freud (Pile 1996) puts 'place' firmly at the centre of subjectivity, whereby space and place are a significant feature of the condition of subjectivity. Space and place are not merely passive backdrops; rather, they are constitutive of relationships between self and others, and are implicated in this relationship in a dialectical fashion (Pile 1996: 104). Psychoanalysis and theories of emotion can be usefully applied because they highlight the affect-laden motivation of all human action (Freud 1930;

Pile 1996; Sedgwick 2003). In psychoanalysis, the source of emotions is the unconscious and the imagination, which are engaged in a relationship between the self and the environment, and connected through dialogic exchange. This process informs subjectivity and the experience of everyday urban life. In the everyday life of cities, we engage with and come to know the metropolis through our sensory, affective and aesthetic modalities, with all the practical interaction and complexity that this experience implies. Our daily encounters with the strangers of the city, along with the sensory phenomenon that assails us – the sights, sounds and smells – activate bodily responses and feed into emotional experiences 'as diverse as pleasure, joy revulsion fear and disgust' (Allon and Anderson 2004: 90).

In this schema, the trope of Other is typically associated with the arousal of negative feelings of fear and disgust because of perceived cultural, sexual or gender differences. The term 'Other' is used broadly to understand the processes by which societies and groups exclude others who are seen as somehow not fitting into a society, and whom a dominant culture attempts to subordinate. In accounting for racial and other prejudices, such negativity is frequently associated with the spatial environment because Others are people who are seen to have transgressed boundaries and are, therefore, 'out of place' (Sibley 1992; Pile 1996: 88). David Sibley points out that the organization of space is an intrinsic part of the outsider problem; it affects the perception of the Other as either a threat, as foreign or simply as different (Sibley 1992). In addition to learning through childhood experiences (Pile 1996: 89), the ways in which spatial boundaries – tacitly or explicitly – are constructed, maintained and policed are related to how people develop boundaries between self and others.

The collective emotional geography of a city produces a psychodynamics of place, its own unconscious life. For Pile (1996) and Michel de Certeau (1985), this involves the psychoanalytic tropes of desire, love, loss and also movement, seeing and meaning (Pile 1996: 228). These are expressed through moments that erupt and disturb civil life, through acts of voyeurism, eroticism, social performance and masquerade that reveal the city's unconscious or emotional life. This chapter now turns to a case study of Brisbane, Australia, a small but rapidly developing city, to explore ways in which urban resources might help provide what Amin refers to as 'collective service, security . . . connectivity and . . . affective commonality' (2010: 2).

Small cities turn into big cities: the case of Brisbane, Australia

> The public realm is a sort of 'civic school' which newcomers (the young, migrants) and outsiders (such as gated communities) can experience and learn key democratic values, such as tolerance, equality of treatment and mutual obligation.
>
> (Gleeson 2005: 2)

Brisbane is a second-tier city and, as an example of a small, provincial city transforming into a place of national significance, it shares characteristics with cities of comparable scale that have been subject to similar forces of urbanization. It is the capital city of the state of Queensland, located on Australia's eastern seaboard, above the larger capital cities of Sydney and Melbourne. It was the country's fastest-growing city from 1986 to 1996 and again between 2004 and 2005, with a population of the greater Brisbane area of 1.95 million (ABS 2007–2008). The scale and pace of Brisbane's recent development situates in between its inward-looking past to an outward-looking future.

Historical circumstance has shaped its difference from other Australian cities, and socio-political features that have developed over many years have the capacity to impact on Brisbane's future development. First, Brisbane's urban cultural development was held back for two centuries following white settlement by the aggressively rural agrarian focus of successive state governments. In the highly regionalized state of Queensland, spending on urban infrastructure and cultural amenity remained low until the late 1980s. Prior to this time, political priorities were aimed at managing the resource-rich regional electorates (Fitzgerald 1984). For most of its history since white settlement, Brisbane was 'a place where urban industrial society is kept at bay' (Whitlock 1984: 80). Second, Brisbane vies for the status as Australia's most suburban city (Salt 2005: 5). Until recently it was a low-density city with very little tradition of apartment living until urban renewal began in 1991. This suggests that Brisbane's development has been based on the suburban ethos of retreat, privacy and seclusion (Davison 1994), a mode of living at odds with ways of living in urbanized, densely populated spaces that require different techniques from suburban living. Finally, from the late eighteenth century and until the late 1980s, Brisbane's population was overwhelmingly Anglo-Celtic. Moreover, until the latter part of the twentieth century, Queensland actively encouraged British migrants over other ethnicities (Fitzgerald 1982: 187). Between 1947 and 1961, Queensland's overseas-born population rose by only 58 per cent, compared with the national average of 139 per cent (Fitzgerald 1982: 187). Brisbane's small, predominantly Anglo-Celtic population and its history of authoritarian governance had earned it a national reputation for being somewhat inward-looking, politically reactionary and with intolerance to difference, a view that was publicly promulgated by politicians and a parochial press that helped maintain the status quo.[1] Yet, living among strangers requires precisely the opposite: a tolerance to diversity and difference and openness towards others.

In the early 1990s, with the introduction of urban renewal and as the forces of globalization played out across the geopolitical landscape, Brisbane's social and cultural climate began to change. This followed Brisbane's hosting of World Expo 88, an event frequently cited as signalling the shift in the city's development. But Expo's impact on the city is not easily disentangled from broader changes occurring across the developed world's cities at the time, and to which most governing authorities were responding. Nevertheless, some twenty or so years later, the city's parochial past is buried among its smart remodelled urban landscape, award-winning cultural venues, growing skyline and new urban amenity. Beneath this new surface, lies the city's palimpsest; culture and values are hard held and take a long time to shift. In the place-making bid of all global cities, Brisbane is reframed in the contemporary rubric of 'creative cities' whose agenda foregrounds culture and creativity, and the promotion of behavioural characteristics such as tolerance and openness to diversity (see, for example, Florida 2002; Johnson 2009). Nigel Thrift observes that this focus employs 'strategic interventions of affect' (Thrift 2000: 56) that emphasize emotive qualities associated with 'buzz, creativity and expressivity'. While creative city strategies can also be seen as attempts to harness the positive emotions of pleasure, joy and hope, the ways in which this aspiration is actually achieved will be evident in citizens' experience of place and of its public spaces.

The Brisbane Urban Renewal Task Force, established in 1991, was the first combined local, state and federal government programme to initiate the revitalization of the city's run-down northern inner-city area. Cultural-led urban revitalization in the city has resulted in the redevelopment of several inner-city areas and the Central Business District (CBD), with an emphasis on the creation of cultural venues such as performance and exhibition spaces. Service industries have flourished in the form of cafés, bars and restaurants, adding to the urban amenity and creative city strategies that encourage markets, festivals and blockbuster exhibitions.

The expansion in Brisbane's cultural amenities parallels the rapid intensification of its residential accommodation across the inner city and, to some extent the suburbs beyond, which house its swelling population. Migration from overseas and interstate has produced a population that is now far more ethnically and culturally diverse than it has been, with over 26 per cent born overseas and external migration exceeding internal migration (Brisbane City Council 2011a). While Brisbane's new infrastructure is vital to its economic and cultural growth, attention to the development of the city's social sustainability is also important as it develops from a low-density suburban place to a city where people live in greater density among strangers. The experience of the city has changed for many people, presenting new ways of being in the city. There is hope that the 'thrown togetherness' (Massey 2005) of the culturally diverse city might offer some potential for a civic culture and commitment to living with difference (Pardy 2011: 8). As social space, the public realm generates opportunities for new encounters, both serendipitous and managed. With the greater range of cultural amenities, activities and places for people to gather and meet in Brisbane, greater attention to *how* people interact in these spaces can help generate a better understanding of the role of urban space in ways that promote a sense of inclusion and participation.

Dalliances with strangers

Brisbane's enhanced public realm is underpinned by a profound shift in networks of sociality, and has transformed how the city is experienced. The proliferation of hospitality and entertainment industries, for example – in the form of cafés, clubs, bars and restaurants – are the consumer-based social spaces in which new forms of sociability and attachment are nurtured and sustained. Prior to the 1990s, there was very limited public or semi-public amenity. The shifts occurring across social networks, with social groupings based on shared affinities and lifestyles rather than kinship ties (Maffesoli 1996), points to new formations in how people connect, gather and meet in urban space. As household size declines and single-person households rise across the country (Brisbane City Council 2011a), urban space and amenity assumes a greater role in the social lives of citizens. The opportunity for places to meet and to be social outside the home is a significant feature of the contemporary city; the city's parks, cafés, bars and restaurants are the places where people gather. For Michel Maffesoli, emotion is the binding element to communities of shared interest or affinities, expressed through 'the exchange of feelings, conversation' (Maffesoli 1996: 13).

The popularity of the city's cultural amenities points to the centrality of sociality in people's lives, but encounters with strangers can test our humanity, tolerance and compassion. The experience of difference may generate negative psychological and affective responses that result in the creation of boundaries and defences. Zygmunt Bauman describes the polarities of responses to this characteristic of city life as 'mixophilia versus mixophobia' (Bauman 2003: 27). In the 'mixophilia' view, the opportunity for learning and knowledge about others, people who are different from oneself, is an enabling and exciting feature of metropolitan life. It is the promise of the unknown, the serendipitous encounter, which is the romance of city life and distinguishes it from a small town or community where people are typically known to each other, often through several generations. Opportunity and serendipitous potential are hallmarks of living among strangers. The competing emotional tugs of fear and hope towards others in increasingly congested urban spaces is a fundamental part of the urban experience, with the current pace of development intensifying this experience.

As smaller cities, such as Brisbane, grow into larger ones, attention to the social and emotional lives of citizens – that is, to the development of social sustainability – should not take a back seat to environmental concerns – something that is 'tacked on' to the bigger picture of infrastructure development. Rather, an understanding of how people engage with and experience the city might help guide the development of urban public space in ways that encourage civil encounters, and a sense of participation and inclusion.

Spaces of hope, joy, compassion

It may sound whimsical to propose that urban planning consider the emotional life of citizens, in particular those emotions of joy, hope and compassion. After all, the modern city developed from the rational principles of eighteenth-century Enlightenment; empirical data provided the principles of reason and order to drive city planning. Efforts to bring order to the chaos and complexity of urban life is the task of the planner, but cities are complex, dynamic organisms, and the imaginative and emotional lives of its citizens are etched into its fabric and played out on its streets and public spaces. For Dominique Moisi, 'the subjective "soft" realities are essential to understanding geopolitics at even the most rudimentary level'

(Moisi 2009: 22). This 'feeling life' is part of what constitutes the somewhat intangible ambience each city has and what we sense on first arrival – whether it's the energy of Manhattan or the chutzpah of Paris. As film-maker George Miller observes, 'approach any city, in any epoch, and at first glance you will know its people and their aspirations' (Miller 2001: 77). A city says something about its inhabitants, their aspirations, hopes and fears, but how are feelings experienced and how do they manifest in the urban landscape? How might anxieties about strangers and urban density be minimized – and hope and social responsibility be encouraged? The subjective nature of emotion can make analysis difficult, but emotion is also a collective experience based on an instinctive, affective driven engagement with the city's sensory triggers. Identifying the ways in which the emotional dimension of urban living is woven into the experience and fabric of the city, and how it is inflected and refracted in the strategies of urban planning, opens a window into opportunities that harness the essential civility of urban citizens. Hope, as an attitude that is underpinned by the affect of desire, is a good place to begin.

Hope

The city a priori is evidence of humanity's optimism and hope. It is the site of technological, architectural and social ambition; the built environment with its towering skyscrapers, elaborately landscaped parks, networks of roads and bridges is a crucible of hopes and dreams. Cities the world over are redolent with stories of people arriving from small towns to 'make good', to escape poverty in the hope of a better life, to find work, opportunities, romance, fame and fortune. Hope is confidence (Moisi 2009: 30). It is trust in one's identity, in one's ability to interact positively with the world; it is 'a form of trust that pushes us towards others, to accept how they differ from us without fear' (Moisi 2009: 31). Hope is future focused, but should not be ignorant of the past.

Demonstrations of hope in Brisbane's recent past, prior to its current period of regeneration, paid little attention to the social fabric of its inhabitants, and hope was manifest almost exclusively in the commercial built form. In 1985 the city vied for the tallest building in the world, and a spate of tall, nondescript buildings constructed during the 1970s and 1980s are dotted around the city, once symbols of Brisbane's entrée into the world of commerce. Many of the city's unique historic buildings were demolished during this period, their destruction a denial of the city's past and a wilful singular vision of the future. The public demonstration of grief and loss were ignored until heritage legislation was finally introduced in 1995.

Utopian thinking is a rich vein that runs through the history of urban planning, the desire to 'get the city right' (Sandercock 1997; Donald 1999). Because hope is future focused, a city that supports the culturally 'new' is perceived as optimistic and forward looking. Richard Florida's (2002) indices of creative cities (those that attract creative workers who contribute to the creativity, dynamism and buzz of the place) have been adopted by many urban administrators who see the social and economic value of culture and creativity in cities. Historically, this is nothing new;

creativity and culture have always found their source in the city, but the extent to which they flourish and engage with the public realm depends on the imagination of its citizens and administrators. Creative city strategies are evident in the development of Brisbane's cultural infrastructure and cultural precincts. These strategies have revitalized Brisbane's inner city and CBD, creating new forms of cultural and leisure consumption in the manner of cities across the world. Yet gentrification is not without contestation and displacement of lower income groups, and when Amin talks about 'the good city' and an 'ethics of care' (Amin 2010) he recognizes our obligations to marginalized and displaced people, so that structures of support are part of an ethos of the socially just city. In Brisbane's quasi-gentrified Fortitude Valley, several charitable organizations have stepped in to provide alternative meeting venues for people pushed out by gentrification, such as Mission Australia's Café One, which is used by clients who may have long-held feelings of belonging to the area, but feel excluded by the new amenity, art galleries and sleek cafés. Other service groups are active in their efforts to provide affordable housing in these localities, but these initiatives require adequate public support and effective legislation to ensure they are developed and maintained in sufficient numbers as the city continues to grow.

Alongside the individual ambitions of city shapers – developers, architects, planners and urban bureaucrats – are citizens' manifestations of hope. When the future of their city relies solely on decisions made by experts, citizens' optimism about their city is dependent on their confidence in their key administrators. Brisbane's administrative forebears did not make consultation with their constituents a priority; for many decades authoritarian governance was the norm (Fitzgerald 1984). Community engagement is a buzzword, but also a strategy that has replaced the old authoritarian model of urban governance. The efficacy of strategies is measured by their outcomes – whose voices were heard and acted upon? Confidence in the democratic process, in which people's voices are heard and, when possible and appropriate, acted upon, empowers people to contribute to their cities' futures. Participatory democracy through consultation, through local government members' accessibility, increasingly aided by the use of technology, are all part of the paradigm of urban hope. Many voices present a diversity of views – often with conflicting interests – but without a forum or process for grievances and opinions, hope is usurped by feelings of frustration and apathy.

Our culture's trend towards individualization cuts across the impetus for community participation, but ample evidence suggests that people are prepared to commit time to activities that involve others in their community with an eye to the future that is built on inclusion and care – of community and environment. One example of this orientation towards the future is the formation of inner-city food farms. As the awareness of the many implications of climate change takes hold, initiatives around the production of food have resulted in the formation of city gardens in some parts of Brisbane and other cities. In a strategy to minimize the travel miles of food, the local cultivation of fruit and vegetables limits the environmental impacts of transportation as food is shipped from one end of the country to the other. In addition to eco-awareness, the activity enables the experience of sociality in which neighbours meet, talk and share ideas. Hope as future focused also recognizes the importance of the earth's resources as finite and allows nature into the city, retaining green spaces that are not compromised by the developer's demands for larger footprints. Brisbane has missed many opportunities for developing the types of small pocket parks that are typical to the larger Australian cities of Sydney and Melbourne, allowing insensitive development to intrude in what could be public space. In the face of increasing environmental and resource depletion, hope for the future is a political imperative.

Joy

Joy, pleasure and sociality are all part of what draws crowds to festivals and markets, to gather with friends, or alone in sidewalk cafés, to promenade along streets and boardwalks, and to congregate and picnic in parks. Such activities generally produce limited exchanges with strangers, but the desire to be among the throng of humanity is nonetheless based on an affective and life-affirming impulse of 'being togetherness' (Maffesoli 1996). Festivals, markets, people-watching from parks and cafés are all activities and arenas that provide one of the essential pleasures of urbanity – that is, of spectacle and performance (Pyle 1996; Sennett 2000). According to Richard Sennett, performance, whether the cajoling of a marketeer or everyday interaction, enables strangers to express themselves to each other in comfort, to communicate emotionally with people whom they do not know (Sennett 2000: 385). Sennett uses the term *teatro mundi*, or theatre of the world, to describe a kind of self-dramatization that is played out on the city streets, where the body – through adornment and display – is central to performance. In acting out or performing in city space, it is the anonymity and the types of encounters to which we are subject – unknown, fleeting and fragmented, yet sometimes corporeal – that encourage the experience of ourselves as actors.

Effectively designed public spaces encourage a variety of interactions and performances, or conversely they allow, in Robert Hughes's elegant phrase, places where 'solitudes may lie together' (in Miller 2001: 79). Despite a programme of improvement and increase to Brisbane's public spaces, there remain many poorly used areas owing to insensitivities related to climate: trees uprooted to save diverting a few yards of drain resulting in insufficient shade, priority given to cars rather than pedestrians, too many mediocre examples of architecture whose buildings fail to adequately address the street, and numerous 'dead' zones, particularly towards either end of the CBD where poor streetscape and heavy traffic fails to invite use.

Strategies that are aimed at harnessing pleasure in urban spaces may be over-dictated by the demands of consumerism, marginalizing those unable or unwilling to participate in consumer culture because they focus on privileged patterns of consumption and lifestyle practices (Zukin 1995; Evans 2003). Among the emergent forms of Brisbane's redevelopment, South Bank Parklands, located adjacent to the river and across from the CBD, stands out as an exception to the consumer-focused model of waterside development seen in many cities around the world. The diversity of non-commercial and commercial uses the parkland offers, and its attention to the local conditions of Brisbane's subtropical climate through the planting of vegetation and the inclusion of a large artificial, landscaped beach, makes it distinctive from waterside developments such as Sydney's Darling Harbour where the focus is principally on consumption. The principal aim of South Bank Parklands 1997 Master Plan was how best to 'get the public space strategy right firstly', with the built environment and commercial uses to follow (Snow 2009). Happily, in this instance, this approach has resulted in a large green space, and accessible and well-used parklands where commercial services do not dominate the public site. The parklands offer the aesthetic, sensory and social pleasures of an urban beach, picnic spots, promenading under a one-kilometre bougainvillea arbour or along a generously scaled boardwalk by the river, a rainforest precinct, and several open, shaded picnic areas. The beach functions as something of a subtropical plaza or enhanced version of the local swimming pool – a place where people gather to seek relief from the intense humidity of Brisbane's summer months. The low-key approach to commercial infrastructure and the heavy usage of the parkland is indicative that the pleasures of the city do not have to be consumer focused.

In jockeying for cultural and symbolic capital, cities compete for stand-out iconic buildings, such as Sydney's Opera House and Bilbao's Guggenheim; technology transforms the urban fabric through digital interactivity, electronic billboards, transport hubs and the vast digital network that connects cities and people across the globe. Here, joy is suggested in the surprise of the new, the unusual, the out of the ordinary. The city's interstitial spaces offer elements of surprise: laneways animated with cafés, art and shops, public art that might invite interaction or comment, buskers and street performers, and electronic billboards upon which citizens can comment or to which they can upload data. All these strategies are what planners call 'urban acupuncture': small-scale and low-cost interventions, aimed to add the experience of pleasure to the urban environment. Such small-scale urban interventions can produce transient moments of joy through a fleeting exchange or encounter, or an emotional, physical or intellectual engagement, helping to form a bridge between people and lessen the threat of their difference (Lorde 1984).

Joy and civility are combined in the spaces of Brisbane's burgeoning café culture; the café as a place that is central to dialogic exchange and civil discourse dates back to its sixteenth-century origins (Ellis 2004). The eighteenth-century coffee house in Britain was the centre of the community for informal discussions and politics, and, unlike all other social institutions of the time, was defined by its inclusivity of people from all walks of life (Ellis 2004: 59). Similarly, the contemporary café is circumscribed by its role as a place of hospitality where the cultivation of civil behaviour, such as courtesy and reciprocity, is coded into its spaces. Although cafés are consumer spaces – and, as some have argued, may be bourgeois spaces (Zukin 1995) – in both contexts they perform important civic functions. Habermas (1984) identified the café as a site that has both socializing and civilizing functions; it is a place where the art of conversation, listening, dialogic exchange and reciprocity are likely to occur. Here, the techniques of conversation assume particular importance because the café is a venue where people frequently meet with others who are less familiar to them. At a broad level, the café can be seen as supporting the growth in networks of sociability and facilitating the cultivation of urban civility. In the increasingly ethnically diverse contemporary city, places such as the café assume importance for people from different traditions to converge and meet. The enthusiastic adoption of cafés and outdoor dining in Brisbane has been accelerated by its subtropical climate, which is conducive to outdoor drinking and dining.

Compassion

It is axiomatic that in order to exercise civic virtues such as tolerance and care for others, we ourselves must feel, at the very least, unthreatened and, at the most, secure in our environment. Australians are living in a time of unprecedented affluence and yet it does not take much to rattle the sabre of fear. While security is in part a perceptual phenomenon, the macro socio-environment informs the micro, everyday and affective experience. Brisbane and other small cities remain unburdened by the inequities that are characteristic of megapolises where overcrowding, major disparities of wealth and large tracts of depleted urban precincts are common. In cities such as Brisbane most of the citizens are optimally placed to attend to the civic obligations of social responsibility and care. Alongside the social responsibility involved in caring for those in need are the realities of a significantly ageing population where physical frailty, memory loss and dependency will make their imprint felt in urban public space. Instability in many regions across the world suggests that the likelihood of people arriving from war-torn regions and who have experienced trauma and hardship will continue to grow. The panoply of behaviours occasionally exhibited in the urban public space, of people who are disoriented, traumatized and simply unwell can be confronting and discomforting, but they demand attention and a humane response. As Amin observes:

> The city that commits to mixed or public housing under pressure to gentrify or segregate . . . to collective services . . . to the vulnerable, disadvantaged and threatened under pressure to invest for the economically privileged and the rich, to open and inclusive public spaces under pressure to privatise or control entry, to multiculturalism and hospitality under pressure to eject and discipline the stranger . . . shows that it is willing to stand by a particular idea of urban living.
>
> (Amin 2010: 10)

Because the public realm is a sort of 'civic school', 'deeply premised on the basic values and obligations of citizenship' (Gleeson 2005: 2), there is greater emphasis on the importance of a public realm that is beyond the immediate reach of private interests, markets, families, and so forth. In liberal democracies, those institutions organized around regimes of care, such as hospitals, social housing, childcare centres and, to some extent, schools, have traditionally been primarily publicly funded institutions or the domain of religious organizations. The best interests of the sick, poor and unwell are usually not met by the market. A public realm in which an ethics of care invites participation may require greater public resourcing.

The mixing of 'the market' into the public realm sends confusing signals to citizens about fundamental rules and values (Gleeson 2005: 2), and while history shows us that the public good is not by default best served by a public authority, it is incumbent on public authorities to practise the democratic principles that involve the care and consideration of those unable to exercise due care for themselves. Whether this translates in a practical sense to small measures such as adequate public seating, good clear signage for visually impaired and the elderly who suffer from memory loss, ramps for wheelchairs, better street lighting and more children's playgrounds, or to the macro level issues of adequate public housing and affordable public transport, these are all amenities that require regulatory measures based on notions of the public good.

The value of 'modelling' has been demonstrated in educational and child-rearing literature, and it is also relevant to the public realm. If public space is one of the arenas in which we learn about the ethics of care in relation to citizenship, demonstrations of care need to be made explicit. How do we know about the lives and needs of the disadvantaged if they are made invisible by inadequate public facilities that prevent them from participating in civic life? How can compassion be extended beyond our immediate circle of family and friends if we cannot bear witness to others in need?

Conclusion

The 'utopian impulse' (Sandercock 1997) is a strong driver in the question of how best to plan and manage cities. From nineteenth-century slum clearances to le Corbusier's ideal housing plan, Radiant City (which was never built), or Ebenezer Howard's Garden City, these are offered as rational, built solutions to the larger question of nurturing and maintaining civility when large aggregates of populations live together. This chapter has proposed that a deeper understanding of the emotional forces that motivate citizens might not be as utopian as the idea first appears. Such an understanding can serve to shine a light on the ways in which the experience of the city is central to feelings of inclusion or exclusion, to participation or retreat to communities of similarity. As the focus on environmental sustainability increases, so too should the focus on social sustainability. Emergent cities that are undergoing periods of rapid development, such as Brisbane, are at a pivotal period in their evolution, with the weight of their civic potential yet to be realized. Brisbane's legacy of provincialism lingers beneath the surface of its recent transformation into a 'new world city' (Brisbane City Council 2011b). The design and management of its public spaces – one that considers the collective, affective life of citizens – is central to its growing development as a cosmopolitan city.

Note

1 For example, the now defunct Australian newspaper *The Sun* ran a headline on 12 October 1989, declaring: 'GANG WAR FEAR – Asian thugs in battle for Valley'.

References

Allon, F. and Anderson, K. (2004) 'Sentient Sydney', in *Passionate City: An international symposium*, Melbourne: RMIT, School of Media Communication.

Amin, A. (2010) 'Cities and the ethic of care among strangers', paper presented at the Department of Geography and Institute of Advanced Study, Durham University, January.

Australian Bureau of Statistics (ABS) (2007–2008) 'Regional Population Growth'. Available at: www.abs.gov.au/ausstats/abs@.nsf/Previousproducts/3218.0MainFeatures6200708?opendocument&tabname=Summary&prodno=3218.0&issue=2 (accessed 8 March 2010).

Bauman, Z. (2003) *City of Fears, City of Hopes*, London: University of London, Goldsmiths College, Centre for Urban Community and Research.

Berlant, L. (2008) *The Female Complaint*, Durham, NC: Duke University Press.

Brisbane City Council (2011a) 'Where did the current residents live five years ago?'. Available at: http://profile.id.com.au/Default.aspx?id=327&pg=230&gid=10&type=enum (accessed 6 November 2011).

Brisbane City Council (2011b) 'Brisbane's growing economy'. Available at: http://www.brisbane.qld.gov.au/about-council/governance-strategy/vision-strategy/economic-development/growing-brisbanes-economy/index.htm (accessed 18 July 2011).

Davison, G. (1994) 'The past and future of the Australian Suburb', in L. Johnson (ed.) *Suburban Dreaming: An interdisciplinary approach to Australian cities*, Geelong: Deakin University Press.

de Certeau, M. (1985) 'Practices of space', in M. Blonsky (ed.) *On Signs: A semiotics reader*, Oxford: Basil Blackwell.

Donald, J. (1999) *Imagining the Modern City*, London: Athlone.

Ellis, M. (2004) *The Coffee House: A cultural history*, London: Weidenfeld & Nicolson.

Evans, G. (2003) 'Hard-branding the cultural city – from Prado to Prada', *International Journal of Urban and Regional Research*, 27(2): 417–440.

Fitzgerald, R. (1982) *From the Dreaming to 1915: A history of Queensland*, St Lucia: University of Queensland Press.

Fitzgerald, R. (1984) *A History of Queensland from 1915 to the 1980s*, St Lucia: University of Queensland Press.

Florida, R. (2002) *The Rise of the Creative Class*, New York: Basic Books.

Freud, S. (1930) 'Civilization and its discontents', in *Civilization, Society and Religion: group psychology, civilization and its discontents and other works*, Vol. 12, London: Penguin.

Gleeson, B. (2005) 'Online Opinion', 6 April. Available at: www.onlineopinion.com.au/view.asp?article=3316&page=2 (accessed 10 June 2009).

Habermas, J. (1984) *The Theory of Communicative Action*, trans. Thomas McCarthy, Boston, MA: Beacon Press.

Johnson, L. (2009) *Cultural Capitals: Revaluing the arts, remaking urban spaces*, Farnham: Ashgate.

Lefebvre, H. (1991) *The Production of Space*, Oxford: Basil Blackwell.

Lorde, A. (1984) *Sister Outsider: Essays and speeches*, Berkeley, CA: The Crossing Press.

Maffesoli, M. (1996) *Time of the Tribes: The decline of individualism in mass society*, trans. Don Smith, London: Sage.

Massey, D. (2005) *For Space*, London: Sage.

Miller, G. (2001) 'A city that works' in *Sydney Papers*, Spring: 77–79.

Moisi, D. (2009) *The Geopolitics of Emotion*, London: The Bodley Head.
Pardy, M. (2011) 'Eat, Pray, Swim – women, religion and multiculturalism in the suburbs' in *M/C Online*, August.
Patton, P. (1995) 'Imaginary cities', in S. Watson and K. Gibson (eds) *Postmodern Cities and Spaces*, Cambridge: Blackwell.
Pile, S. (1996) *The Body and the City: Psychoanalysis, space and subjectivity*, London: Routledge.
Robins, K. (1996) *Into the Image: Culture and politics in the field of vision*, New York: Routledge.
Salt, B. (2005) *Cinderella City: A vision of Brisbane's rise to prominence*, Sydney: Austcorp.
Sandercock, L. (1997) *Towards Cosmopolis: Planning for multicultural cities*, London: John Wiley.
Sedgwick, E. K. (2003) *Touching Feeling: Affect, pedagogy, performativity*, Durham, NC: Duke University Press.
Sennett, R. (1970) *The Uses of Disorder: Personal identity and city life*, London: Routledge.
Sennett, R. (2000) 'Reflections on the public realm', in G. Bridge and S. Watson (eds) *A Companion to the City*, Oxford: Blackwell.
Sibley, D. (1992) 'Outsiders in society and space', in K. Anderson and F. Gale (eds) *Inventing Places: Studies in cultural geography*, London: Longman.
Simmel, G. (1950). 'The metropolis and mental life', adapted by D. Weinstein from Kurt Wolf (trans.) in *The Sociology of Georg Simmel*, New York: Free Press.
Snow, M. (2009) 'A better Brisbane' Talk at The Brisbane Institute, 25 May 2009. Available at: http://www.udal.org.au/search?updated-max=2009-06-14T15%3A51%3A00%2B10%3A00&max-results=18 (accessed 24 October 2010).
Thrift, N. (2000) 'With child to see any strange thing: everyday life in the city', in G. Bridge and S. Watson (eds) *A Companion to the City*, London: Blackwell.
Whitlock, G. (1984) 'Queensland: the state of the art on the "last frontier"', *Westerly*, 29(2): 85–90.
Zukin, S. (1995) *The Culture of Cities*, Cambridge, MA: Blackwell.

11

BUILT ENVIRONMENT, DESIGN AND ETHICS

The social responsibility of educational institutions

Paul Sanders, Shannon Satherley and Kuniko Shibata

> Why design matters: The history and culture of a nation are written in its buildings, public spaces, towns and cities. Through their design and how we live our lives in them, we recognize what is special about our society and communities. Every new building and public space is an expression of our values and aspirations. How places are looked after speaks volumes about our self-esteem and sense of national and local pride and identity.
>
> (Simmons 2009: 1)

Introduction

In a contemporary society in which the liberal market principle and individualism pervade, the subjects of both ethics and design are likely to be reduced to a subjective moral code and personal preference. Despite this conventional view, design of the built environment, which considers the principles of access, social justice and equity, has been central to the development of civilization. In particular, the design of the built environment has shaped the public realm of human life and corresponds to the progress of citizenship rights and democracy (Simmons 2009: 1). Therefore, it is not surprising that the concept of 'design ethics', which surfaced in nineteenth-century Europe, paralleled an awakening sense of citizenship rights among working-class populations in industrial cities (Engels and McLellan 2009).

Industrialization, since the late eighteenth century, has enabled an ever-increasing growth in the production and consumption of designed products, catering for mass clienteles. Mass production, brought about in the Industrial Revolution, has made aspects of good design accessible to most populations in advanced economies. Indeed, the progress of design in the modern period is inseparable from industrialization and the subsequent democratization in developed economies. Ultimately, designed products were once only accessible to those who had power in a society; the major benefactors of designed products were limited to royalty, aristocracies or religious institutions, wealthy merchants, industrialists and the professional classes. However, democracy and social advancement has enabled the majority of the population to enjoy quality design in the modern state. During this period, conventional aesthetic standards of design have been considerably challenged, a development that parallels the transition of ethical norms in society from feudal autocracy to the establishment of equal citizenship.

The relationship between design and ethics has once again become a subject of intellectual inquiry brought about by social and environmental change. First, the principles of environmental sustainability have been established as new criteria for most designs, and second, accessibility has become an increasingly apparent ethical issue whereby access to 'good' design in remote communities is a core ethical challenge. Furthermore, some products and places have not been properly considered for their ease of access and use by the disabled, elderly, children and women. Third, there is a growing awareness that the concept of 'design ethics' should be critically addressed, as design requirements vary depending on climate, environment and cultural specificities. Finally, although mass production has lowered the prices of designed products, affordability is still another barrier for the poor. This is particularly true in the built environment design fields, which require the significant resource inputs of skill and time, and thus finance.

Despite considerable increases in democracy and citizenship rights, the market economy has continuously failed to provide universal access to a quality built environment. Responding to this apparent failure to fulfil the practice of ethics in design, there has been a growing awareness of how built environment design professionals can contribute to protecting the environment, as well as increasing accessibility to a quality built environment for the broad community, in particular disadvantaged groups. In terms of promoting environmental ethics and sustainability, there are now a number of regulations and incentives in the construction of new built environments. These new standards have been implemented by international, national and local governments. However, advancing social cohesion, another important criterion in design ethics in the built environment, has not been fully articulated by design professionals.

The development of ethics in design has been advanced by a number of visionary professionals, social reformers and educators, as will be described later in this chapter. In the early twentieth century, educational institutions played significant roles in making design more democratic and accessible to the population by setting new ethical discourses and social responsibilities for design professionals (Pevsner and Weston 2005: 168–169). Nonetheless, these institutions' role in contributing to the development of design ethics has been increasingly fragmented by the demands of the market, a phenomenon of commercial culture that has penetrated into the management of educational institutions, thereby influencing how design is taught.

Institutional ethics has been referred to as corporate social responsibility (CSR), which was born out of the bitter acknowledgement that all institutional behaviours are not inherently ethical. A burst of corporate scandals (for example, the collapse of Bank of Credit and Commerce International in 1991 and of WorldCom in 2002) has posed a question of the ethics of institutions, as well as of the professionals working for them. This institutional malpractice was epitomized by the 2001 collapse of Enron, the United States' energy and commodities company, against claims of corruption and professional malpractice. Despite a growing public scepticism about institutional and governmental integrity, the role of educational institutions in practising professional ethics has been scarcely discussed. In universities, all faculty members are required to satisfy the criteria of research ethics, and to exercise social responsibility by contributing to the wider community in their professional capacity. Curriculum development in professional education also deals with the issue of ethics in business practice, yet students themselves are rarely asked to explicitly play a part in institutional ethics during their time of study at university.

This chapter, while addressing itself to the relationship between ethics and built environment design, aims to contribute to discussions of practice within the design professions and the academy, specifically around students' involvement in ethical practices. The aim of the chapter is threefold. First, it charts a history of the relationship between built environment design (primarily of urban amenity) and ethics, in particular the roles of design professionals and educators. Second, it explores the issue of professional and institutional ethics in relation to design, with a focus on the role of the educational institution as a place of training and as an organization capable of providing design services to communities. Finally, the chapter examines the practice of institutional ethics in facilitating quality built environment design by outlining a recent design project in the remote community of Karumba, Queensland. The project was carried out by students and staff from Queensland University of Technology (QUT) as an illustration of the university's commitment to community service as an expression of ethical social responsibility. It also highlights how educational institutions can contribute to the development of quality design in the built environment. This project is an example of how design professionals and educational institutions can use their expertise to enrich community life by exploring a connection between ethics and design.

Social reform, built environment and ethics in the nineteenth and twentieth centuries

Ethical concerns for the built environment in the Western world can be linked to nineteenth-century social reform movements in Britain, as cities became industrialized. Industrialist Robert Owen (1771–1858) was one of the first people to realize the connection between the environment and the health and well-being of the populace at his factory workers' settlement in New Lanark, Lancashire in 1800. Owen inherited the cotton-spinning mill and its workers' residential settlement from David Dale (1739–1806), a philanthropist who had shown concern for the condition of his workers' children (New Lanark Trust 2009). Under Owen's management between 1800 and 1825, New Lanark's housing conditions, shop facilities, amenities and urban design, as well as the children's education and the health of residents significantly improved (New Lanark Trust 2009; 2011a).

Workers' housing was equipped with generous communal and living spaces and improved hygiene standards (New Lanark Trust 2011b). Owen built a children's school for the mill workers as well as a community education centre and introduced a new type of community shop, *the village store*, which sold quality goods at cheaper prices to residents (New Lanark Trust 2009, 2011a). The village store formed the foundation of subsequent cooperative movements in Britain, a model that later expanded worldwide (Garnett 1972). New Lanark became the model for the Garden Cities (Howard 1902) of the early twentieth century, as well as model workers' villages such as Port Sunlight (1887) and Bourneville (1879) in England.

Owen is now considered an early social reformer, indeed a founder of socialism in Britain. He was deeply convinced that industry had a significant impact on human life, and therefore it should fulfil social and ethical responsibilities for communities (New Lanark Trust 2011b). He was a pioneer who introduced the idea of social amenity within the built environment for the welfare of the working class, and practised it in his own industrial village. His ideals and innovations have had a great influence on forming relationships between built environment design and citizenship rights, as well as the discussion of business ethics. The experiment in New Lanark proved how built environment design could have positive impacts on human conditions and help foster social cohesion, and thus benefit the public interest. Nevertheless, his ideas were too far ahead of the times to be fully accepted by society (New Lanark Trust 2011a).

As industrialization progressed in the nineteenth century, governing authorities became increasingly concerned about the harmful effects of overpopulation, dreadful living and working conditions, and of a lack of open spaces affecting the health of the working-class population in major industrial cities (Hall 2002: 13–46; Engels and McLellan 2009: 36–86). A number of government committees were set up to improve these conditions in the UK during this period (Hall 2002: 19–23). The Public Park Movement was one of these reform initiatives, and gained public acceptance in the UK and North America. The reformers believed that the provision of open spaces for public use improved both the health and 'morale' of the industrial workforce (Walker and Duffield 1983; Stormann 1991; Jordan 1994).

From the eighteenth century in Britain, privately owned walks often became available for public usage in spa towns, increasing their amenity for commercial reasons (Jordan 2003: 3). These public walks gradually developed into public gardens and parks during subsequent years. In 1833, the Select Committee on Public Walks recommended that the British Parliament secure more public open spaces in the vicinity of crowded towns for the working-class population (Thornton 1983: 3). During this period, the importance of public parks as 'lungs' had been widely recognized in industrial cities and towns in the UK and North America (Walker and Duffield 1983; Stormann 1991). Therefore, the provision of public open spaces for the health and well-being of all citizens was considered essential in the mid-nineteenth century. Nevertheless, although other similar recommendations followed, by the 1840s no British public authority had undertaken action (Thornton 1983: 3).

It was not until Birkenhead Park, in Wirral near Liverpool, was opened in 1847 as the first public park for 'the working classes created by a municipality in the world' (Metropolitan Borough of Wirral 2009), that the built environment and its role in social reform was taken seriously. Designed by Sir Joseph Paxton, the success of Birkenhead Park was in its design, innovation in financing landscape design fees through the sale of upper-class properties, and open access to the general public (Thornton 1983). Its success became iconic to the Public Park Movement across the Atlantic – for example, having significant influence on Olmstead and Vaux's design for Central Park, New York (Metropolitan Borough of Wirral 2009).

From this period onwards, the social and ethical dimension of the built environment became inseparable issues for debate of design. Ethics in this context lay in the assertion that all human beings are entitled to benefit from 'good' design. Design could no longer be just a matter of pandering to the aesthetic preferences of the privileged; consequently, utility and accessibility became important criteria as 'democracy in design' emerged as a key tenet of modernism within industrial society. This idea was spread by outstanding educators of the schools of arts and design, which were established during the nineteenth and early twentieth centuries.

The Arts and Crafts Movement, initiated in the UK by artist William Morris (1834–1896) during the latter half of the nineteenth century, rejected the lavish designs of the Victorian era and attempted to introduce simple design and craftsmanship for everyday use (Pevsner and Weston 2005: 36–48). 'Design Reform', one of the principles proposed by Morris, intended to improve the design of objects consumed by the public instead of the privileged (Crawford 1997: 22). He passionately promoted the view that art was an expression of the ideas of designers who should serve to promote ethics and equal citizenship in society. Morris's ideas about re-establishing the lost connection between art, ethics and society in the industrial world were inspired by social reformer and educator John Ruskin (1819–1900).

The twentieth century produced a general consensus that everyone has an entitlement to enjoy well-designed products. Design in the built environment is no exception. Design professionals believed that design democracy would contribute to forming an egalitarian society. The Bauhaus (1919–1933), one of the first schools of design and founded in Weimar, Germany, in 1919, produced a number of outstanding forms of architecture, art and new media (Bauhaus Dessau Foundation 2010). The spirit of the Bauhaus, encapsulated in the following statement, frames another definition of good design: 'to design a better world, to increase international communication through design and to use the modernity of materials, techniques and forms to promote an egalitarian, democratic society' (Aynsley 2009: 76). Despite the inspirational manifesto that the Bauhaus set for architects, landscape architects and planners to follow, their vision was only partially achieved. One of the reasons they failed to achieve their social vision was that their view on society and the mass population was elitist, even repressive. The new generation of designers were autocratic and failed to understand that people have individual preferences and desires regarding how they live their lives (Jacobs 1972). By this failure, architects not only lost their social vision of democracy by design, but also clients of ordinary classes, other than the bourgeoisie for whom (landscape) architects have always catered (Crawford 1991: 29–31).

There has been an enduring disparity between the reality of what is actually built and the sometimes lofty ideals underpinning the design of the built environment. This disparity is evident in, and characteristic of, both architectural and town planning professions. One of the criticisms levelled against the architectural professions and their capacity to design with social reform agendas in mind is that an architect's professional status has largely relied on 'artistic' qualities, while other professionals rely on science/technology/law for their exclusive professional status (Crawford 1991: 28–31; Crawford, 1997: 16–17).

The problem with an architect's identity as an artist is that the built environment is always relational and social in contrast to other art works such as paintings and sculptures (Hall and Ward 1998). A building and garden cannot be autonomous; it is never isolated from the surrounding environment, infrastructure, users and the socio-political economy. From the 1960s onwards, state-sponsored built environment projects, as well as privately commissioned architecture design, were severely attacked by the public, by civil organizations and academics, as architecture was seen to become increasingly alienated from social reality. Ethical concerns for the design of the built environment have once again surfaced as an important area of academic inquiry.

Contemporary issues of ethics and the built environment

> Ethics asks: in what manner shall I live? What is good? What is excellence/virtue? What is right action? What is Just?
>
> Architecture may ask: what is 'good' architecture? What constitutes virtue in architecture and in the practices of architecture?
>
> Is there an ethical connection between the 'goodness' and 'virtues' of architecture and the greater 'social good'?
>
> (Wasserman *et al.* 2000: 32)

The values of contemporary built environment design professionals are inscribed in codes of professional conduct that govern the activities of the various design disciplines and their members. In Australia, members are expected to advance the public interest through engagement in public service. Ethical standards include raising the quality and public appreciation of the environment and, consequently, quality of life and social cohesion. Fundamental to these ideals is improving the accessibility of disadvantaged groups to well-designed environments. A core aim is to maintain general well-being by upholding commonly agreed values of ethical behaviour, equality of opportunity and social justice (Australian Institute of Landscape Architects 2005; Australian Institute of Architects 2006). The Royal Institute of British Architects (RIBA), however, excludes any specific mention of ethics in its Code of Professional Conduct, but adopts three principles of acting with integrity, competence and respectful professional relationships (Royal Institute of British Architects 2005). It refers to the conduct of the individual while avoiding a commitment to acting in the interests of the public good.

However, professional ethical values often sit in a tension between the demand for profitability from design projects and the ethics of the design practitioner. In many instances, the priority of market forces has promoted the interests of private enterprise over the 'greater public good'. We have already noted the professional institutes' declaration of upholding ethical standards in social justice; but to what extent are the professions genuinely enacting these ethical principles? Eeva Berglund argues:

> Architects are seemingly not considered necessary to daily life in the way that doctors, lawyers and teachers are . . . The debate on how to salvage architecture from marginalization is not new, but so long as urban culture is media driven and in thrall of 'starchitecture', the problems are unlikely to go away.
>
> (Berglund 2008: 107)

The crisis in the commodification of the built environment can be in the self-serving aestheticism of designers who exploit opportunities created by the new mode of production and consumption in the 'post-modern' capitalist economy (Harvey 1990: 285–290). As Neil Leach observes, this kind of narrow aestheticism of design has led to a 'rinsing of social, political and economic concerns' (Leach 2005: 137). Tatjana Schneider and Jeremy Till warn that, 'as long as priorities lie in the [superficial] aesthetic and technical [aspects of built environment design] . . . it is all too easy to turn one's attention away from the social and political' (Schneider and Till 2008: 109). When design is bereft of an ethical purpose, and absent of a social dimension, it is too often reduced to merely a stylistic exercise. There is a fundamental paradox to the activity of designers in the buildings and places they design, between what is intended as 'ought to be' and what is 'right in the circumstances' (Spector 2001: 9; Ray 2005: 1). This quite often translates as the tension between the public good versus the client needs. This further unravels to a question of whether designers deserve a privileged position or enact a greater responsibility to society (Ray 2005: 1). While the debate for new and reflective definitions for built environment design practice (including those of design as an ethical practice) gains currency, the stasis in the current professional ethical malaise continues. To recast the purpose of built environment design thus requires understanding the tenet of a design ethic in terms of what is good, right and wrong, virtuous, just and fair; what is good design, and ultimately what is worth designing (Wasserman *et al.* 2000: 20; Fewings 2009: 12).

> Architecture, in its many manifestations, is as much an ethical discipline as a design discipline . . . Architecture is concerned with the future state of the environment to suit human purposes; the consideration of what we ought to make, how we should make it, and the places made.
>
> (Wasserman *et al.* 2000: 32)

Such is the limited role that design professionals have in many sectors of the built environment that projects falling outside the commercial scope of fee-based practice place design professionals in danger of becoming irrelevant to the wider community. This is most apparent in sectors such as the broad housing market where architects' involvement is less than 10 per cent (Murray 2007: 43), and more generally where only a fraction of building around the world involves architects (Berglund 2008: 106).

If a successful community is judged by its investment in, and accessibility to, public services (health, education, technology and basic infrastructure), then should we not value 'good design' accordingly? If so, should this in turn be measured by the level of availability and access to quality design in disadvantaged and/or remote communities? 'Good' built environment design here is not a saleable commodity or a packaged 'artistic' product, but is defined as well resolved ethically, with sound design provided by experts whose services are widely accessible. The remainder of this chapter focuses on the ethical practice of social responsibility, wherein design that fulfils these criteria is made accessible to all members of society.

Bridging the gap

To some extent the gap in the availability of design services beyond the limited scope of professional activity in areas of socio-economic need is being addressed by a number of non-government organizations such as Architects without Frontiers, Architects without Borders and Emergency Architects. These groups have demonstrated an orientation framed around ethical concerns arising directly from the global crises of poverty, health and homelessness, often caused by natural disasters.

The critical and ethical framework of these groups reflects Clare Cumberlidge and Lucy Musgrave's notion that a project is locally relevant when created from: 'multiple visions, frameworks where differing meanings and cultures can coexist. Adaptive transformations, which use, reuse and shift existing infrastructures, become more appropriate forms of vision – visions building on and working with existing contexts and meanings and cultures' (Cumberlidge and Musgrave 2007: 13). Architects without Frontiers, for example, aims to mobilize the resources of the Australian design profession, providing design services to assist communities in need through delivering built projects (Architects without Frontiers 2009). Such organizations rely heavily on voluntary participation and the support of public and private funding agencies. In many respects, the pioneering work of such groups has highlighted the inadequacies of mainstream professional bodies in addressing the social dimension of design practice. Nevertheless, the outreach of design services to centres of great need is a prime example of how an ethics-based approach can operate. With professional institutes falling short of their own ethical missions, and in the wake of the neglect to address social justice and uphold the public interest in the built environment, an important role emerges for higher education institutions. By training the next generation of professionals to enact their social responsibility in built environment design, universities can play a leading role in providing design services to marginalized communities, and also fulfil their own institutional ethical missions.

Ethics and educational institutions

> It is about the struggle between universities and professional bodies over who are the appropriate guardians of ethics in public life and the professions.
>
> (Strain *et al.* 2009: 1)

Peter Jarvis sees the same dilemma in the evolution of universities that has afflicted the professions: the relativity of the capitalist values inherent in the contemporary world is reflected in the loss of a distinctive ethos within universities, which have themselves been forced to become corporations (Jarvis 2009: 13). Consequently, some universities have de-emphasized their civic missions (Checkoway 2000). Contrary to this predicament, many universities do still maintain a traditional mission of public service, and discussion is intensifying as to how universities can become 'more relevant to the rest of society . . . [and] reinvigorate the public purposes and civic mission of higher education' (Hollander and Saltmarsh 2000: 29). A review of the mission statements from some internationally renowned universities in the US, for instance, reveals widespread affirmation of public and community service. Harvard University, Massachusetts Institute of Technology and the University of California all highlight service to their community and society in their charters, a value that is representative of most universities worldwide. The claims made for the social responsibility of universities is evident from these mission statements, and 'as social institutions, universities must actively help build social cohesion and no longer be content simply to look after their own development' (Descoings 2006: 24). Universities can lead, enacting their ethical missions, to be a major part of building a more ethical future (Sethna 2006: 109).

Ethics and design: a role for universities

The focus on ethical principles being brought to bear in the design process is most paramount among disadvantaged people and communities who are already marginalized by mainstream structures. By their nature, remote and disadvantaged communities generally experience a lack of contact with professional and institutional services, and people living in these communities will be unfamiliar or wary of professional practitioners. Projects that aim to satisfy social needs within these communities require sensitivity through careful discussion and negotiation, which ideally should involve all stakeholders. The socially responsive consultative process requires the involvement of a range of stakeholders for the effective identification and management of priorities, resources and processes.

Patrick Hamlett observes that universities are ideally placed to engage as arbitrators of processes of public deliberation, bringing 'expertise to the people' (Hamlett 2003: 15). The university can be usefully engaged in the democratic steering of public deliberation, providing resident expert knowledge, and articulating an independent, autonomous and non-partisan position, which is void in conflicts of interest. It can also engender a wide range of views from their multidisciplinary constituencies, be able to disseminate expertise to public forums in a manner understandable to non-experts, and act as professional facilitators (Hamlett 2003: 17).

Consequently, it is now quite common for design-based academic departments in universities to fulfil their ethical expectations through engaged participation in community design, making the design skills of staff and students available to remote and disadvantaged communities. The university may also make educative use of these opportunities to advance the skills and sense of social responsibility of students. In an effective community-based project, a community acts as a full partner in design development, thus investing in the *process* as much as in the finished design work (Dawes and Satherley 2008: 31–32). This outcome is best achieved through two means: an ongoing conversation between the differing forms of knowledge and capacities embedded within community and those within the university (Armstrong 1999: 19; Thomas 2006: 5), and through student immersion in the whole 'place' (Relph 1976: 46–48) – its ecological processes, built forms, social systems and cultural values.

Case study: 'Linking Karumba'

On the Gulf of Carpentaria, Karumba (population 600) and the adjacent small town of Normanton (population 1,600), are the most remote towns in Queensland. The nearest service centre, Cloncurry, is almost 400km away, and electricity is supplied over a distance of nearly 800km from Townsville. Karumba's economy is based on tourism, fishing and mining. Carpentaria Shire has a low ratepayer base and high annual maintenance and development costs associated with remoteness and the extremities of the wet and dry seasons.

In 2008, 16 QUT students from the fields of landscape architecture, architecture, industrial design and environmental engineering undertook a design project in Karumba that was a response to the geographical disconnection of the town into two main sections. In such an isolated town, the students were confronted with a landscape, climate and community that was dramatically different from their base in urban Brisbane. Part of the problem of Karumba's disconnection is that it has extremely limited access to professional design services, and thus the experience of a participatory design process with university students and staff was a unique opportunity. The project did not operate as a paid consultancy: rather a variety of stakeholders covered costs, and the benefits to students were educational and experiential.

The project brief

Karumba has two centres: the 'Point', where the Norman River meets the Gulf, and the 'Town' which lies 2.5km upriver. The journey between is only achievable by boat or a 9km drive, as the intervening wetland is not traversable. This lack of physical connectivity was identified by the Karumba Progress Association (KPA) and Carpentaria Shire Council (CSC) as representing a deeper socio-cultural disconnect within the town. Karumba also faces the possible introduction of new mining infrastructure on the wetland, which would physically compound the town disconnect and damage its unique ecological setting at a time when ecotourism expansion is a high local priority.

Economically, the town is keen for the new infrastructure, but would prefer it to be situated near an existing facility. Initial work on a wetland traverse was undertaken by a private design firm, but professional fees limited its scope simply to a boardwalk, which failed to address a wider range of issues. KPA and CSC wished to widen the scope to a more holistic plan for the future, but had limited resources with which to do so. Through consultation, QUT School of Design staff, KPA and CSC identified the need for a strategic approach to ensuring a strong, connected basis for shaping the town future and agreed to embark on a design project. Accordingly, a design brief was developed that identified four priorities to foster.

- Sustainable social linkages, encouraged through a common purpose towards a more unified town identity and increased social interaction.
- Sustainable local economic development, especially through enhanced tourism opportunities and connections, and niche industries celebrating Karumba.
- Ecological sustainability to protect the sensitive gulf ecosystems while providing opportunities for increased awareness of this subtle environment.
- Cultural sustainability to enhance and respect the participation of all cultural groups and stakeholders in maintaining and strengthening the cultural character of Karumba.

Pedagogy and process

The corresponding pedagogical aims of the project were for students to develop not only their design skills, but also their ethical sense of social responsibility as designers, as representatives of the institution and as citizens. Specifically, the curriculum's aims were that the students should develop an understanding of a different place and culture from the one in which each currently lives and works, and to extend their design reflexes in these fresh circumstances; a sensitivity to specific physical, social, economic, ecological and cultural contexts, and the role of local identity in an increasingly global operating environment; an understanding of the complexities of ideas of 'sustainability' in a real world setting, and a corresponding sense of ethical responsibility.

Four teaching strategies were used to achieve these goals: a reflective journal comprising drawing and writing exercises guiding student reflections on their immersion in the unfamiliar Karumba landscape and community; formal and informal community engagement sessions to facilitate community deliberations; traditional design studios to give the students the security of the familiar; and students using exclusively manual drawing techniques and media, as the majority of the community did not actively engage with digital media.

The students impressed community members who became involved, such as council members, members of the town's Progress Association, indigenous elders and business owners, with their sensitivity, open-mindedness to difference, and ability to articulate future scenarios responsive to community priorities. The students brought to Karumba their urban-based design skills, and over a fortnight learned how to listen to, arbitrate between, talk with, work on, and communicate visual designs with, and to, people with environmental, social and cultural experiences, and values both similar to, and very different from, their own.

Project outcomes

As well as having an outstanding educational experience, the students produced four highly resolved strategic planning options toward creating sustainable linkages, both within Karumba and with the wider region. Proposals included consolidation of tourism and industrial land uses; zoning of ecological conservation areas with supportive access and management programmes; enhancement of local and regional culture and heritage; and localized designs for traversing the wetland zone. Community responses to the final exhibition of this work were overwhelmingly positive, although as in any democratic situation, not all parties were pleased with every outcome. A popular strategic plan was 'Linking Karumba: make the switch', which tackled the core of the community's concerns regarding future mining development. Pared-back design drawings with an uncluttered, logical layout clearly and accessibly illustrated that land use distribution is not fixed and can be 'switched' to achieve community aims and create the linkages that Karumba needs.

The student work was exhibited in Karumba, and soft and hard copies provided to KPA and CSC. A total of AUD $830,000 in government funding has been secured to implement aspects of the designs, and the community is currently debating their priorities for construction. The intent of the project was not to dictate a single design solution to this community based on the subjective preferences of the academic designers, but to offer a range of socially, economically, ecologically and culturally responsible options that they could debate, adopt or reject as they saw fit. This exemplifies a model of design practice bridging the gap between good (ethically sound) design and disadvantaged or remote community needs. It is a model not tied to the business imperatives of private enterprise, but enacting the goals of good, ethical, universally affordable design. 'Linking Karumba' received the 2008 Far North Queensland Regional Partnerships Award, impressing judges with the level of productive social engagement between the community and university. This successful relationship continued with a second project undertaken in 2010 in the Carpentaria Shire town of Normanton.

Conclusion

The history of the built environment is inseparable from changes in social values and ethical concerns through particular periods of time. In fact, built environment design has been advanced through constant challenges to existing understandings of what constitutes ethical approaches to designing products and places that people use and inhabit. Despite this, design professionals' capacity to advance public benefit and social reform became increasingly marginalized during the course of the twentieth century. One of the key problems identified in this chapter is the fragmentation of ethics and values in design practices operating in the modern capitalist economy.

Access to 'good design' in the built environment is still problematic for many communities who are remote, marginalized and/or disadvantaged. There are many obstacles confronting design professionals working in the public or private sector to fulfilling an ethic of social responsibility, yet equally, the design pioneers and social reformers in the nineteenth and twentieth centuries were faced with many challenges in attempting to realize their vision. Part of the problem for contemporary designers is that engagement in community design is no longer a part of mainstream professional activity. As such, architects, landscape architects and urban designers, through their own business imperatives, have become increasingly alienated from the social and environmental realities facing many citizens. Thus the current status of design services is that they are largely reserved for those who can afford them, or dependent upon the largesse, vision and economies of governing authorities who chose to sponsor public buildings.

Universities face a similar dilemma. They are increasingly asked to operate as business corporations, characterized by the dual functions of mass-education production and externally sponsored research projects sometimes at the cost of promoting scholarship, dissemination and social service. In the early twenty-first century, the social purpose and public benefit of the academy, which is declared throughout their mission statements, has been de-emphasized, and so too their own moral credibility has diminished.

Despite the problems surrounding current practices, there are attempts to address the broader benefits to social and public interest as evidenced by the various community outreach projects that have been undertaken by design schools in some higher education institutions. Through the design skills of academic staff (who are often practitioners themselves) and students, a number of projects have been identified and undertaken in partnership with communities.

Staff and students of QUT succeeded in providing a model solution in the reported case study. Without such initiatives communities may continue to suffer from the absence of affordable 'good design'. The Linking Karumba project shows that design professionals in university communities can contribute to remote or disadvantaged community development through making good built environment design more accessible. The experiment in Karumba is an excellent model project reconnecting ethics and design, academics, students and professionals in built environment design; it revives the legacy of early modern design professionals and embraces the high ideals enacted by those pioneering schools towards 'designing a better world' (Aynsley 2009: 76).

An overview of the social history of built environment design reveals that design professionals and schools can enhance the way we live by encouraging high ideals and practices among trainee design professionals. Universities and educators need to be aware of their capacity to facilitate change by reconsidering their social responsibility and the role of the curriculum in effecting change.

References

Architects without Frontiers (2009) *Vision and Mission*, Melbourne. Available at: www.architectswithoutfrontiers.com.au/site/index.php?option=com_content&view=article&id=177&Itemid=152 (accessed 29 December 2009).

Armstrong, H. (1999) 'Design studios as research: an emerging paradigm for landscape architecture', *Landscape Review*, 5(2): 5–25.

Australian Institute of Architects (2006) *RAIA* 'Code of Professional Conduct'. Available at: www.architecture.com.au/i-cms?page=442 (accessed 18 July 2011).

Australian Institute of Landscape Architects (2005) 'Code of Professional Conduct'. Available at: www.aila.org.au/codeofconduct (accessed 29 December 2009).

Aynsley, J. (2009) *Designing Modern Germany*, London: Reaktion Books.

Bauhaus Dessau Foundation (2010) *Bauhaus History*, Dessau: Bauhaus Dessau. Available at: www.bauhaus-dessau.de/index.php?history (accessed 7 January 2010).

Berglund, E. (2008) 'Exploring the social and political: Are architects still relevant to architecture?', *Architectural Research Quarterly*, 12(2): 105–111.

Checkoway, B. (2000) 'Public service: our new mission', *Academe*, 86. Available at: www.aaup.org/AAUP/pubsres/academe/2000/JA/Feat/chec.htm(accessed 3 January 2010).

Crawford, A. (1997) 'Ideas and objects: the arts and crafts movement in Britain', *Design Issues*, 13: 15–26.

Crawford, M. (1991) 'Can architects be socially responsible?' in D. Ghirardo (ed.) *Out of Site: A social criticism of architecture*, Seattle, WA: Bay Press, 27–46.

Cumberlidge, C. and Musgrave, L. (2007) *Design and Landscape for People: New approaches to renewal*, London: Thames & Hudson.

Dawes, L. A. and Satherley, S. D. (2008) 'Sustainable futures by design: enriching the balance between engagement processes and outcomes', *The Australasian Journal of University Community Engagement*, 2(3): 28–37.

Descoings, R. (2006) 'Universities: a social duty', *OECD Observer*, 255. Available at: www.oecdobserver.org/news/fullstory.php/aid/1900/Universities:_A_social_duty.html (accessed 23 June 2011).

Engels, F. and McLellan D. (2009) *The Condition of the Working Class in England*, Oxford; New York: Oxford University Press.

Fewings, P. (2009) *Ethics for the Built Environment*, London: Taylor & Francis.

Garnett, R. G. (1972) *Co-operation and the Owenite Socialist Communities in Britain, 1825–45*, Manchester: Manchester University Press.

Hall, P. G. (2002) *Cities of Tomorrow: An intellectual history of urban planning and design in the 20th century*, Oxford: Blackwell.

Hall, P. and Ward, C. (1998) *Sociable Cities: The legacy of Ebenezer Howard*, Chichester: John Wiley & Sons.

Hamlett, P. W. (2003) 'Universities and public deliberation: bringing expertise to the people', *On the Horizon*, 11(4): 15–24. Available at: www.emeraldinsight.com.ezp01.library.qut.edu.au/Insight/viewContainer.do;jsessionid=907BECBDCAAE4A8B48057DB842D1FB7F?containerType=Issue&containerId=11386 (accessed 23 June 2011).

Harvey, D. (1990) *The Condition of Postmodernity: An enquiry into the origins of cultural change*. Oxford: Basil Blackwell.

Hollander, E. L. and Saltmarsh, J. (2000) 'The engaged university', *Academe*, 86. Available at: www.aaup.org/AAUP/pubsres/academe/2000/JA/Feat/holl.htm (accessed 3 January 2010).

Howard, E. (1902) *Garden cities of tomorrow: being the second edition of 'Tomorrow: a peaceful path to real reform'*, London: Swan, Sonnenschein.

Jacobs, J. (1972) *The death and life of great American cities*, Harmondsworth: Penguin.

Jarvis, P. (2009) 'Ethics, values and higher education' in J. Strain, R. Barnett and P. Jarvis (eds) *Universities, Ethics and Professions*, New York: Routledge.

Jordan, H. (1994) 'Public parks, 1885–1914', *Garden History*, 22(1): 85–113.

Jordan, H. (2003) *Public Parks Review: A summary*, London: English Heritage.

Leach, N. (2005) 'Less aesthetics, more ethics', in N. Ray (ed.) *Architecture and its Ethical Dilemmas*, New York: Taylor & Francis.

Metropolitan Borough of Wirral (2009) 'Birkenhead Park', Wirral: Metropolitan Borough of Wirral. Available at: www.wirral.gov.uk/lgcl/100006/200073/670/content_0001109.html (accessed 2 January 2010).

Murray, S. (2007) 'Housing', *Architecture Australia*, 96(3): 43–45. Available at: www.architecturemedia.com/aa/aaissue.php?issueid=200705&article=15&typeon=3 (accessed 23 June 2011).

New Lanark Trust (2009) 'New Lanark – an introduction', About New Lanark Resources, New Lanark: New Lanark Trust. Available at: www.newlanark.org/download/upload.46.rtf (accessed 29 December 2009).

New Lanark Trust (2011a) 'Robert Owen and New Lanark: A man ahead of his time', New Lanark: New Lanark Trust. Available www.robert-owen.com (accessed 12 July 2011).

New Lanark Trust (2011b) 'A Quest for Universal Harmony: Extracts from Robert Owen's published works', New Lanark: New Lanark Trust. Available at: www.robert-owen.com/extracts.html (accessed 17 July 2011).

Pevsner, N. and Weston, R. (2005) *Pioneers of Modern Design from W. Morris to W. Gropius: Revised and expanded edition*, New Haven, NJ: Yale University Press.

Ray, N. (2005) *Architecture and its Ethical Dilemmas*, London: Taylor & Francis.

Relph, E. C. (1976) *Place and Placelessness*, London: Pion.

Royal Institute of British Architects (2005) 'RIBA Code of Professional Conduct', London: RIBA. Available at: http://www.architecture.com/Files/RIBAProfessionalServices/ProfessionalConduct/Constitution/CodeOfConduct/2005RIBACodeOfProfessionalConduct.pdf (accessed 23 June 2011).

Schneider, T. and Till, J. (2008) 'Alternate currents: an introduction', *Architectural Research Quarterly*, 12(2): 109–111.

Sethna, B. N. (2006) 'Ethical leadership in a global society: (how) can universities lead?', in J. C. Knapp (ed.) *For the Common Good: The ethics of leadership in the 21st century*, Santa Barbara, CA: Praeger.

Simmons, R. (2009) *Good Design: The fundamentals*, London: CABE. Available at http://www.designcouncil.org.uk/Documents/Documents/Publications/CABE/good-design.pdf (accessed 28 June 2011).

Spector, T. (2001) *The Ethical Architect*, New York: Princeton Architectual Press.

Stormann, W. F. (1991) 'The ideology of the American urban parks and recreation movement: past and future', *Leisure Sciences: An Interdisciplinary Journal*, 13(2): 137–151.

Strain, J., Barnett, R. and Jarvis, P. (2009) *Universities, Ethics and Professions*, New York: Routledge.

Thomas, G. S. 'Poona futures: students respond to a community cry for help', Embedding University Community engagement: The good, the bad, and the ugly: Australian Universities Community Engagement Alliance National Conference, Perth, July 2006.

Thornton, C. E. (1983) *The People's Garden: A history of Birkenhead Park*, Williamson Art Gallery & Museum: Metropolitan Borough of Wirral.

Walker, S. E. and Duffield, B. S. (1983) 'Urban parks and open spaces – an overview', *Landscape Research*, 8(2): 2–12.

Wasserman, B., Sullivan, P. and Palermo, G. (2000) *Ethics and the Practice of Architecture*, New York: John Wiley & Sons.

12

RETHINKING PRACTICE

Architecture, ecology and ethics

Marci Webster-Mannison

Preamble

Architectural practice, in Australia and globally, currently faces a serious choice of a future characterized, on the one hand, by the passage through the trend for uniformity to the satisfaction of the individual's perceived desires, and on the other, by a manifestation of individualism to the pragmatic recognition of a new environmental ethic. These choices are curiously entwined. Both require a design approach that not only integrates the concerns of building users, owners, designers and community, but also recognizes the environmental consequences inherent in the design process. Given the nexus between knowledge and values in dealing with environmental issues, the process of changing our design approach may be as important as the change itself.

Despite a well-established need for the architectural, design and construction professions to embrace more environmentally responsible practices, there are limitations inhibiting this transformation. This chapter is a culmination of ideas about the integration of ecological concerns into the architectural design process acquired through thirty years of practice and research.

The discussion is centred on the understanding of a particular body of work, designed by the author over a ten-year period, at Charles Sturt University's Thurgoona campus, Australia, where 'continuity and the slow evolution of architectural thinking, in built form over time, transforms into an iterative maturity of ideas' (Mackenzie 2005: 86). The Thurgoona campus developments exemplify an innovative approach to design and construction that integrated ecological concerns.

Identified are the key limitations and barriers to integrating environmental ethics into architectural practice, before exploring new understandings and lessons about integrating such ethics into design and construction. To begin, the author's approach to architecture will be outlined briefly in the context of the Thurgoona campus development, which will feature throughout the discussion, as will the philosophical approaches to architecture.

Situated in Albury, New South Wales, an hour's flight out of Melbourne and Sydney, the architecture of Thurgoona's 87-hectare campus, which stretches over wetlands, demonstrates the creative possibilities of environmentally sensitive design, even in rural Australia.

Thurgoona campus

The author has developed a distinctive architecture committed to the synthesis of ecological responsibility and innovation, and perhaps above all to the creation of meaningful environments. Meaningful architecture is architecture with a narrative.

At the Thurgoona campus, the use of rammed earth and recycled timber, glass and steel invite questions about materials and construction. Buildings oriented for optimal solar access and covered with extensive solar arrays speak of energy and renewable resources. The careful use of space and materials and the forty-six composting toilets at Thurgoona teach about waste. The integration of rainwater tanks, the meandering constructed creeks and wetlands animate the importance of water in the dry, arid continent of Australia. The deliberate alignment of significant vistas to stands of remnant trees, and the 'living museum' of local vegetation planted along the waterways and supporting habitats give a voice to biodiversity and ecosystems. The use of natural ventilation, abundance of sunlight and non-toxic materials breathe comfort and health (Figures 12.1–12.4).

A visit to the Thurgoona campus will reveal how the built environment influences how people live in these surrounds, socialize with one another, plant permaculture gardens, maintain free bicycles for transport and use the site as a learning laboratory. These observable outcomes reflect the builders and designers who have used the Thurgoona development to (re)discover their craft and work collectively to improve each project. The overt articulation of ecological competence is teaching the local community about an ecological ethic and impacting on the wider systems serving the buildings. Despite lamenting the difficulty in finding examples of sustainable architectural design, Paola Sassi nonetheless identifies the Thurgoona campus as one of the few cases where a comprehensive approach has been achieved (Sassi 2006: 2).

Caitlin McGee and Cynthia Mitchell also point to the Thurgoona campus as a model for future design demonstrating a fundamental design and decision-making principle: integrity. They then identify the key barriers to sustainable development as the perceived risk of innovation, lack of financial incentive, lack of public interest, available industry skills or resources and the lack of an integrated approach to decision making and design (McGee and Mitchell 2002: 4).

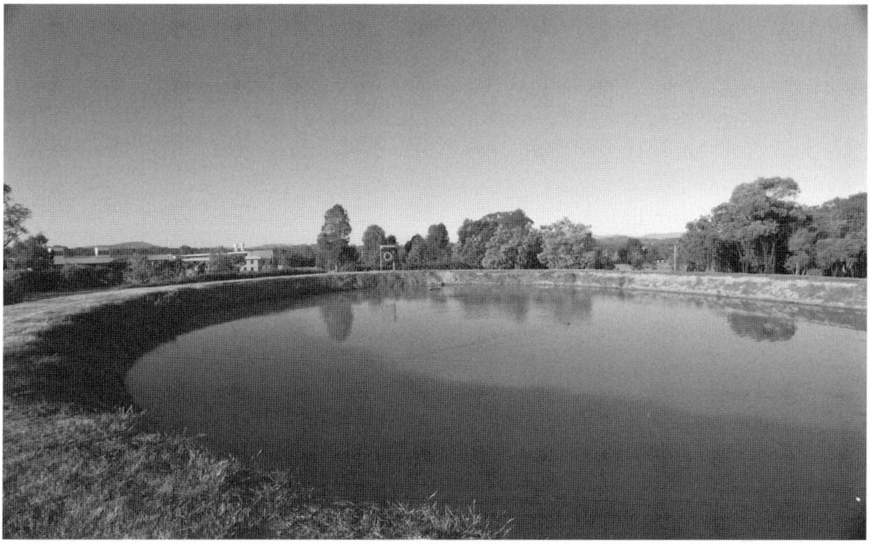

FIGURE 12.1 Turkey's Nest Dam (© Dirk HR Spennemann 2011).

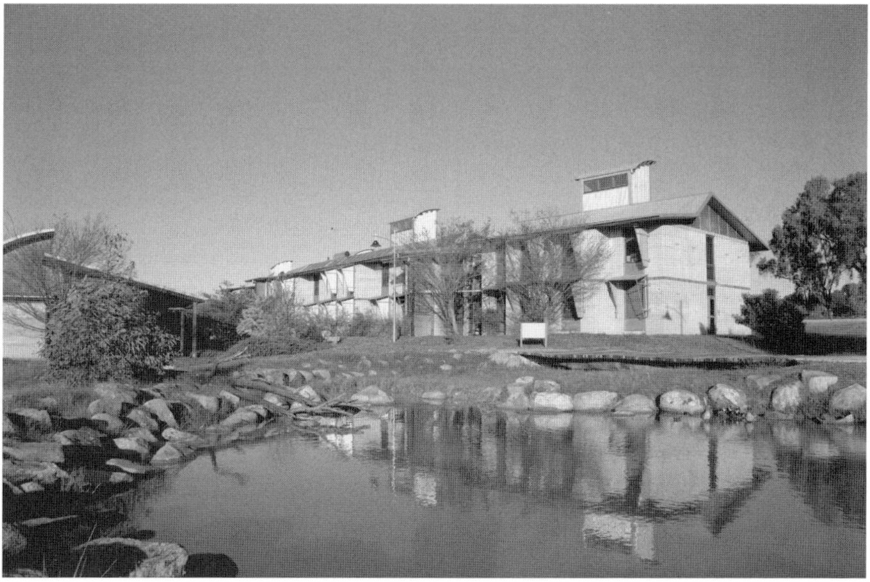

FIGURE 12.2 School of Environmental and Information Sciences (© Dirk HR Spennemann 2011).

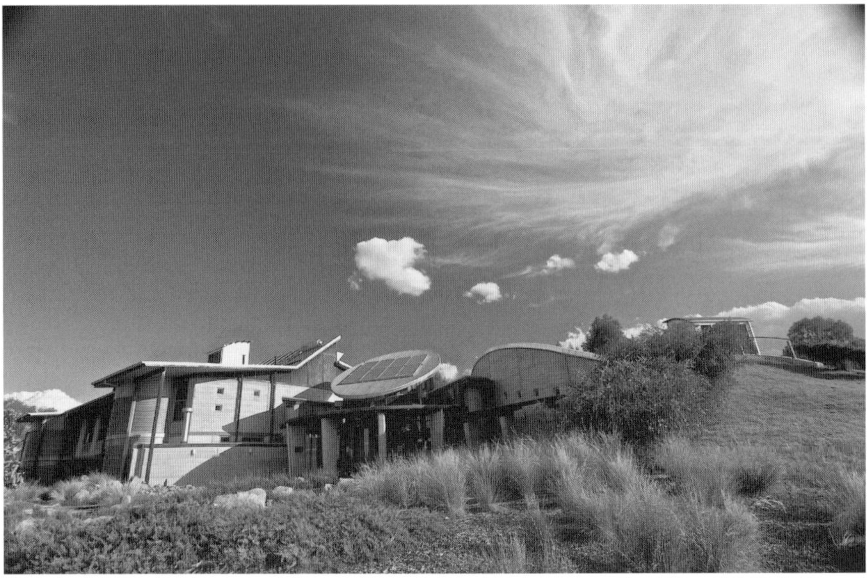

FIGURE 12.3 CD Blake Lecture Theatre Complex (© Dirk HR Spennemann 2011).

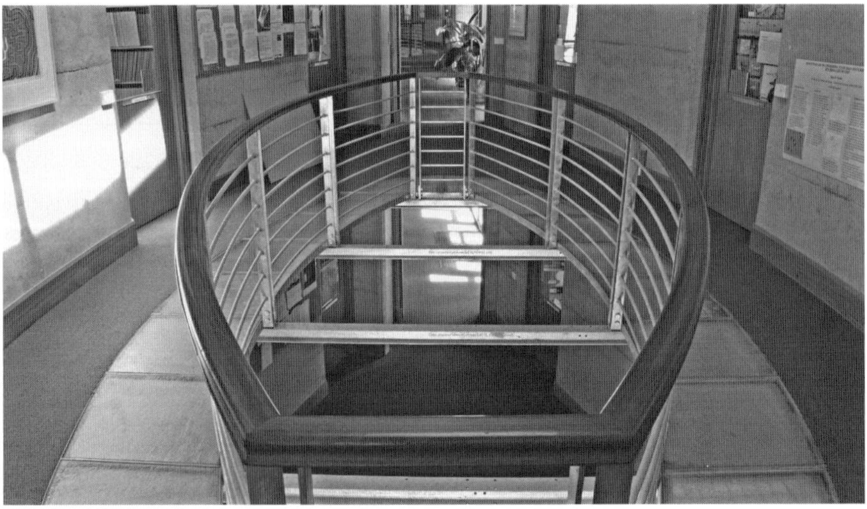

FIGURE 12.4 School of Environmental and Information Sciences interior (© Dirk HR Spennemann 2011).

Context

In the 1950s and 1960s, designers began to reconsider the social, cultural and ecological roles of architecture. When the Australian architect Robin Boyd said 'architecture makes a statement with its motive' (Boyd 1963: 247) and spoke ironically of efforts to 'correct' the Australian landscape, was he supporting an environmental ethic? He was certainly proposing something like a bioregional approach to design.

A culmination of the previous ten years of research by Victor and Aladar Olgyay, *Design with Climate: Bioclimatic approach to architectural regionalism* (1963) is seen by Victor Olgyay as only a first exploratory step in the debate about more appropriate architecture. Although focused on bioclimatic design, Olgyay touches on a wider appreciation of environmental architecture when he draws an analogy between natural formations and architecture: 'In natural history the rule is universal that only species are fit to survive which are in harmony with their environment, balanced with their tissue materials, and adapted to all internal and external forces to which they are exposed' (Olgyay 1963: 84). Traditional approaches to architecture have involved the creation of a setting, based on metaphors, rather than a considered analysis of the ethical inferences of environmental considerations to design decisions (Birkeland 1994).

It has been argued that to make ethically valid, aesthetic decisions, there is a need to combine the quality of subjectivity with a sense of the cumulative effects of actions of the past and positive strategies for change in the future. A new environmental ethic involves a major reconceptualization of space from a new political, social, economic and aesthetic standpoint. With potentially unknown and different outcomes presenting a threat to established space organization and conception methods, such as ethic challenges, the existing systems of planning governance and procedures, which are becoming obsolete in a rapidly changing society once accustomed to a very determinate planning and design context, now demand flexible and indeterminate decision-making processes (Gibson and Watson 1995).

It is clear that the consumption patterns of development in industrialized countries are thoroughly stressing the global ecosystem, creating huge inequities with the developing world which, on a basic level, needs more raw material, energy and economic development to overcome critical economic and social problems. Agenda 21 points to depletion of the natural resource base, degradation of fragile eco-zones, chemical pollution and the use of building materials harmful to human health caused by the construction sector as a major source of environmental damage. Compounding the harmful side effects for human health and the biosphere by the construction industry is the lack of integration of economic, social and environmental concerns in decision making at the policy, planning and management levels.

It is too easy to shy away from acknowledging that any design process is value-laden and to present an 'objective' approach. By the inclusion of an ethical framework upfront, the subjectivity and indeterminacy of a design process concerned with equity and ecological integrity is brought to the forefront of the design process and elevated as a goal.

Responsibility of architects

The architectural professional associations of America, Europe and Australia all make a commitment to environmental responsibility in the use of materials and design process. In 1994, the Royal Australian Institute of Architects (RAIA) introduced an environment policy that reinforces the urgent need for architects to act on their environmental responsibilities. It includes specific attention to concerns about non-renewable resources and the restoration of biodiversity (RAIA 1994: 87–88).

These policies indicate the growing recognition by architects of their responsibilities for the contribution of building development to environmental problems. Only when this is coupled with, and legitimated by, an emphatic ecologically sustainable design policy by the federal government, will specific ecologically sustainable development design strategies for large buildings, among other things, be in order. Meanwhile, difficulties of the individual's isolated efforts of implementation hinder significant change. The urgency of Louise Cox's (RAIA former president) call for architects to 'make a stronger, clearer commitment to ecological sustainability' is paralleled by other voices, such as Susan Coldicutt, former Head of the Department of Architecture, University of Adelaide, whose statement regarding the status of the RAIA's environment policy seems to invite a 'conscience vote':

> let us use the policy for the many good things it can achieve, but remember that since policy generalises, and design is particular, no policy, no matter how excellent, can substitute for the creative leads that can truly inspire a new understanding of the interrelationship of ourselves and our environments.
>
> (RAIA 1994: 93)

Almost ten years on, there is little indication of change. Emerging trends in environmental law may force designers, regardless of our individual stance, to adopt a more morally defensible position. The challenge for the design professions is how to make a difference when they are frequently confounded by the ebb and flow of expediency at governmental levels (Jones 1998: 243).

Limitations and barriers

Political framework and professional identity

There are historical instances of grass-roots action and change that have had a significant impact on the built environment in Australia. In the 1970s, when Jack Mundey, the Builders Labourers' Federation (BLF) and green bans were at the forefront of environmental activism in Australia, it appeared that the nation was about to change. The social conscience and political force of the New South Wales BLF that contested indiscriminate development and the exploitation of marginalized groups such as women, indigenous peoples, prisoners, and gays and lesbians, provided a powerful lesson in responsibility.

However, architecture was still generally considered as a 'profession' rather than an art, and implicit in this highly focused view was the lesson that ethical concerns likewise did not matter. Certainly, architecture was not thought of as a political act and its legitimate form was confined to the rendering of services to the client, the client being the one who pays. This narrow conception of architecture subjugates the ways in which architecture is a material expression of social, economic and political values. The wider public good, which one may naïvely assume was ultimately what architecture was about, didn't get the attention it deserved. The roles of the designers and the combination of organizational techniques employed on a particular project were largely dictated by individual circumstances.

Nevertheless, as Tony Fry puts it, the role of the professional designer, in practical terms, is 'embracing the material, social or symbolic environmental consequences of the impact of our actions' (Fry 1999: 290). The significant presence of architecture that philosopher Roger Scruton highlights in the following argument strengthens the pressure for designers to change their approach: 'Architecture is public; it imposes itself whatever our desires and whatever our self image. Moreover it takes up space: either it crushes out of existence what has gone before, or else it attempts to blend and harmonize' (Scruton 1979: 15). Traditionally, humans' relationship to the environment has been mapped out – assuming the exploitation, or at best, the management of nature. According to American architect William McDonough, 'our present systems of design have created a world that grows far beyond the capacity of the environment to sustain life into the future' (William McDonough Architects 1996: 407). Such approaches to design are based on the principle of total use, implying that every natural area or thing should be cultivated, resourced or otherwise used or enjoyed by humans. Such views and practices are inconsistent with an environmental ethic, and are ultimately unsustainable for the well-being of future generations.

Market drivers

Market drivers present a significant barrier to the ability of the architectural profession to adopt environmental ethics. The short-term, speculative nature of the construction industry in Australia, and the lack of statutory environmental performance measurements or criteria that reinforce a standard of building design, shows disconcertingly little regard for environmental quality. In Northern Europe, where there are many more examples of innovative, ecologically sustainable design, quite a different pattern of development of owner-built and occupied premises may be observed that stem from a longer-term view of the building as an investment and the staff as people. By urging designers to operate outside of the vacuum of the current market-driven nature of architectural services Jeffrey Cook thus points towards opportunities for architects to exercise environmental ethics (Cook 1991: 5).

Motivation

The lack of care about the built environment obvious in many designs merely reflects the anthropocentric nature of our market economy, which fails to recognize the ecological effects of pollution or the value of natural resources. An understanding of an ecosystem will catalyse change in value systems, thus framing the longer-term ecological implications of our strategic choices (Lawrence and Raar 1996). Therefore, if social and ecological responsibility is to be incorporated in design decision-making, organizational and technical support must be combined with individual resolve.

The importance of a shared vision and rationale is becoming a distinct concern of architects who are rejecting the individualistic, patently unsustainable values that have so dominated development of the built environment in favour of societal values that respect all life. The emergence of 'green buildings', designs that foreground environmental sustainability, can help change the way that architects and those involved in the building and development industry think about buildings so that their environmental impact is reduced.

Hand in hand with a changed attitude to design, a more enlightened view of development is required. The owners and users of green buildings are not just 'doing the right thing'. As Kateshi Matsunawa observes, if a building is designed well, the benefits are observable for their social and economic benefit, such as higher rental values and reduced costs of maintenance (Matsunawa 2000: 20).

The present close and 'enormously beneficial symbiotic relationship' among architects, the construction and real-estate industries stunts the development of a social or greater community conscience, posing a challenge to designing and developing environmentally responsible buildings (Ghirardo 1996: 387). Design decisions examined as part of a recursive process demand design leaders who can step outside this nexus to provide models for sensitive and environmentally sustainable architecture.

Organizational management

For organizations, the duty of tackling ethical dilemmas of environmental management requires commitment from management to proactively assimilate ethical reasoning into strategic decision-making processes. Implementation involves integration of shared values in policy and staff selection supporting environmentally ethical behaviour.

Taking on social and ecological responsibility is fraught with intellectual, material and financial obstruction. In response, environmental activist Robert Bullard advocates a decision-making framework that takes on responsibility rather than simply managing and distributing the risks, with the founding principle of rights to equal protection from environmental degradation that attempts to uncover the underlying assumptions that may contribute and produce differential exposure and unequal protection. It also brings to the surface the ethical and political questions of 'who gets what, when, why and how much' (Bullard 1999: 34–35).

With a precautionary approach of instituting a preventive public health model, Bullard targets action and resources as problems with the greatest impact. An essential characteristic of his recommended strategy is the shift of culpability of detrimental effects to those responsible, regardless of intent.

In the context of architecture and the built environment, designers must explore their role in environmental injustice and explore the multiplicity of ways to recognize justice and think out some pragmatic guidelines for their action.

Design process

The architectural interpretation of environmental science is not plainly a technical exercise, but a process influenced by many interests. Overcoming roadblocks to technical change calls for bridging obviously important research with all levels of the industry. John Goulding and J. Owen Lewis suggest '[demonstrating] the [compatibility] of energy-conscious buildings with the highest standards of architectural design, and highest quality living and working environments' (Goulding and Lewis 2000: 10). Mechanical air-conditioning systems that defy bioclimatic principles are a very recent invention that illustrates how mainstream architecture was dominated by passive techniques of daylighting and natural ventilation until around 1950 (Cook 1991: 21).

The challenge of engaging the wider construction industry in realizing appropriate change to traditional practice is further magnified by its fragmented nature; project initiation, design, materials manufacture and supply, building trades and construction management are usually undertaken by separate companies. The sequential nature of conventional planning procedures limits the overview and influence of individuals upon final outcome; yet, an integrated planning process where all those involved have input from the project's conception through to planning and construction stages creates a synergistic outcome.

Ecodesign necessitates a change in lifestyle and social relations that the designer can only facilitate. For buildings and systems to operate successfully, they must be maintained and fine-tuned, and people need to think more about their interaction with their surrounds and with others. Ecodesign, therefore, grapples with the wider issues of climate change, energy consumption, resource depletion, pollution, waste and health, and at the same time takes into account the source of the problem, not just the effect, and ensures that the proposed solution does not lead to greater detrimental environmental impact.

Once designers are certain of their environmental ideals, and are aware of the radical changes implied by these ideals, they need to adopt a design approach that is sensitive to the web of interrelationships between issues and that can chart the path from environmental ideals to everyday realities. Designers need to fill the gap between theory and technology with a structure for design analysis that is aligned with an ethical stance concerned with social well-being, equity and ecological integrity.

The sorts of problems that the designer is likely to face in following through with green principles are political and technical. Both manifest themselves throughout a project's initiation, design, documentation, construction and occupation phases.

Definition of architecture

How we define architecture may be a further impediment. Simply put, environmental architecture is a way of designing buildings and manipulating the environment within and around buildings by working with eco-justice principles, which spotlights environmental impacts, and responsible use of resources while utilizing passive design as the foundation of benign comfort conditions. However, such a technical definition does little justice to the practice of environmental architecture. The whole story views architecture as a work of art, where the architect must visualize and define the quality of the spatial interpretive experience before it is realized, orchestrating the many disparate elements to a harmonious whole.

The biggest barrier to the widespread adoption of an ecodesign approach will be our own commitment and abilities, and education will play a role in overcoming this. Architectural and engineering education need to foster a professional concern and intellectual approach to built responses to the issues of climate change, energy-source depletion and environmental impact. This may involve addressing the vocabulary and meaning of environmental language in architecture – to look at the stories that have already been written with this language. Ecocentric ethics needs to form the core of critique for existing and new works, and should be taken as an environmental paradigm around which much of the discussion must occur.

Bottom line

Directly contributing to the process of biospheric degradation, our social and technological history reveals a human-centred focus within our cultural identity through the inappropriate use of technology, and permitting of the wealthy to continue profiting at environmental expense. Operating within such a disparately amoral political, social and economic context perpetuates ecological destruction. As argued,

> We need to understand that we are not just dealing here with an absence of ethics in the animal sphere, but also with a disempowerment of ethics and communicative experience generally in neo-liberal societies, and hence with something that affects both humans and non-humans . . . The growing exclusion of justice, care and responsibility from the economic sphere in the interests of global competition affects all of us in different ways, but these different ways can still bring us together in the struggle for a fair and just form of economic life as it affects both human and non-human spheres.
>
> (Plumwood 1999: 208)

Examining the value and belief systems that generate unsustainable behaviour will go some way to addressing an ethics of design. Such questions are typically avoided owing to complexity and a lack of sensitivity to other members of the ecological community. We lack both a detailed understanding of environmental systems and our interaction with them, and the ability to accept an affordable level of comfort that values social and ecological health. What, then, defines an acceptable quality of life? Who will get it, why, and what are the implications?

New understandings

Given the range of limitations identified here, what lessons from the Thurgoona development, introduced at the beginning of the chapter, can help integrate environmental ethics into the practice of architecture?

Aesthetic

Architectural expression of a new environmental ethic may well inspire a new aesthetic, or a reinterpretation of the vernacular tradition, or seemingly present little change to the look of buildings. A balance between functional, organizational and technical requirements, and individual needs may lead to a built form of recognizable human scale – a place that people may be happier to work in and even be more productive.

Recognition of variable cultural and economic influences may lead to buildings capable of continual adaptation in terms of physical planning and environmental performance, or with a deliberately long life. The architectural interpretation of environmental principles may establish an expression based on a response to climate. From responsible resource management, a more pleasing synthesis between architecture and construction and architecture and land use may emerge. The role architecture plays in shaping our thinking about the environment is also important if, as Scruton suggests, 'architecture becomes new by creating new expectations' (Scruton 1979: 15).

Values

The values inherent in the Thurgoona campus design were initiated by the design architect through a process of educating key stakeholders of the detailed rationale behind design decisions. Participation in the design process helped ensure a level of understanding that was essential to gaining support of the key decision makers. Facing design parameters – namely, budget constraints – the Thurgoona campus experience of cutting-edge design within limitations valued the process as much as the technical outcomes.

Uniquely for a university, the new Thurgoona campus was delivered through an in-house design and construction process; that is, all brief preparation, and most design and documentation, construction management by trade packages and some construction was undertaken by university design staff. This overcame the barriers faced by practitioners working with a disparate group of consultants, suppliers and contractors, and thereby benefited the project.

The establishment of a shared set of values for the design and construction team is a process of negotiation. The team must judge issues, debate options, plan activities, reach decisions, establish standards, resolve differences, change patterns, exert influence and decide right from wrong. Values must not only be reinforced through explicit teaching and resources, but also be espoused by practice. An architectural practice can greatly influence the individual's decisions and actions by providing a benchmark for appropriate or acceptable behaviour.

Although a practice's values are critical components in shaping the individual's behaviour and providing some ethical and moral direction, how is this process implemented in a way that supports ethical decision-making?

Assuming and incorporating moral responsibility into the economic system by managerial actions and decisions is not easy. Ian Thompson's research (2000) on the integration of ecological values with social and aesthetic values among design practitioners found limited examples of landscape projects that demonstrated successful integration of all three values as a foundation for design. Rather, ecological values were more commonly seen as secondary to the aesthetic of the design, and this view is similarly reflected in architectural practice.

Design practice

How we conceive boundaries dictates our perception of architecture (Colomina 1996: 6). Current building design, construction and management methods tend to be insensitive to contemporary environmental understandings and commitments. Understanding how designers' ideas are shaped by social assumptions and values might mean a greater examination and responsibility towards the decisions that shape the work of architects.

Modelling itself on an integrated planning approach, the design of the Thurgoona campus was the outcome of a comprehensive and ecologically sensitive design strategy. The open setting sculptured by artificial creeks and wetlands, native vegetation, a windmill, solar collection panels, buildings articulated in rammed earth, and recycled timber clearly express the university's approach to environmental practice. Solar hydronic heating and cooling, earth thermal exchange, night cooling, innovative use of natural ventilation, daylighting, non-toxic, recycled, low-impact materials, composting toilets, greywater treatment wetlands and stormwater reuse place the development on the leading edge of sustainable design.

Architect Lyndsay Johnston's description of the campus reflects on the design process as well as the outcomes:

> The Thurgoona campus buildings are in the lineage of 'eccentric' architecture – Bruce Goff, Herb Greene, Paolo Soleri, Ton Alberts, Kota Kawasaki, Gregory Burgess. On my thorough visit to the site, on a glorious sunny cold winter

> day, the depth of understanding of environmental issues, the rigorous commitment to closing the resource loops, and the functional performance of the whole complex were most impressive. The conceptual integrity and many of the details of the exteriors and interiors were, in my opinion, delightful.
>
> (Johnston 2001: 95)

Integrated design approach

Design is very much a cyclical transdisciplinary process of projection, practice and testing; it involves continuing collaboration and interaction with academics and researchers as an important aspect of this process and to refining one's skills. Therefore, part of what is argued here is that architectural change can only occur when designers attain a level of ethical responsibility and better understand their relationship to the process of design.

Among the twenty-eight pre-selected projects of excellence in Peter Barda and Tom Crow's in-depth study of the drivers of industry best practice was the Thurgoona campus. The study points to 'improved relationships, both within . . . and between the industry and clients' as a key challenge to both the building and construction industry, and a catalyst to the most important 'drivers of excellence' – behavioural – through 'effective and informed client leadership' (Barda and Crow 2001: 5). Project performance was consistently the worst in process improvement, supplier-driven relationships and information use. Professionally, behavioural and attitudinal change were inherent in the design thinking about the Thurgoona campus, and this was recognized by qualitative research conducted among staff, managers, construction workers and designers (Willis 2000).

The success of the campus design is established in its acclaim through awards and publications, but more importantly in its reception by the client body and people who live and work in these environments. The real joy, and certainly an indication of the significance of this body of work, is the ongoing and daily users' satisfaction of enjoying the spaces they inhabit, be it a childcare centre, green space, laboratory, office or home.

Many of the awards for the campus have been given by professional bodies allied to architecture. This recognition reflects the adherence to an inclusive and integrated approach to design that acknowledges the concerns of engineering, construction and environmental planning in the technological, social and ecological innovation of design solutions. In contrast, the traditional architectural process focuses on the isolated pursuit of a technological or stylistic artefact that is contrary to new understandings that the built object cannot rightly be separated from its local, regional or global context.

Urgently required is an approach to architectural design that can deal with multifaceted questions, dissect the problems and examine them from as many perspectives as possible; an interdisciplinary approach that includes the concerns of building users, owners, designers and the community, along with the consideration of ecological consequences.

Experiential learning – architecture as critical process

As an experiential learning experience, the Thurgoona campus embodies what architecture can be all about. Occupied and operational, people are happy to be there and want to talk about it – clearly, something significant has happened.

Immediate feedback facilitates behavioural changes, and by making the environmental choices highly visible, building users are challenged to examine the underlying social, scientific and cultural connections that operate, and how we cause environmental degradation. More than routine or practice, architecture is a critical process. Ultimately, architecture is a public art, with the associated obligation and responsibility to draw out the kind of possibilities and potential that it has to shape discourses.

Architecture is public

Architecture is inherently in the public sphere, although this is not to deny that the personal is also very political. Thus, a cautious approach is necessary, especially when architects seem to be looking either to leave their mark on the environment or 'to enhance what is there', observe Robert Venturi and Denise Scott Brown as they challenge architects with a paradigm shift (Venturi and Scott Brown 1996: 310).Their argument is without value judgement in the provocative presentation of the Las Vegas strip as a model of architectural communication. By recognizing the strength of the political and cultural climate in determining architectural persuasions, their work addresses the emerging 'manifestation of an opposite direction of architectural theory' (Venturi and Scott Brown 1996: 320). As the philosopher John Ferguson remarks, 'the ideal city lives in its citizens, here and now' (1975: 187).

In many large projects, social and cultural benefits are largely add-ons – aesthetic improvements to the built environment, better street lighting, increased safety, maybe the provision of a park, and so on. Thurgoona's social and cultural ambitions are far higher, with the university aiming to provide an exemplary environment for low-impact living. Through its carefully integrated systems of energy, water and waste management, it sets out to influence behaviour and thus contribute to cultural change towards more sustainable ways of living and working.

Operating in the public sphere, architecture demands a rigorous and consistent theoretical examination where architects must be prepared to acknowledge the risk that we may get it wrong. Another aspect of the public nature of architecture is to avoid translating everything into our own terms.

Conclusion: call for action

Many designers are working around the edge of change, but fundamental shifts are required to build a sustainable future. For Robyn Eckersley, in adopting an ecocentric view, we have two choices of action: either bringing about the peaceful and creative disintegration of industrial society or inviting 'change through education and exemplary action' (Eckersley 1992: 182–183): put another way, an eco-archi- 'terrorist' role versus the best practice model.

That few architects appear to have taken on the eco-archi- 'terrorist' role perhaps reflects the conservative and apolitical historical nature of the profession, combined with its socio-economic background. Dianne Ghirardo claims that 'avoiding the risk of antagonizing moneyed interest' is the key reason architects take the 'safer course by designing buildings that evade issues of substance' (Ghirardo 1996: 390).

Architect Philip Bess (1996) points to examples of advocacy planning, environmental design and socially responsible design as indicators of an ethical shift towards communitarian values in architecture. He cites the Mad Housers, a guerrilla group that constructs portable individual shelters for the homeless, as an example of growing recognition of the need for an ethical stance in the practice of architecture. Bess's positioning of the 'building's proper place in an urban hierarchy' (Bess 1996: 382), although based on the spatial formalities of traditional architecture, is largely a recognition of the power of the built environment to reinforce a particular way of life. He radically denounces the themes of individualism and emotivism as promoting the 'relentless stroking of consumer passions' (Bess 1996: 377), deconstructivism as an unresolved 'retreat from accountability' (Bess 1996: 378), and neotraditionalism as class-specific aestheticism (Bess 1996: 380).

Suggesting the Australian political climate 'lacks bite', Johnston notes 'the "green agenda" at both intellectual and practical levels . . . among individual architects and smaller practices' failed to translate into substantial examples of green architecture (Johnston 2001: 59). Among the most ambitious ecological developments in Australia, the Thurgoona campus is a pioneering larger-scale development to comprehensively and rigorously pursue autonomy and sustainability, providing an appropriate case study to further our understanding of an ecodesign process in practice.

The challenge posed by the almost inconceivable scale of environmental problems to all those who shape the built environment is for attitudinal change in terms of natural and cultural systems as well as to the interactions between the participants in the design process. Within the 'cyclical process of projection, practise and verification' that is design, Eiji Maki and William McDonough stress continuing collaboration and interaction with academics and researchers, where the 'solution to multi-faced environmental problems' is a 'collective, multi-disciplinary' approach (Maki and McDonough 2000: 11).

With a vital tension building for architects to take critical action on the political front, whether through archi-'terrorism' or persuasion, an ecocentric architectural practice may be typified by research activities, analysis of materials and processes, innovative applications of technology, new aesthetics and a social and political profile. Where process and outcome are inextricably linked, tackling the challenge of change will manifest the enduring rewards of an eco-effective design.

References

Barda, P. and Crow, T. (eds) (2001) *Projects as Wealth Creators: Drivers of project excellence,* Sydney: Property Council of Australia.

Bess, P. (1996) 'Communitarianism and emotivism: two rival views of ethics and architecture', in K. Nesbitt (ed.) *Theorizing a New Agenda for Architecture: An anthology of architectural theory 1965–1995,* New York: Princeton Architectural Press.

Birkeland, J. (1994) 'A critique of ecological architecture', paper presented at the Protecting the Future: ESD in Action, National Conference on Successful Strategies for Ecologically Sustainable Development, Wollongong, New South Wales.

Boyd, R. (1963) *The Australian Ugliness*, Mitcham, Victoria: Penguin Books.

Bullard, R. (1999) 'Environmental justice challenges', in N. Low (ed.) *Global Ethics and Environment*, New York: Routledge.

Colmina, B. (1996) 'Battle Lines E1027' in F. Hughes (ed.) *The Architect: Reconstructing her practice*, Cambridge, MA: MIT Press.

Cook, J. (1991) 'Global indigenous architecture', in Y. Kodama, J. Smart and S. Yannas (eds) *Passive and Low Energy Architecture*, Tokyo: Process Architecture Publishing.

Eckersley, R. (1992) *Environmentalism and Political Theory: Towards an ecocentric approach*, London: UCL Press.

Ferguson, J. (1975) *Utopias of the Classical World*, London: Thames & Hudson.

Fry, T. (1999) *A New Design Philosophy: An introduction to defuturing*, Adelaide: UNSW Press.

Ghirardo, D. (1996) 'The architecture of deceit', in K. Nesbitt (ed.) *Theorizing a New Agenda for Architecture: An anthology of architectural theory 1965–1995*, New York: Princeton Architectural Press.

Gibson, K. and Watson, S. (eds) (1995) *Postmodern Cities and Spaces*, Oxford: Blackwell.

Goulding, J. R. and Lewis, J. O. (2000) 'Research networking for energy efficient building', Energy Research Group, Dublin: School of Architecture, University College Dublin.

Johnston, L. (2001) 'The view from Australia: green limits in the land of plenty', in B. Edwards (ed.) *Green Architecture*, London: Wiley & Sons.

Jones, D. L. (1998) *Architecture and the Environment: Bioclimatic building design*, London: Laurence King Publishing.

Lawrence, A. and Raar, J. (1996) 'Environmental management: an ethical dilemma', Proceedings of the Second Annual Conference of the Australian Association of Professional and Applied Ethics, Wagga Wagga, New South Wales, September.

McGee, C. and Mitchell, C. (2002) *A New Model: The city as ecosystem . . . postcard from 2050.* Available at: www.aila.org.au/nsw/greeningcities/papers/proc_mitchmcgee.pdf (accessed 16 June 2011).

Mackenzie, A. (2005) 'Learning through example', *Architectural Review Australia*, 79: 84–89.

Maki, E. and McDonough, W. A. (2000) 'Sustainable architecture: an East–West perspective', in A. Ray-Jones (ed.) *Sustainable Architecture in Japan: The green buildings of Nekken Sekkei*, New York: Wiley-Academic.

Matsunawa, K. (2000) 'The Nikken Sekkei Approach to Green Buildings', in A. Ray-Jones (ed.) *Sustainable Architecture in Japan: The green buildings of Nekken Sekkei*, New York: Wiley-Academic.

Olgyay, V. (1963) *Design with Climate: Bioclimatic approach to architectural regionalism*, Princeton, NJ: Princeton University Press.

Plumwood, V. (1999) 'Ecological ethics from rights to recognition: multiple spheres of justice for humans, animals and nature', in N. Low (ed.) *Global Ethics and Environment*, London: Routledge.

RAIA (1994) 'RAIA Environment Policy', *Architecture in Australia*, September/October: 87–90.

Sassi, P. (2006) *Strategies for Sustainable Architecture*, Oxford: Taylor & Francis.

Scruton, R. (1979) *The Aesthetics of Architecture*, London: Methuen.

Thompson, I. H. (2000) *Ecology, Community and Delight: Sources of values in landscape architecture*, London: Spon Press.

United Nations Environment Programme (2004) *UNEP Annual Report 2004*. Available at: http://earthwatch.unep.net/agenda21/UNEP/DEWA/Earthwatch (accessed 26 December 2004).

Venturi, R. and Scott Brown, D. (1996) 'A significance for A&P parking lots or learning from Las Vegas', in K. Nesbitt (ed.) *Theorizing a New Agenda for Architecture: An anthology of architectural theory 1965–1995*, New York: Princeton Architectural Press.

William McDonough Architects (1996) 'The Hanover principles', in K. Nesbitt (ed.) *Theorizing a New Agenda for Architecture: An anthology of architectural theory 1965–1995*, New York: Princeton Architectural Press.

Willis, A. M. (2000) *Australian Building Energy Council Building Case Study: Charles Sturt University, Thurgoona campus*, Australian Building Energy Council. Available at: www.abec.com.au/studies/studies (accessed 15 November 2003).

13

SUSTAINABLE HOUSING

Family experiences with supply chain ethics

Wendy Miller and Laurie Buys

Introduction

Sustainability and houses

Climate change, resource depletion and increasing urbanization are converging global issues that are challenging the way we design, construct and operate buildings. The housing sector is a significant contributor to these global issues through consumption of limited resources, waste generation and disposal (solid, liquid and atmospheric waste), and negative human health impacts (Senick 2006). Although the design and construction of 'sustainable housing' would appear to be an obvious and technically feasible solution, there remains multifaceted issues affecting the delivery of sustainable housing (Holloway and Bunker 2006). Two fundamental issues – what makes a house sustainable and to what extent regulation should be used to deliver sustainability – have been, and continue to be, debated at multiple levels in society. Despite personal, professional and political views on these issues, three key characteristics of the whole housing supply chain require fundamental change if we are to successfully address sustainability challenges (Birkeland 2008). These include: fragmentation; established methods, practices and processes; and the relationships between players. A more in-depth understanding of the role of ethics (values, beliefs and standards) and the potential ethical conflicts within the supply chain will assist in better defining the nature of the fundamental changes required.

Sustainability, housing and ethics

There is a plethora of research into the moral and physical need for changes in the way humans view their relationship with the environment (Hobson 2003; Russell and Albright 2008). Numerous researchers discuss environmental ethics, the importance of ecological design, the need for 'positive development' and the sustainability implications for the entire building construction supply chain (Ding 2008; Essa and Fortune 2008).

The essence of existing research can be distilled into two key foundations. First, from an ethical viewpoint, there is a need to reconceive relationships with each other and to reconsider human relationships individually and collectively with the natural environment, and the value and status assigned to it and its non-human content (Nalukenge 2009). Second, from a social change viewpoint, to recognize that design professions play a critical role in assisting this transformation (Birkeland 2002).

The role of the end consumer

There also exists a large and rapidly growing body of research in both housing technologies and the roles and challenges of various potential change agents: governments; professions such as engineering, design, banking and finance; manufacturing and construction industries; and various environment and community advocacy groups (van Hal 2007). Much of this research has been from a top-down approach or has focused on one particular 'segment' studied in isolation to the entire housing supply chain (Revell 2007; Shi 2008). The supply chain in the delivery of a 'sustainable house' includes the codes and regulations that place parameters with which the product must legally comply; the designers of the product; the construction industry that must interpret and implement that design; the manufacturers and suppliers of building products; the industries that value, finance and insure the product; and the purchaser/user of the product over its life (Spiegel and Meadows 2006). While acknowledging various failings in this supply chain, many governments and professional and industry sectors continue to give the impression that a key barrier to the uptake of sustainability is lack of consumer demand (McGee *et al.* 2008). However, surprisingly little research has explored the experiences of consumers who specifically request sustainable housing outcomes, as the end-users' role in the building supply chain is rarely examined. For example, Katie Williams and Carol Dair, in examining barriers to sustainability in housing, did not include interviews with residents (Williams and Dair 2006).

The purpose of this subset of the broader research topic is to gain a deeper understanding, from an end-user perspective, of the extent to which conflicts between professional and family ethics influenced the sustainability outcomes of family homes. A *transformative perspective* (Lofland *et al.* 2006) has been adopted to discuss the implications of the research and to re-evaluate these relationships and practices.

Method

Our broader, extended case study utilizes both quantitative and qualitative approaches to better understand the role that design and construction professions play in the 'successful achievement' of a sustainable house from the perspectives of the end client (the household). This component of that larger research study adopts a qualitative approach to explore the interactions between end users and design and construction professionals within the context of the design and development decisions of the Ecovillage, with a focus on the decision-making processes and ethics.

Housing context

The physical context of the case study is a residential Ecovillage in subtropical Queensland, Australia. The area zoned for housing (20 per cent of estate land) is divided into lots of various sizes to encourage a mixed demographic; lots are organized into small hamlets (about ten homes) to encourage social interaction. Hamlets are linked with cycling and walking paths, as well as vehicular laneways. The vision of the developers of this estate was to inspire sustainable living and inform further ecologically sustainable developments (Landmatters Currumbin Valley Pty Ltd 2006). To understand the context in which the participating families were building and to formulate the outline for the semi-structured interviews, the building codes of the Ecovillage were analysed. All houses are constructed off-ground (that is, on stumps or stilts) and incorporate a hybrid approach to the building envelope (high thermal mass and lightweight materials).

TABLE 13.1 The extent and complexity of the Ecovillage building code.

	Ecovillage architectural and landscape code	
	Ethos, purpose, considerations, requirements	
Environment protection/ enhancement	*Resource management and monitoring*	*Social cohesion*
Buildings (size and scale to minimize site impacts)	*Energy* (energy efficiency, renewable energy)	*Community* (enhance casual and organized social interaction)
Land (protection, restoration and stewardship)	*Water* (self-sufficiency, rainwater; recycled water)	*Home office* (lifestyle, reduce transport needs)
Soil (protection of the ecological integrity of the site)	*Waste, re-use, recycling* (e.g. construction management)	*Accessibility* ('adaptable' and 'universal' design for life)
Landscape (sustainable landscaping, light pollution)	*Materials* (embodied energy, life cycle, toxicity)	*Privacy, security, safety* (visual, physical and acoustic)

The practical application of the Ecovillage vision, with regard to the design and construction of houses on individually owned residential lots within the estate, is managed through the Architectural and Landscape Code (the Codes), part of the by-laws of the registered Community Management Statement (CMS) as allowed under the Queensland Body Corporate and Community Management ACT 1997 (BCCM ACT). This has the effect of creating a binding mutual covenant between all members of the body corporate on the signing of the land deed for each lot (BCCM ACT, Section 59). The estate-level building codes also form part of the Development Approval of the estate. The Codes, then, are in addition to, but cannot be in conflict with, state building regulations. The environmental, social and economic principles and objectives that underpin the development and decisions of the Ecovillage are 'premised on the interconnectedness of all things' and 'embrace both local and global concerns' (Architectural and Landscape Code 2006: 2). The issues and intent of the Code can be broadly categorized into three areas that it attempts to promote: environment protection, resource management and social cohesion. The extent and complexity of this Code (Table 13.1) demonstrates that these sustainable homes are not merely standard houses with solar panels and rainwater tanks.

Participants

Participants were eight volunteer families (fifteen individuals), representing approximately 17 per cent of completed residences in the Ecovillage at the time of the study (early 2010). Each family had been through the design, construction and occupation phases of 'sustainable homes' in the period 2007–2010. The range of demographic, experiential and construction variables represented by these eight families is shown in Table 13.2. The income level of these families can be broadly classified as lower to upper middle class.

In-depth interviews

Family experiences through these processes were recorded through semi-structured interviews undertaken in their homes. Additional data sets and supplementary documentation were collected at a later stage for the purpose of data triangulation. This chapter focuses on the interview data, supporting correspondence and demographic and contextual information.

The semi-structured interviews incorporated global environmental issues and personal responses to these issues, overall goals for their home and their design and construction experiences within each of the categories of the Ecovillage building code. The recorded interviews were transcribed and coded to condense and categorize the data into key themes. Further axial and selective coding was used to identify key themes and subthemes relating to ethics. Quotations from families are indicated by F1, F2, etc. after each quotation.

TABLE 13.2 Demographic, experiential and construction variables of case study families.

Indicator	*Range/variables*	*Individuals/ (families)*
Age bracket of adults	24–34	1
	35–45	4
	45–60	6
	60–75	4
Education level	Year 10: 3	
	Trade/industry/professional qualifications: 6	
	Degree: 4	
	Post-graduate studies: 2	
Family size	Single	(1)
	Couple with 1 child	(2)
	Couple (no children at home)	(3) working; (2) retired
'Designer'	Owner, with draftsperson	(1)
	Owner (professional designer)	(1)
	Contracted registered architect	(3)
	Contracted registered building designer	(3)
Construction management	Owner-builder (i.e. self-built/managed)	(2)
	Building contractor (minimal owner involvement)	(2)
	Building contractor (high level of owner participation)	(3)
	Composite: building contractor and owner	(1)
Previous build experience	No experience	(3)
	Experience with 1 or more houses previously	(5)
Approximate construction costs ranged from AUD \$1200 to \$3000 m^2		

Results

Two key themes emerged from the data: first, ethical differences among families and the design and construction professionals engaged in their homes affected sustainability outcomes, and second, these differences were most evident at four key decision points.

Theme 1: ethical positions affecting sustainability goals

Families and design/construction professionals held different and often conflicting values and beliefs on issues of environmental ethics, social responsibility and sustainability. In some instances the family was able to assert its values, while in other instances the family's values became subservient to the design/construction professional's values and/or work practices. The families often felt that their relationship with the designer and other professionals was not necessarily collaborative, but rather based on an uneven sense of power, with decisions being out of their control.

> I suppose we could have got our straw bale professional to provide an engineer for [a structural] assessment, but the architect did not want to work with anyone other than his engineer, and neither of them had straw bale experience . . . We all had a round table: the designer, engineer, builder, straw bale consultant and us: none of them had any straw bale experience before, except the consultant, and no one else would listen to him. We are disappointed that we got pushed in a certain direction, and in hindsight they were not for good design or economic reasons . . . we had to do a lot of mucking around with the straw bales that in the end cost us tens of thousands more. Looking back now we were just railroaded into a particular direction.
>
> (F7)

> There were so many times when solar access was about to be compromised and I got in the way. While I deferred to [the architect] in things like, say, size for instance, I was absolutely adamant and bold about the passive solar stuff.
>
> (F2)

The uneven sense of power appeared to be among professionals as well as between professionals and families (perhaps considered non-professionals). One family pondered that this sense of power was possibly due more to ego than to professional risk.

> That was putting [the architect] in an awkward situation professionally to have their client with more information on particular things . . . whereas [the architect] would ordinarily be identified as being the knowledgeable one.
>
> (F2)

Theme 2: ethical differences at four key decision points

These differences in values and beliefs among families and their design and construction professionals were revealed most prominently at four key decision points: acceptance of the context in which the sustainable house will be built; defining who is the designer; determining cost and value; and implementing professional practices.

Sustainability building Codes: decision to accept or dispute

In order for houses in this development to meet the required Code, the families, and the design and construction professionals, need to deal with the complex interactions and interdependencies of each of the twelve areas (see Table 13.1). Despite the fact that the Codes for this estate are contractually binding, the families described two opposing approaches to these Codes that represented a value judgement on the authority and legality of the Codes. First, most families (and their designers/builders) were comfortable with working within the parameters established by the Codes. For them, the Codes were seen as a 'set of rules' that provided a relatively consistent standard and uniformity. This consistency and uniformity of the overall end result (conceivably all of the homes in the estate) was valued even though individuals sometimes disputed specific sustainability requirements. These families used the Codes as a source of guidance and information; it gave them an opportunity to learn more about sustainability issues in the built environment. They had a sense of trust in the process of Code development.

> we went with the Ecovillage recommendation . . . I accepted the fact that the [developer team] had done their research . . .
>
> (F5)

However, an alternative approach was taken by a few families and design/construction professionals who were in opposition to the Codes. While not registering a legal challenge to the authenticity of the estate Codes, some owners and designers disagreed on 'what is sustainable'. They agreed with some/most of the requirements, but vehemently opposed other requirements:

> Part of it was about those issues which are not cut and dried. What is sustainable in one direction is not necessarily so in another. And as someone who is reasonably well informed about the factors, it's . . . [a weighing up of the sustainability factors, and deciding, if there is a conflict, which one takes precedence]
>
> (F2)

The Codes were seen as restricting and limiting to the design process, and there was a non-acceptance of the authority of a developer to impose sustainability codes on individuals and, by default, their designers. While some objections related to the obligatory nature of the Codes as a whole (that is, a view that the Codes should be advisory only, allowing each family and designer to implement their own version of sustainability), other objections were quite specific (for example, against the mandatory installation of an Intelligent Metering and Control System to monitor and control water and energy usage, or for living areas of homes to have good views of, and access to, community greenways). Apparently, some designers encouraged lot owners to work against the Codes under the premise that 'covenants' in other developments are negotiable and that there were 'ways around the rules'. These families did not use the 'alternative pathways' option provided in the estate's design approval process, which allows for variations to the prescriptive sustainability requirements provided that the ethos and objectives are met.

Both supporters and deniers of the Codes perceived each other as impacting on the achievement of their sustainability goals: supporters viewed the deniers as devaluing the sustainability standards outlined in the community contracts; deniers viewed supporters as restricting personal or professional rights to implement their own values of sustainability or as limiting design creativity. The personal and professional decisions to accept or reject the legality of the building Codes was one key element in determining the speed at which the building design and construction progressed through the various approval and implementation stages.

Who is the designer?

The twelve areas of sustainability indicated in the Codes (see Table 13.1) added multiple design complexities and interactions not usually considered in homes in the general market. There were also potential 'conflicting priorities' between environmental, social and economic sustainability parameters. The families did not assume that any one designer would have sufficient knowledge to cover this complexity and all used a range of additional people who were integral to the design of their homes, including: the Village Design Panel; building sustainability assessors; 'experts' in specific technologies; structural engineers; specialist trades such as builders, plumbers and electricians; and the householders themselves. Each family also described difficulties that arose when either their designer or their builder would not take sustainability advice from alternative sources. The hierarchies of relationships between professional groups as well as between professionals and householders, rather than the validity of technical information, appeared to be used as the criteria by which design/construction decisions were made.

> Our architect used a particular engineer to do the footing design, as he had worked with rammed earth walls before. He could do this part, but this engineer had not ever seen screw-in piers used directly as the stumps for off-ground houses before. We had seen this, and requested this type of footing because it would mean lower embodied energy, less site impact and the ability to restore the site at the end of the life of the house. The engineer insisted on capping the steel piers with cement piers, then adding steel stumps. We lost all of the environmental benefits the piers were meant to provide, as well as adding an extra level of complexity, time and cost. He refused to do it any other way, and didn't consult with the screw-in pier company for advice.
>
> (F8)

Some families had a high level of specialist knowledge in one or more areas of sustainability, but mentioned being patronized or ignored by their designers.

While some families expressed concern about professions 'taking control' of the building project, others were confident in managing the relationship, ensuring that they remained in the 'driver's seat' regarding design decisions.

> There's a balancing act throughout the entire build process, not just by industry standards, but also by budgetary constraints and environmental considerations. There's this constant balancing act with all of the professions, whether its designers or plumbers or anyone else, of trying to work out when to take their advice; yeah, this is great advice and I should take it . . . and when to go, nuh, even though I am not the plumber, I have actually researched this topic, and I'm not going to stand for it, and they're wrong and I'm right, and I'm going to do it. That's just an impossible line to navigate . . .
>
> (F2)

Money and value

One commonality shared among all families was their long-term approach to their homes. They designed homes to meet both immediate and long-term family needs, and immediate and lifetime sustainability goals. All families indicated that they considered this to be their 'forever' home and, therefore, meeting current market expectations was not a priority. Another commonality was the need to ensure that the resultant home had low operational costs, particularly in terms of energy and water. While the immediate construction costs of the homes was important, most families had a longer term cost/benefit framework, expecting the lower operating costs of the home to compensate to some extent for the possibility of slightly higher upfront costs. Limiting the size of the home, rather than the sustainability features of the home, was seen as a legitimate cost control mechanism as well as a good strategy for lowering the home's ecological footprint. Other families placed a very high value on overall resource management, a value that did not need to be expressed in actual dollar terms. Each of these families perceived that they were forced into accepting design decisions without being fully informed of all alternatives and implications, or they felt coerced into making compromises to their ideals.

> We commented to [the designer] after we saw the neighbour's tinted glass, and he said: 'Well, that's very expensive', so that was the end of that. [The completed house does not perform as well in summer as the family wanted/expected.]
>
> (F7)

> It was meant to be a lot smaller. We became vulnerable to the advice of architects and others . . . that we needed a certain size [bigger].
>
> (F2)

Differing perceptions of building form and aesthetics among design professionals and families also impacted on the families' sustainability goals. While a visually attractive house was taken as a given (that is, no one wanted to live in an unattractive house), other issues such as affordability and resource minimization were equally important. In various ways, most families expressed concern that some design decisions were made on what they perceived to be purely aesthetic or 'artistic' reasons of the designer, which in turn compromised environmental or economic performance.

> We were basically told we had to have one room wide, for good ventilation, so that's what we've got: our whole house is one room wide, but it uses a lot more colourbond, a lot more rammed earth, a lot more concrete, a lot more recycled timber . . . it cost a lot more.
>
> (F1)

> the roof's gone from one reasonably even rectangle to five different sections and it's just hugely more expensive and hugely more risky in terms of its waterproofness – a huge drama to execute.
>
> (F2)

A fourth area of conflict regarding money and value was evident in common industry practices on a building site. Particular trades did 'what they always do', with little regard for the clients' wishes or the documented building approval documents. For some families, it was the highly inflated prices (sometimes as much as 300 per cent) charged by subcontractors compared with equivalent jobs in other estates. Electrical contractors were a key example, typically charging three to five times more for electrical fit-out within the Ecovillage than for similar sized, innovative and sustainable homes in the same region at the same time (personal correspondence with builder).

No justification of these inflated prices was provided. For other families, it was the deliberate or careless substitution of alternative products that did not meet the environmental performance criteria of the original specification. Some families also experienced a deliberate ignoring of alternative work processes that had been requested, or a lack of respect for the physical and financial input of the householders.

> I had marked every stick of timber [salvaged from a demolition site], marked it with its length and where it was to go [marked on the construction detail plans] . . . and then the builder rings up and says I need to get more timber . . . that we've run out . . . and it turns out he had picked up any piece, and cut it to fit the first post, and worked his way along, and then there were no pieces long enough left for the end posts.
>
> (F4)

Professional practice

While everyone experienced some challenges in the design and construction process, families who had never been through a design and construction process before experienced numerous 'dilemmas' that reflected a lack of knowledge and understanding of the overall processes. This lack of understanding led to perceptions of unethical behaviour by the various professionals involved in the design and build process, even if the actions were within defined Codes of Conduct and standard practices of the various professions. To varying extents, each family experienced the feeling of being locked out of, or peripheral to, 'the system', and that this alienation sometimes 'forced' them into accepting solutions that were not in line with their original intent. They had five key areas of misunderstanding or lack of knowledge of professional practice:

- Who is involved: the players, their roles and their interconnections.
- Language: professional terminology (for example, plans, full plans, BA documents).
- Processes: time frames, sequence of events, professional responsibilities.
- Contracts: what is, and is not, included in the respective service contracts.
- Relationship management: communications protocols.

Discussion

Existing social science design theory research on the role of clients in design identifies a range of issues, such as establishing shared meanings and understandings, imbalances of power, the time cost of participation for users, and the different 'lifeworlds' inhabited by designers and their clients (Weedman 2008). While being consistent with existing research in this area, the experiences of these case study families reveal additional complexities that are elicited when sustainability criteria are added to the design brief, bringing into play ethical considerations. The values and beliefs that design and construction professionals hold on issues of environmental ethics, social responsibility and sustainability often conflict with the values of households, and this conflict impacts on the sustainability of homes. These differences in values and beliefs were revealed through four key decision points that have implications for the design and construction professions.

Sustainability codes and by-laws

The fundamental issue of whether, and to what extent, regulation should be used to deliver sustainability in the built environment is hotly contested at political, professional and industry levels, as well as in the general community. This debate is likely to be ongoing as we decide how best to solve myriad increasingly urgent environmental and social challenges facing the built environment. The developer-led Codes of this particular housing estate include prescriptive measures far beyond current government regulations in Australia. Arguably, these requirements address areas in which many design and construction professionals currently have little knowledge or experience, and some of these requirements may be hotly disputed. Despite these differences, design and construction professions have a legal and professional responsibility to abide by the relevant parameters of projects. Clients have a right to expect that professionals will conduct themselves in a lawful manner, and arguably a right to refuse to pay for services that are not legally compliant.

Redefining 'the designer'

In homes requiring the balancing of complex sustainability considerations, there is a strong case for moving beyond the protective exclusivity of traditional practices of residential design professionals to a more relational, collaborative and reiterative approach. Much of this change has already occurred in the commercial building sector, but the project team approach used in 'green' commercial buildings does not appear to be transferring to the residential sector (Koebel *et al.* 2004). The achievement of sustainable housing is inarguably beyond the expertise and responsibility of any single profession. The concept of 'the designer' needs to be replaced by the concept of 'the project team' that utilizes the expertise of many players to optimize the sustainability outcomes of residential dwellings through design, construction and operation. Such a project team would conceivably include building sustainability assessors (using building simulation tools as a design optimization and decision support tool); specific technology and sustainability specialists; building and construction trades (bringing practical application knowledge); and the commissioning households. Traditional residential design professionals could very well take a coordination and project management role in such a team. The project team would approach the design and construction task with a collaborative, reiterative process that would seek to explore and evaluate design solutions and develop decision support tools and post-construction feedback mechanisms for the optimization of the environmental, social and economic sustainability of the dwelling.

Money and value

There are obvious tensions in the value systems that inform design decisions and the factors that contribute to these. There is also a pervasive industry, government and market perception that, to achieve sustainability outcomes, some 'sacrifice' (for example, of aesthetic appeal or affordability) is required (Crabtree and Hes 2009). Continuation of this mindset of 'trade-offs', 'sacrifice' and 'compromise' does not address the core issue and is unlikely to result in industry transformation. Perhaps redefining the value of a sustainable house would be more beneficial to all stakeholders. These families stated they did not want 'value' to be determined by market forces, nor do they want sustainable outcomes to be approached in an adversarial manner. Design and construction professionals need to enhance their knowledge of sustainability solutions and integrate these solutions into their technical and artistic decision-making frameworks, which would result in win–win solutions.

Professional practice

There appears to be a need for some of the traditional design and building practices and processes to reflect the more collaborative, reiterative approach required to engage with the complexities of sustainable homes and a higher level of involvement from the client. Such changes, relatively easily implemented at both professional association and individual business level, could include better client engagement processes and documentation, such as:

- A lexicon/glossary of terms.
- A reiterative and inclusive, rather than linear, design process.
- A diagrammatic representation of the design/construct process.
- A relationship and responsibility chart showing all players in the supply chain.
- An explanation of the design process, including timelines and expectations.
- A communications protocol.
- A 'product' operations manual.
- A 'services contract' between clients and designers that clearly defines the processes, expectations and decision-making protocols.

Conclusion

These eight families exhibited a range of environmental ethics and a sense of the importance of individual action in solving environmental issues. They demanded, from the design and construction industries, homes that exhibited sustainability considerations in advance of current building regulations. The homes are now built; they are occupied and are certainly more 'sustainable' than the market standard. However, the houses themselves, and the families occupying them, bear the consequences of the ethical tensions inherent in the decision processes of the design and construction professions involved – that is, decreased social, economic and environmental sustainability. Design and construct decisions compromised the sustainability goals of the households: in comfort levels, in operational costs and in life-cycle environmental impacts; some professional decisions significantly and unnecessarily increased the cost of the homes, affecting the long-term debt and disposable income of the families, and the failure of the design and construct professionals to actively seek and accept the involvement of others who could contribute to complex sustainable solutions was a contributing factor to higher costs and the loss of optimal performance.

The purpose of this research was to gain a deeper understanding, from an end-user perspective, of the extent to which conflicts between professional and family ethics influenced the sustainability outcomes of family homes. The findings of this research provide a deeper understanding of the social interactions implicit and explicit in the process of designing and constructing homes, in particular the role of ethics (values, beliefs and standards) and potential ethical conflicts within the housing supply chain. This understanding will assist in better defining the nature of the fundamental changes required in the whole housing supply chain in order to enhance the performance outcomes of sustainable homes and aid the diffusion of sustainability throughout the housing market.

Acknowledgements

The author wishes to sincerely thank the eight families for generously sharing their personal stories for the purposes of research into sustainable housing. Their openness, sincerity and insights are invaluable.

References

Architectural and Landscape Code (2006) 'The Ecovillage at Currumbin', *Community Titles Scheme No. 35580.*

Birkeland, J. (2002) *Design for Sustainability: A sourcebook of eco-logical solutions*, London: Earthscan.

Birkeland, J. (2008) *Positive Development*, London: Earthscan.

Crabtree, L. and Hes, D. (2009) 'Sustainability uptake on housing in metropolitan Australia: an institutional problem, not a technical one', *Housing Studies*, 24(2): 203–224.

Ding, G. K. C. (2008) 'Sustainable construction – the role of environmental assessment tools', *Journal of Environmental Management*, 86(3): 451–464.

Essa, R. and Fortune, C. (2008) 'Pre-construction evaluation practices of sustainable housing projects in the UK', *Engineering, Construction and Architectural Management*, 15(6): 514–526.

Hobson, K. (2003) 'Consumption, environmental sustainability and human geography in Australia: a missing research agenda?' *Australian Geographical Studies*, 41(2): 148–155.

Holloway, D. and Bunker, R. (2006) 'Practice reviews: planning, housing and energy use: a review', *Urban Policy and Research*, 24(1): 115–126.

Koebel, C. T., Papadakis, M., Hudson, E. and Cavell, M. (2004) 'The diffusion of innovation in the residential building industry', Report for Department of Housing, USA.

Landmatters Currumbin Valley Pty Ltd (2006) 'Seller's Disclosure Statement: The Ecovillage at Currumbin', *Community Titles Scheme 35580.*

Lofland, J., Snow, D., Anderson, L. and Lofland, L. (2006) *Analyzing Social Settings: A guide to qualitative observation and analysis*, Belmont, CA: Wadsworth.

McGee, C., Partridge, E., Carrard, N. and Milne, G. (2008) 'Mainstreaming sustainable housing: policies and programs that work', paper presented at the World Sustainable Building Conference (World SB08), Melbourne, 21–25 September.

Nalukenge, H. (2009) 'Environmental ethics is key to sustainability in a contemporary society', in E. L. Weber (ed.) *Environmental Ethics: Sustainability and education*, Oxford: Inter-Disciplinary Press.

Revell, A. (2007) 'The ecological modernisation of SMEs in the UK's construction industry', *Geoforum*, 38(1): 114–126.

Russell, R. and Albright, B. (2008) *Federal Research and Development Agenda for Net-Zero Energy, High-Performance Green Buildings*. Available at: www.bfrl.nist.gov/buildingtechnology/documents/FederalRDAgendaforNetZeroEnergyHighPerformanceGreenBuildings.pdf (accessed 15 May 2010).

Senick, J. A. (2006) 'An analysis of green building best management practices: implementation recommendations to the New Jersey Meadowlands Commission', Rutgers Centre for Green Building.

Shi, Q. (2008) 'A responsibility chart of realising sustainability for housing construction', *International Journal for Housing Science and its Applications*, 32(3): 231–238.

Spiegel, R. and Meadows, D. (2006) *Green Building Materials: A guide to product selection and specification*, Hoboken, NJ: John Wiley & Sons.

van Hal, J. D. M. (2007) 'A labeling system as stepping stone for incentives related to the profitability of sustainable housing', *Journal of Housing and the Built Environment*, 22(4): 393–408.

Weedman, J. (2008) 'Client as designer in collaborative design science research projects: what does social science design theory tell us?' *European Journal of Information Systems*, 17: 476–488.

Williams, K. and Dair, C. (2006) 'What is stopping sustainable building in England? Barriers experienced by stakeholders in delivering sustainable developments', *Sustainable Development*, 15: 135–147.

PART IV
Fashion

14

FASHION, ETHICS, ETHOS

Paula Dunlop

Introduction

Most ethical critiques of fashion focus on questions related to production and consumption, and centre on the determination of apt or functional outcomes in terms of environmental or social responsibility. Notions such as 'ethics' and 'right action' therefore place primacy on a teleological end point – the premise being that we can 'design' our way out of ethical dilemmas by determining the correct rules or behaviours needed to reach a particular end. This belief is consistent with conventional understandings of design, which emphasize planning, forethought and decisive action as key to design thinking. This outcome-centric focus, however, risks restricting 'design ethics' simply to becoming 'designed ethics'. As such, it overlooks ethics as something perpetually lived, made and remade through ethos – our located experience of the world. This chapter argues that, on the contrary, considerations of design ethics must take into account the fundamental place of ethos in ethical thinking. Rather than centring all considerations on the teleological outcome (waste reduction, for example), this alternative focuses design ethics on questions of recognizing and attending to our place in the world. This is especially important for fashion because, as a field concentrated on ideas of the autonomous, 'visionary' designer who transcends the everyday, any connection to the complexities of location dramatically alters not only how we perceive the very question of ethical practice, but it also transforms understandings of fashion and the practice of the fashion designer.

In this chapter I first adopt a polemical stance in order to explore the predominant notions of fashion, design and design ethics. The first section outlines conventional outcome-oriented understandings of fashion design and fashion design ethics. It then follows with an overview of Anne-Marie Willis's 'Ontological designing' (2006), suggesting that it offers an alternative theoretical model of design practice. I show

how, by formulating design as an ongoing interaction with and negotiation of our physical and conceptual location in the world, we begin to sense the shortcomings of models that position design as teleologically driven activity determined by an autonomous creator. To further illustrate this point, I explore domestic dressmaking as offering both an alternative history and conception of practice. I position domestic dressmaking as an intrinsic site of contemporary fashion practice and as an example of an activity invested in location. I argue that home sewing, as an activity inextricably linked with the home, makes apparent one's physical location as well as one's location within quotidian histories, traditions and cultural ideologies. This more domestic conception illuminates the relationships and connections that are otherwise hidden in predominant models of fashion practice.

This alternative approach to fashion design draws on a feminist reading of ethos as location – the identification and articulation of our historical, geographical and cultural positioning – as well as Cameron Tonkinwise's (2004) exploration of ethos and design to question the predominant outcome-centric conceptions that tend to govern the idea of ethical design practice. I assert that an interrogation of ethos – of location – is fundamental to an alternative ethical design thinking because, if we understand ethics as grounded on a responsibility of self in the world, it follows that ethical practice must therefore constitute an ongoing appraisal of our location in the world. Furthermore, when we self-consciously attend to our ethos, we move towards a responsibility for its continuous making. By offering this consideration of ethos as never finished, the usual understandings of fashion design practice and design ethics are shifted from an end-object focus to an activity that continues, is ever-shifting and always in the making – embedded and invested in the 'locatedness' of everyday lived experience. I therefore consider dressmaking practice as an example of handling ethos in the sense that it reconfigures the practitioner away from the privileged concept of an autonomous figure to one that is made, and makes, within larger stories of making and doing. In addition, by placing the emphasis on ethos, discourse in design ethics shifts from a concern for just outcomes derived autonomously to reconceiving design practice as a fundamental way of creating, identifying – and being responsible for – our presence in an interconnected world.

The designed object, fashion and ethics

Regardless of their scope and disciplinary application, theoretical definitions of design generally emphasize schematic planning and problem solving – the intellectualized management and rational ordering applied towards an intended outcome. In contrast to artistic or intuitive creation, design has settled itself largely in the domain of concepts and outcomes – a focus that orientates both aesthetic and functional elements towards a practical solution. In keeping with this model, traditional understandings of modern fashion design centre on this ontology of design as a preconceived system determined by its end product. Likewise, the designer (as the one who preconceives these ends) is positioned akin to the *auteur* – as an autonomous and isolated design authority.

Modern fashion is founded on notions of visionary design authorities and inspired, decisive creation. For Gilles Lipovetsky, the advent of haute couture in the late 1800s signalled a significant disconnect between the 'professional and private spheres' of clothes-making practice with couturiers claiming special authority and social distinction as innovators and taste-makers (Lipovetsky 1994: 83). The prestige attached to the work of the couturier has continued with the ready-to-wear industry; fashion designers are celebrated as iconic and visionary individuals who transcend the 'everyday' with decisive and inspired visions of the future. Regarded as dislodging the world from static perceptions and old conceptions, their creativity remains associated with originality and the orchestration of innovation as initiating a discontinuity from the mundane world of the wearer (Lipovetsky 1994: 85). This privileging of the 'original' and 'new' has allowed fashion designers to work under an assumption of autonomy with the ultimate value of designed garments lying in their perceived separation from the past. This ideology of individual creativity, inseparable from a culture of modernity, regards both producers and consumers as motivated by a desire to signify difference and individual freedom through creativity and innovation (Lipovetsky 1994: 84).

The term 'fashion designer' thus continues to weigh heavy with connotations alluding to a position as cultural arbiter, particularly in the high-end segment of the ready-to-wear market. The physical reality of the production of fashionable clothing encompasses a vast range of creative exchanges between people in various professional roles (Rissanen 2007) and therefore also involves a complex interplay between various sites of cultural and material production. Yet, a combination of branding and the prestige of celebrity designer continue to position the fashion designer as a sole creator with a unique perspective, someone who controls and shapes from on high. This attenuated understanding is compounded by the lack of discussion around the idea of process (particularly when discussing approaches to practice) in fashionable clothing production (Griffiths 2000). While designers of high fashion work within a complex system of both material and immaterial constraints, they have traditionally been positioned outside of the constituent limits and conditions of design practice as a lived activity. Within this context, the nuances of process – the way we make – are either simplified or rendered invisible.

It is my argument that the privilege placed on the planned outcome extends to the treatment of ethical discourse in fashion design. To be clear, it is my contention that the influential individualist, teleologically focused conception of fashion design circumscribes its range of possibilities, and this limited conception is transferred to its ethical discourse. Inevitably, fashion's ubiquitous presence as a symbol of modern mass production and profligate consumption sees it targeted – often with good reason – as an industry and social practice in need of a greater moral conscience. These ethical critiques centre largely on industry settings and on the negative impacts of either the product life cycle or the cultural systems of production and consumption. The result is an almost exclusive focus on establishment of standards for enacting social or environmental responsibility, either through a redesigning of the clothing itself or the systems through which it is made and distributed.

The design of 'better' products is promoted, for example, by contrasting with an awareness of the perils of material cultivation, waste and pollutants during production, or the by-products of use and disposal (Brower *et al.* 2005; Hoffman 2007; Fletcher 2008; Hethorn and Ulasewicz 2008).

Alternatively (or in addition), the transformation of fashion systems is proposed through discourses centring on issues such as Third World manufacture and exploitation, questioning planned obsolescence and excess (Rosen 2002; Fletcher 2008; Hethorn and Ulasewicz 2008; Timmerman 2009) or issues of beauty and gender (Evans and Thornton 1991; Church Gibson 2000). In all cases, the discussion of ethics still centres on a teleological end point – the determination of the 'right action' towards a just outcome. While I do not dispute the importance of achieving a 'right' outcome in ethical action, the risk involved is that it perpetuates the focus on an end point, which has the effect of overlooking the place of ethics as ethos – what Tonkinwise refers to as 'an essentially lived culture' (Tonkinwise 2004).

It is not the case, of course, that all existing fashion discourse ignores notions of the lived culture of design – the relationships or connections through which design functions. Many accounts of sustainable fashion practice note connectedness or a transparency of process as central to ethical discussion. For example, Kate Fletcher's article 'Clothes that connect' calls for systems that emphasize and 'advance relationships' between individuals, communities and environments (Fletcher 2007: 123). Nonetheless, these relationships are largely discussed in terms of a teleological paradigm. Positioned as an outcome fostered through planning or decisive action, ethical living is seen as something created through 'good' design. I wish to build on these commentaries by considering lived relationships as something through which design itself already functions. In contrast to viewing design and ethics as exclusively planned or intentioned to a correct and predetermined outcome, I wish to emphasize design ethos as inherently lived, thus opening up design thinking to a different consideration of the inherent and ongoing engagement between design and ethics. To fully appreciate this, it is essential that both practitioners and theorists move beyond a simple inversion of the product/process dichotomy in order to consider the complexities of our engagements with the world of design and designed things. Given the tenor of our times and the urgency with which we have come to realize the importance of ethics in considerations of best (design) practice, it seems imperative that we begin to examine the very foundations of our design thinking.

Ontological designing

Some of this work has begun. The project of rethinking design practice has been taken up by design theorists who take the debate beyond the designed object to encompass conceptions of design practice as an ongoing, lived activity, which is capable of transforming our lived experience both in terms of the objects we use and also the way we operate in our world. In her paper 'Ontological designing', Willis explores design as a relationship between 'human beings and lifeworlds'

(Willis 2006). Working in collaboration with colleagues (including Fry and Tonkinwise), and drawing on the work of Heidegger and Hans-Georg Gadamer, Willis articulates a theory of design that goes far beyond fulfilling commercial ends to embrace design as a fundamental way of thinking, making and being that constitutes who and how we are in the world. I have reservations about a theory that seems to position design as instrumental to our living – a position that seems to omit a consideration of chaos, or the unknown at play in the world – in short, a position that omits the aesthetic dimension of making and creating. Still, Willis offers a model of design that usefully complicates the subject–object division as a necessary requisite of teleological accounts of design. In place of a one-way movement from subject to object – with distinct beginnings and ends (that is, humans making objects) – Willis construes design as a 'circularity' of design presences. By this she means that not only do we design in and *through* a multitude of pre-existing conditions, but also are ourselves designed *by* these conditions (see also Fry 2009). Therefore, our movements and our agency – our ability to enact outcomes – in the world are, in part, directed by the limits and possibilities of our physical and conceptual locations in the world.

Willis points out that this is not simply a reiteration of environmental determinism. It is not a case of environments, or objects producing the subject – a configuration that would adhere to neat subject–object causal distinctions. Instead, it reconsiders design as a 'subject-decentered practice' (Willis 2006) involved in a complex system of pre-existing relationships. In this conception of ontological designing, 'human' and 'world' are viewed as inseparable. Design is rather the result of a complex interplay of subject and object, material and immaterial, or what Donald Schön calls, the 'conversation with the situation' (Schön 1983: 23). In short, there is a simultaneous engagement between our being designed, our interpretations and our designs:

> we design, that is to say, we deliberate, plan and scheme in ways which prefigure our actions and makings – in turn we are designed by our designing and by that which we have designed (that is, through our interactions with the structural and material specificities of our environments).
>
> (Willis, 2006)

The things that surround us, design us; we come into a pre-existing, prefigured world and create (and are created) through an interpretive engagement with this world. By framing design as ontological and embedded, rather than autonomous, we are not only able to reconsider the broad reach of the design object and its touch on (and place in) our everyday life, but we can also begin to recognize our designing as conditioned by our located (physical and conceptual) being. This alternative formulation suggests that design is embedded in, and constituted by, an engagement with the world as located within historical, geographical and sociocultural conditions. It disrupts the conventional notion of design as a more or less straightforward, teleological movement of designer over world, of active subject over passive subject.

Dressmaking

I would now like to return to fashion by way of an exploration of domestic dressmaking as a model for this different understanding of design as ontological, and thus as an activity embedded in pre-existing historical, geographical and social-cultural conditions and relationships. As I mentioned at the start of the chapter, histories of Western fashion as an industry dominate understandings of clothing's modern production and consumption, which are founded on a divorce between the professional and private spheres of clothing production. In this model, the designer is perceived as an autonomous agent who envisages and carries out plans geared towards a decisive end outcome.

The presumptions governing the canon of Western fashion design generally overlook design practices undertaken in non-professional sites of production. These are sites that have co-existed with professional practice, yet rarely receive attention within surveys of fashion design history. Part of the complexity lies in the accommodation of such diverse practices within generalized understandings of design. Its production encompasses a wide range of activities, nuanced by specificities in consumption, therefore making neat demarcations difficult to pin down. From the replication of high-end apparel to the making of garments from purchase or online sharing of home-made patterns to DIY subcultural style, it is actually a broad and diverse area of practice. Significantly, it exists as a practice that is inextricably linked with the home.

In 'On the margins: theorizing the history and significance of making and designing clothes at home', Cheryl Buckley writes:

> the activities of the home dress-maker and the products which resulted do not correspond neatly to 'typical' design methods or archetypal objects. Also the designer's role is much more negotiated and divergent than the usual 'model', and the value and significance of the designs cannot be assessed using criteria which stress innovation, commercial success or viability, and uniqueness. Instead one could argue that dress and dress-making are cultural sites where identity, place and memory figure prominently.
>
> (Buckley 1998: 160)

Design in the home therefore happens amid 'everyday' activities and, as such, jars with the predominant notion of design as the conception of an original object. It also disrupts the view of design as produced according to a teleologically distinct plan and by the autonomous designer. Its intrinsic link with a sense of location is therefore the most telling difference because it is here that the nuances of *habitus* come to the fore – constraints of place, time, skill base and the availability of tools and materials bear upon the work and highlight the specific, conditioned nature of design activity. The home sewer makes by 'finding space on the kitchen table, and squeezing sewing between other domestic responsibilities' (Buckley 1998: 157). Similarly, Irene Brin's article '*Fanno loro la vera moda* [They make the real fashion]' of 1949 evokes a physically embedded activity that is overshadowed by the more illustrious accounts of professional design: 'Dressmakers sew in the bedroom, take measurements in the dining room, use movie stars as their models. Their charges are very modest, and so their glory is more definitive than that of Fath or Dior' (in Caratozzolo 2006: 56). Design in the home places the emphasis on the materiality of design and design as an embedded (and embodied) activity. When grounded within the circumstances of site and embodiment, we begin to acknowledge the pre-existing situations through which design functions, which in turn unsettles the assumption that design is an original creation or under the unmitigated control of the sovereign designer.

The historical process that saw the professional male practitioner assume dressmaking under the banner of design meant that design lost these connotations. The 'everyday' was resisted, seen to mitigate the authority and skill of professional practice. Of course, dressmaking practice itself did not disappear. The term 'dressmaker' continues to connote one who is able to create a garment in its entirety. This prevailing definition leaves dressmaking as an activity that encompasses and integrates the entire material and immaterial aspects of a garment's creation. Limiting histories of design only to commercial sites of production, then, risks losing knowledge of a large cross-section of varied design activity. Indeed, widening the focus to include non-professional design practices does not automatically deny the particular character of design practice in the professional spheres. Rather, it presents an opportunity to explore a long history and co-existence of complementary activities and practices, which have shaped so much of modern design culture (Pacey 1992: 217).

Acknowledging design in the home reveals that modern fashion comprises a complex mix of contributions on a vast range of fronts. Dressmaking, and in particular domestic dressmaking, presents an interesting historical and practical counterpoint to conventional histories of modern fashion design because producing garments in the home is an activity openly invested in, and even conditioned by, its site or location. Home dressmaking is a practice that points distinctly to an ontology of design founded in an unabashed belonging to the everyday lived circumstances of making and exposed to the contingencies of such a location. It is an activity grounded in the 'everyday' circumstances of production, and which actively participates in a world of fashionable clothing, but resides on the absolute periphery of conventional understandings of design. Making clothes in the home thus discloses larger stories of fashion making and reveals ongoing stories of cultural production bound up in the nuances of 'identity, place and memory' (Buckley 1998: 160).

The ethical implications of this line of thinking lie in the inherent sense of connectedness suggested by the emphasis on active and ongoing relationships as central to both our activities and our lived experience of the world. When considering design ethics, the vitality of connections within this relational model of practice emphasizes ethical design practice as not simply the concern for just outcomes, but as something constantly lived, made and remade in (and through) the very practice of making.

Ethos as location

The importance of location in reconceptualizing design practice helps to clarify the concern with ethos because it involves an ongoing negotiation of lived situation and experience. Theories of ethos, however, largely derive from studies in rhetoric and are primarily conceptualized in terms of linguistic communication. If this were to remain the exclusive concern of ethos, then it would undermine the importance of material culture in the formation of ethos. Our engagement with the world of material things is significant for, as Tonkinwise notes, 'an immaterial culture is an impossibility' (Tonkinwise 2004).

Tonkinwise's paper 'Ethics by design, or the ethos of things' (2004) is a discussion of ethics and ethos in relation to design and the world of designed things. Following a track similar to Fry's and Willis' ontological design (which question distinct separations between designer and world), he explores the idea of an ethics that is materialized in design – that is, the possibility for designed things as simultaneously reflecting, fostering and sustaining ethics. Tonkinwise points the way toward a consideration of ethics in relation to material things. Ethics, he argues, should be discussed in terms of material as well as social relations, and, following this, design needs to be scrutinized as it contributes significantly to our material culture. Tonkinwise therefore posits ethics as concerning not so much a fixed set of rules to guide towards ethical ends, but as something materially lived, 'a way of being, not a knowledge about that way of being' (Tonkinwise 2004). It is this notion of awareness – of ongoing, reflective critique of our lived situations – that I would like to focus on and extend; it has parallels with feminist theories of ethos as location.

Feminist understandings of ethos focus on site and embodiment. Nidra Reynolds regards issues of 'site' as crucial to understanding ethos in the poststructuralist sense – where 'the subject is the "site" on which language becomes meaning, where meaning is constituted and thereby constitutes the subjectivity of the individual' (Reynolds 1993: 326). The currency of site, she writes, has 'long been important to the rhetorical concept of ethos' because it 'encompasses the individual agent as well as the location or position from which that person speaks or writes' (Reynolds 1993: 326). To demonstrate the importance of location to ethos, she returns to the term's etymological complexity as meaning 'space, place or haunt' – a complexity that conventional translations have failed to acknowledge (Reynolds 1993: 327). Furthermore, its translation either as 'character' or 'habit' stems from the meaning of the word in the Greek lexicon as 'a habitual gathering place' (Halloran 1982: 60; Reynolds 1993: 327–329; see also Jarratt and Reynolds 1994: 48). The etymology of ethos therefore refers to a relationship between habit, character and place, from 'the classical ideal of character pointed toward public life, the life lived in that gathering place' (Halloran 1982: 62). Following this translation, Reynolds interprets ethos spatially – that is, as an aspect and locating of the self within broader social contexts (Reynolds 1993).

According to this understanding of the term, the subject does not hold themself as an autonomous individual, but recognizes their subjectivity as operating at the intersection of a multitude of (largely unknowable and ever-shifting) contexts (Jarratt and Reynolds 1994). Ethos marks 'the position of the self, to the admittedly limited extent that it can be articulated by the author, making no claim that this speaking self is completely known or stable'; it is 'the admission of a standpoint, with the understanding that several other standpoints exist and that they change over time' (Jarratt and Reynolds 1994: 53). Ethos is 'never finished'; it is always in the making through our immersion in the particular circumstances of our embodied, lived experience. We do not have complete control over our ethos – we are, after all, born into pre-existing circumstances – but nor is ethos untouchable or unchangeable. We are able to locate our subjectivity at points and 'attend to our own ethos' (Schmertz 1999: 89) through a critical engagement with our immersion in the world. Similarly, a community's ethos is never singular or fixed, but rather formed through the influx interrelations, which are always in the making but are able to be arrested and named at points for scrutiny in retrospect. Ethos is always a negotiated construction in the making. By identifying our ethos – our location – we also identify a subjectivity that acknowledges not just our conditioned experience, but subjectivity is something always negotiated and never completely 'ours'. 'Character', writes Reynolds, 'is formed by habit, not engendered by nature, and those habits come from the intersection of a plurality of discourses within a community or culture' (Reynolds 1993: 329). The perpetual making of ethos is thus 'a shared enterprise among members of the community', and the responsibility of ethos rests on the 'negotiation or mediation' between the individual and the community (Reynolds 1993: 328).

Conclusion: fashion, design and ethos

I have argued that in following teleological models of design, ethics is conceived as a goal to be reached. This understanding assumes that an ethical designer is one who plans for ethical design outcomes. Planning for ethics in this way, I have argued, seems to miss the point when we consider ethos. It fails to recognize that the fundamental condition of our existence is embodied and that we live in terms of an ongoing engagement in a shared cultural environment. Instead, I assert that the responsibility that comes from recognizing this interconnectedness is at the heart of the concern for ethical living.

A focus on the ethical in terms devised exclusively 'through design' therefore overlooks the fact that a move towards the ethical requires a more rigorous appraisal of one's place in a cultural situation. This sentiment is shared by Tonkinwise, who argues that in following a design for ethics, we risk our desire for ethics becoming a desire for ethics as an end. A 'designed' ethics also risks the sort of habitual response that comes from instrumentalist approaches that can lead to a falling back on abstract principles or moral conventions (Tonkinwise 2004). If the whole point of ethical behaviour is living decently and justly in the world, then an automatic or 'unthinking ethics' that relies on planning or rules for ethical conduct actually undermines the ethical to the extent that it does not acknowledge differences between particular situations, nor does it facilitate an awareness of our location within an interconnected world.

This notion of recognizing and being responsible for our place in the world is central to conceptions of ethos as location. When we attend to our ethos (that is, when we seek to locate ourselves amid broader social contexts), we are taking responsibility for ourselves (the sites or locations from which we speak or act). Furthermore, the responsibility engendered by an ethos as location can serve as a platform for understanding ethical engagement (being just).

Domestic dressmaking is an activity that emphasizes an investment in ethos by serving as a model for understanding design ethics as an embodied, conditioned and located activity. It positions design as situated in time and place. This is because dressmaking involves thinking through bodily engagement with the material and immaterial conditions of making and doing. Its histories are inextricably linked with the home. It therefore makes apparent one's physical location as well as one's location within histories, traditions and cultural ideologies. While emphasizing being located or embedded, the focus on ethos does not suggest a position that is totally fixed, but rather malleable and changing in time and place. The sense of continuous making – of no decisive end point – highlights the long life of design objects and reinforces the constitutive place of both design and ethics in our lives. Ethics becomes not just a goal or end point, but something continuously lived, made and remade – making us, and made by us, in all aspects of our living.

References

Brower, C., Mallory, R. and Ohlman, Z. (2005) *Experimental Eco Design*, Switzerland: RotoVision.

Buckley, C. (1998) 'On the margins: theorizing the history and significance of making and designing clothes at home', *Journal of Design History*, 11(2): 157–171.

Caratozzolo, V.C. (2006) *Irene Brin: Italian style in fashion*, Venice: Marsilio and Fondazione Pitti Discovery.

Church Gibson, P. (2000) '"No-one expects me anywhere": invisible women, ageing and the fashion industry' in S. Bruzzi, and P. Church Gibson (eds) *Fashion Cultures: Theories, explorations and analysis*, London: Routledge.

Evans, C. and Thornton, M. (1991) 'Fashion, representation, femininity', *Feminist Review*, (38): 48–66.

Fletcher, K. (2007) 'Clothes that connect' in J. Chapman and N. Gant (eds) *Designers, Visionaries and Other Stories*, London: Earthscan.

Fletcher, K. (2008) *Sustainable Fashion and Textiles: Design journeys*, London: Earthscan.

Fry, T. (2009) *Design Futuring: sustainability, ethics and new practice*, Sydney: University of New South Wales Press.

Griffiths, I. (2000) 'The invisible man', in N. White and I. Griffiths (eds) *The Fashion Business: Theory, practice, image*, Oxford: Berg.

Halloran, M. (1982) 'Aristotle's concept of ethos, or if not his somebody else's', *Rhetoric Review*, 1(1): 58–63.

Hethorn, J. and Ulasewicz, C. (eds) (2008) *Sustainable Fashion: Why now?* New York: Fairchild Books.

Hoffman, L. (ed.) (2007) *Future Fashion White Papers*, New York: Earth Pledge.

Jarratt, S. C. and Reynolds, N. (1994) 'The splitting image: contemporary feminisms and the ethics of *ethos*' in J. S. Baumlin and T. F. Baumlin (eds) *Ethos: New essays in rhetorical and critical theory*, Dallas, TX: Southern Methodist University Press.

Lipovetsky, G. (1994) *The Empire of Fashion: Dressing the modern democracy*, Princeton, NJ: Princeton University Press.

Pacey, P. (1992) '"Anyone designing anything?" non-professional designers and the history of design', *Journal of Design History*, 5(3): 217–225.

Reynolds, N. (1993) 'Ethos as location: new sites for understanding discursive authority', *Rhetoric Review*, 11(2): 325–338.

Rissanen, T. 'Types of fashion design and patternmaking practice', Nordic Design Research Conference: Design Inquiries, Stockholm, 27–30 May 2007.

Rosen, E. (2002) *Making Sweatshops: The globalization of the U.S. apparel industry*, Berkeley, CA: University of California Press.

Schmertz, J. (1999) 'Constructing essences: ethos and the postmodern subject of feminism', *Rhetoric Review*, 18(1): 82–91.

Schön, D. (1983) *The Reflective Practitioner: How professionals think in action*, New York: Basic Books.

Timmerman, K. (2009) *Where am I wearing?* Hoboken, NJ: John Wiley & Sons.

Tonkinwise, C. (2004) 'Ethics by design, or the ethos of things', in *Design Philosophy Papers*. Available at: www.desphilosophy.com/dpp/dpp_journal/back_issues/paper4_TonkinEthics/dpp_paper4.html (accessed 11 October 2009).

Willis, A. (2006) 'Ontological designing', in *Design Philosophy Papers*. Available at: www.desphilosophy.com/dpp/dpp_journal/back_issues/paper1_WillisOnto/dpp_paper1.html (accessed 11 October 2009).

15

NOURISHING OR POLLUTING

Redefining the role of waste in the fashion system

Alice Payne

Introduction

The creation, destruction and shifts of value of garments in the fashion system produces waste that is both tangible and intangible: the excess of physical waste generated by the garments of the fashion system, and the excess of creative ideas developed and expended season by season. Once the material garment loses its lustre of novelty, thus rapidly diminishing its aesthetic value, it necessarily loses its material value, instantly converting it to waste. Although individual garments may hold a longer-lasting emotional value to the wearer, fashion's creative cycles inexorably move on. Waste and excess are key determinants of the value system that drives consumer capitalism. In particular, the logic of fashion – characterized by constant change and creative destruction – is deeply implicated in the wasteful consumption practices of the West. The excesses of fashion have a material consequence, whether through the release of toxic chemicals into the soil and groundwater, or in the tonnes of textile products sent to landfill. In this context, labelling a practice or behaviour 'wasteful' implies a moral judgement. For all practitioners of fashion – whether designers or consumers – the waste and excess inherent in the fashion system is a difficult ethical terrain to negotiate. However, inverting the wasteful phases of the production cycle can help reframe waste from pollution to a source of nourishment for future practice. While creative excesses of designers may be 'wasted' after a season, fashion styles and tropes are recycled and reinvented, with the once passé styles and design ideas from previous years revalorized and returned into the fashion system. Similarly, material garments acquire new value through entering or re-entering the second-hand or vintage markets. Design processes can utilize pre- or post-consumer textile waste, or eliminate waste through design. In these processes, waste becomes the primary source of nourishment for future fashion cycles.

Fashion as a site of 'senseless destruction'

Fashion is a system based on change, engaged in what Ted Polhemus calls, 'the perpetual pursuit of novelty' (Polhemus 1994: 8). While clothing is a material object that provides for our decency and physiological need, fashion is a system supported by continuous innovation. This system, in turn, produces a set of symbolic codes, and thus creates an intangible value, often briefly, within a garment. Joanne Entwistle frames the fashion system as an aesthetic marketplace in which 'aesthetic value is *the* value generated around the commodity and the business of selling it' (Entwistle 2009: 28). Here, fashion is not so much the marketing of garments; rather, it is the marketing of the aesthetic values that the garment embodies. By implication, the design of the physical garment is governed first by aesthetics. These aesthetic values are not stable; they shift as dictated by the views of actors within the fashion system. Once fashion trends move on, the aesthetic value of a garment declines. It becomes waste.

The capitalist logic of perpetual growth motivates fashion's increasing speed of production and consumption. Thus, our market economy is deeply implicated in fashion's cycles of aesthetic valorizing and devalorizing. This increase in consumption and profit is fuelled by moving production to the developing nations, a widely accepted practice that offers the 'benefits' of cheap and unregulated labour. As an additional by-product of the globalized and cost-effective fashion trade, trends and styles can be disseminated through global digital communication, prompting consumers to make purchases more often and for a lower price. In turn, consumers perceive garments as disposable. However, economic profit is not the only driver of fashion's change; as Gilles Lipovetsky writes, capitalism promotes individualism, so that novelty and a 'surfeit of choice' become a means to personal liberation (Lipovetsky 1994: 155). Consumption may be framed as an individual's freedom of choice, but consumption brings with it 'the freedom to waste, to discard things that are still perfectly useful' (Hawkins 2006: viii).

Beyond profit and individualism, fashion's excesses may be more fundamental. Patrizia Calefato writes that 'senseless destruction is celebrated by fashion' (Calefato 2004: 123), referring not only to the creation and destruction of value within a fashion garment. She cites Georges Bataille's notion of the 'accursed share', the leftover energy inherent in all biological and human systems. In Bataille's theory of the general economy, more of everything is produced than is needed, as in the excess of sunlight falling on the earth, or the excess of blossoms on a cherry tree. If this excess cannot be absorbed into the growth of the system, then it must be expended somehow, whether in a force of unnecessary consumption or destruction (Bataille 1988: 21). Hence, the 'accursed share' in human activity may be spent as gifting rituals, or as an outpouring of creative energy in the arts that, as Pasi Falk argues, may otherwise be expended in an act of war (Falk 1994: 98). Thus the constant, irrational flux of fashion can be framed as a necessary outlet for frivolity and play, a joyful expenditure of surplus energy. If fashion exists in this space of excess, then the designed garment is waste before it is even manufactured or consumed.

Intangible waste: creative waste as nourishment

The intangible excesses of the fashion system can be witnessed before the garment exists in material form. These excesses are found in the super-abundance of design ideas, of print developments, of mood boards, colour palettes and trims that designers develop in response to the multiplicity of lifestyle, cultural and street trends. This creative abundance is not necessarily bound to the profit motive of companies – fashion and abundance can be witnessed in the playful mismatching of vintage clothing by users, or in the teenager who customizes their jeans, or in the style-leader who chooses to wear a sweater upside down. This creative waste is a form of excess that may enrich the cultural landscape. Within the fashion system, even trends that are superficially similar appear in many mutations. A youth mass-market trend for skull motifs in recent seasons saw endless variations on the theme: skulls as cassette tapes, skulls as appliqué, screen-printed skulls in a myriad of scales, colours and placements. In fashion design practice, a practitioner can vary from the haute couture designer to the mass-market product developer, from the independent avant-garde designer to the craftsperson or dressmaker. To different degrees, all are generating, imitating and regenerating more creative designs, season after season. Many design ideas will be wasted, discarded on the design room floor and never realized in material form. The restless excesses of the trend cycle may be creative waste, but they fulfil a human need for expression, creativity, beauty and change.

Once the season is over, the collection released and the trend exhausted, those designs are discarded as they have lost their aesthetic value because trends and tastes have moved on. However, this creative waste of energy and design ideas will go on to provide nourishment and inspiration for future designers. Designers cherry-pick from the past, from other cultures and subcultures, reinventing and restyling (Craik 1994: ix). Fashion designers, buyers, journalists and users collectively revalorize the dead trends. This recycling of ideas is necessarily disguised by irony, play or subversion, to present the latest incarnation of the idea as novel. The designer, the stylist or the wearer on the street takes the old idea and reinvests it with value. At this point, their transformation is adopted by others and a 'new' trend emerges. As such, in the 1990s the styles and tropes of 1970s fashion re-emerged, with crocheted tops and platform shoes reappearing. As Calefato notes, the platform shoes of the 1970s were themselves referencing 1940s styles (Calefato 2004: 125). The grunge styles of the 1990s were reborn in 2008, as flannel shirts became a mass-market trend, reinvented as tailored shirt dresses with luxe silver threads. In this sense, there is an organic process of creative waste, as the excess of design ideas are later reclaimed and recycled. The spent trends, the outmoded colour palettes, the 'daggy' silhouettes, or the 'done-to-death' detailing will one day resurface and provide creative nourishment.

Tangible waste: from waste as pollution, to waste as food

The movement of tangible waste in the fashion system inevitably mimics the movement of creative intangible excess. A high environmental and social cost is paid to bring the designer's vision to the public. Polluting waste can be witnessed in all stages of the supply chain, beginning with inputs: wasteful practices within fibre and textile production through to design and manufacturing processes. Waste can be seen in the arable land destroyed by the pesticides used to grow cotton, or in the pollution of waterways, such as the poisoning of the Aral Sea owing to intensive cotton production (Allwood *et al.* 2006: 45), or in the groundwater poisoned by dye factories and tanneries (Fletcher 2008: 8, 52–53). Within design and manufacturing, cut-and-sew production methods see an estimated 100,000 tonnes of textiles wasted per year in the UK owing to textile offcuts alone (Rissanen 2008: 187). This waste raises an ethical question as to the duty designers and manufacturers have towards the environment and towards society.

Waste can be witnessed in the outputs of a garment. High volumes of clothing are sent to landfill once their value is exhausted. An unfashionable garment may be thrown away while still serviceable, or at the very least, recyclable. In the UK, an estimated 1.8 million tonnes of unwanted clothing and textile products go to landfill each year (Allwood *et al.* 2006: 16). As textiles decompose in landfill, they form leachate (a groundwater contaminant), release the highly toxic pollutant ammonia and emit the greenhouse gas methane (Caulfield 2009). Here, the waste is not only in the discontinued utility of the garment, but in the waste of valuable tangible resources such as fibre, water and fuel used to produce its textiles and trims, as well as in the wasted less tangible resources of labour, energy and creativity expended in its design and manufacture. A sustainable approach to this waste would require a reckoning of the true value of the physical inputs of the garment in financial, environmental and social terms. This approach would necessarily flow on to a higher value being placed on the less tangible inputs of a garment.

Conversely, second-hand clothing provides a way into rethinking an ethics of waste within fashion. The aesthetic value of a garment will fall but can potentially rise again, as 'value is a product of social process, not the intrinsic properties of things' (Hawkins 2006: 78). Hence, discarded objects can undergo a transformation in value, moving from the wasted to the wanted. In the second-hand market, the movement of the tangible waste may mimic that of the intangible, as 'old' garments nourish 'new' creative trends. Essentially, the second-hand garment will enter another fashion cycle, to be re- and devalorized several more times, in different cultural and subcultural contexts (Gregson and Crewe 2003: 200). The value of a vintage or retro garment may be higher than that of a new garment because of its individuality and authenticity. Likewise, an old or second-hand garment may hold great and particular emotional value to a wearer, based on its story and its history. A consumption approach on the part of users recognizes the value of clothing as cyclic, rather than linear. In this sense, a garment can go on to have many lives with a number of wearers, deferring its eventual disposal as waste.

Within fashion design practice, designers are developing cyclic responses to waste. Some aim to eliminate waste from the design process via pattern-making innovations (Rissanen 2008; McQuillan 2011). Similarly, a growing trend among independent designers has been the 'upcycling' of second-hand garments (post-consumer waste) and textile remnants (pre-consumer waste) through deconstruction and reconstruction into new, desirable garments. For instance, Junky Styling in the UK source second-hand men's suits and remake them into bespoke garments for their customers (Junky Styling 2011). The label 'From Somewhere' collects pre-consumer textile waste from other fashion companies to produce their garments (From Somewhere 2011). Upcycling is underpinned by an environmental ethics, aiming to protect the natural environment through redirecting textile waste from landfill in preference to using virgin fibre. Part of what makes these garments desirable is the new values they invisibly hold; their story, origins and ethics.

These approaches to managing fashion's waste owe much to William McDonough and Michael Braungart's Cradle-to-Cradle (C2C) concept, a closed-loop manufacturing system in which waste is eliminated by design. The core concept of 'Cradle-to-Cradle' is to develop a life cycle for products that emulates the life cycle of nature. In their model, waste equals food (McDonough and Braungart 2002: 92). The 'biological nutrients' of a product, that is, those from a natural source, should be safely composted to nourish the soil. For instance, the Climatex fabric is safely dyed and finished to ensure that it can be composted without polluting the soil (Fletcher 2008: 112). Valuable 'technical nutrients' (synthetic resources) can be reclaimed and reused for new products with no loss in quality. For example, Teijin textiles developed the closed-loop recycling of polyester, in which polyester textiles can be melted down to produce new near-virgin quality polyester. This approach has been used with some success in outdoor wear company Patagonia's 'Common Threads' programme (Patagonia 2010), as well as the more fashion-forward Nau (2011). Both offer a take-back service to their customers to encourage the recycling of their used products in this closed-loop system.

Cradle-to-Cradle thinking is a powerful paradigm for managing the ethical concerns of waste within the fashion system. Although converting to closed-loop manufacturing is a monumental challenge for the industry, C2C promotes a broader cyclical thinking and a reconceptualization of waste as food. When McDonough and Braungart describe their system, they use the analogy of a cherry tree. A tree grows, develops blossoms and fruit, drops the fruit into the soil, a seed grows and in time a new cherry tree emerges. There is no waste, no grave. The tree that may wither and die nourishes the soil as it rots; the new tree that takes its place feeds wildlife and sequesters carbon (McDonough and Braungart 2002: 72). There is a conceptual parallel here to Bataille's notion of excess. The excess of blossoms on a tree would never be deemed 'wasteful' in a negative sense; rather, it is an excess to be delighted in. In much the same way, the creative excess of design ideas in fashion cannot be deemed inherently 'bad'; rather, it enriches and beautifies our lives, going on to nourish the next generation of designs. If the physical waste of the fashion industry could be managed as the creative waste is, in a Cradle-to-Cradle way, then we would be closer to a sustainable fashion system.

However, C2C arguably skates over the more fundamental problem of excessive consumption in the West, whether of fashion products or other consumer goods. Design theorist Tony Fry acknowledges C2C as a progressive model of product design (Fry 2009: 189). However, he believes that the model propagates the same consumption patterns that led humanity to its current state of unsustainability (Fry 2009: 189–190). In Fry's view, the C2C approach can 'easily fold into sustaining the unsustainable' as it may be unproblematically mobilized without questioning the volumes of the designed product, its underlying position within a capitalist economy based on perpetual growth, or whether the product needs to exist in the first place, whether it 'should or should not be eliminated by design' (Fry 2009: 190). The fashion industry faces a dilemma as its processes of production embody Fry's concept of defuturing, or 'sustaining the unsustainable'. Increasingly, there is a need for a view of fashion that is not so closely bound to capitalism's planned obsolescence. Kate Fletcher addresses both users and designers when she says:

> we have to become activists, skilful producers and consumers of garments, our actions exploding some of the mystique, exclusivity and power structures of the fashion system to break the link between fashion and material consumption and to offer alternative visions of fashion's future.
>
> (Fletcher 2008: 126)

The intangible, creative waste that provides much of the delight, spectacle and novelty of fashion need not be rejected for strict frugality. However, when this creative waste is solely employed to propel wasteful, polluting volumes of product through the system, its ethics must be questioned.

Towards an ethics for fashion's waste

Despite recent shifts in designer or consumer behaviour towards fashion's sustainability, waste remains an intractable problem. Rather than suggesting a solution, I suggest an ethical framework through which an individual can engage with questions surrounding fashion's waste. Already, ethical or sustainable fashion has emerged as a worldwide movement to respond to the polluting and wasteful practices of the fashion system. As a design practice, ethical fashion takes a holistic view of the garment life cycle by examining the garment's impacts through fibre and textile choice, manufacturing, supply chain, use phase and eventual disposal (Fletcher 2008; Gwilt 2011). Designers involved in ethical fashion take responsibility for the waste of their products' past, present and future, while ethical fashion wearers select their garments based on the degree of manufacturing and ethical practices: how they were made, who made them and what materials were employed? The ethics underpinning this movement can be understood through a deontological framework, where ethical action is framed according to notions of moral duty and rights. This begins with the acceptance that the natural world has an intrinsic value and, therefore, a moral right to the protection of its biodiversity (Rolston 1989). Likewise, consumers have a right to protection from polluting chemicals, workers have a right to fair pay and safe working conditions. Following from this, ethical designers have a duty to protect the natural world through eliminating wasteful and environmentally polluting practices. Consumers have a duty to consume ethically, to select garments that did not generate undue tangible waste or pollution. All users of fashion have a duty to ensure that when their garment becomes waste, they dispose of it through inserting it into a waste cycle where it can become food for the next cycle of clothing.

A solely deontological ethical approach to waste and excess in fashion provides only a partial answer. A more nuanced approach to ethical fashion can be understood with the addition of environmental virtue ethics, in particular the notion of *eudaimonia*, often translated as happiness, well-being or human flourishing (Cafaro 2005). Arising from Aristotelian virtue ethics, eudaimonia is the happiness one attains through living a virtuous life. Rather than an ethics that critiques actions as moral or not, virtue ethics looks to the character of the actor and asks the question, 'what is the best life for a person and how can I go about living it?' (Cafaro 2005: 31). In environmental virtue ethics, character traits, such as respect, tolerance, greed or envy, can be positioned as virtues or vices. The question of 'what is the best life I can live?' is then framed around what are the moral virtues to aspire to and which vices should be shunned. Vices or virtues are defined not only through their effect on people's well-being, but also on the well-being of the environment (Sandler and Cafaro 2005). Hence, when reframed within the context of sustainability, eudaimonia is human flourishing and well-being that occurs when we live respectfully with the natural world and with others. In engaging ethically with fashion's waste, whether as a designer or a consumer, a notion of well-being allows for an ethics in which a waste that nourishes can be assessed as to its virtuous value, while a waste that pollutes can be shunned.

However, the identification of which forms of waste are virtues and which are vices is highly problematic as it bears the question of who determines what is good and what is bad. As a way forward, an individual can assess the effect of the waste on well-being in both an environmental and social sense. Fashion designers have the power to 'diminish environmental well-being through waste and pollution', but also they 'can improve it through lowering carbon emissions and improving bio-friendly practices' (Hethorn 2008: 57). A set of basic criteria against which garments are assessed by both designers and consumers can be established. These criteria can include, but not exclusively, the well-being of individuals, which can be promoted with garments that meet their aesthetic and functional needs; garments that embody the virtues of temperance, respect for nature and for others; degrees of creativity; and reuse and reinvention. Ideally, a fashion system that places these virtues as central sustains people and allows them to flourish. Fashion's creative waste can be part of this flourishing through a profound engagement with its tangible waste. Hence, within fashion design practice, physical waste can be a food for reinvention and renewal. Within fashion consumption, the discarded can be reclaimed, repaired, reworked and revalorized.

Conclusion

Fashion and waste are entwined at a number of levels. Fashion exists in a space of excess and abundance, a spending of creative energy, to be consumed, destroyed and rebuilt again. The result is a proliferation of design ideas, styles and imagery that has an equivalent in physical waste. The inherent wastage of the fashion system can be witnessed in unsustainable agricultural practices or through the flow of pre- and post-consumer waste to landfill. Managing this waste raises an ethical question regarding the duties of users and makers towards the environment and towards each other. Fashion's excesses are both intangible and tangible, producing a waste that may be physically polluting yet culturally nourishing. For this reason, an ethics resting solely on duty needs to allow some room for the joyful waste of fashion to be celebrated. Eudaimonia, the notion of human well-being and flourishing within ecological boundaries, provides a pathway towards a fashion ethic for users and makers. In this framework, waste is not framed as morally wrong in and of itself, but instead the various forms of waste can be analysed as to whether they contribute to human and environmental well-being or detract from it. Currently, while the ideas and creativity of the fashion system may be regenerated to provide creative nourishment for future designs and trends, the actual artefacts – garments, trims, fabric offcuts, samples – become physical detritus of which only a portion goes on to a useful second life. Solutions to manage this tangible waste, such as resale and reuse, closed-loop recycling and upcycling, all move the system closer to a point where the polluting waste can be used for nourishment. The great challenge for fashion as an industry and a cultural practice is to ethically manage these two forms of waste, or excess, in order to move towards a more environmentally responsible way of creating and living with fashion.

References

Allwood, J. M., Laursen. S. E., Malvido de Rodriguez, C. and Bocken, N. M. P. (2006) *Well dressed?: The present and future sustainability of clothing and textiles in the United Kingdom*, Cambridge: University of Cambridge – Institute for Manufacturing. Available at: www.ifm.eng.cam.ac.uk/sustainability/projects/mass/uk_textiles.pdf (accessed 10 June 2010).

Bataille, G. (1988) *The Accursed Share: An essay on general economy*, New York: Zone Books.

Cafaro, P. (2005) 'Thoreau, Leopold, and Carson: toward an environmental virtue ethics', R. D. Sandler and P. Cafaro (eds) *Environmental Virtue Ethics*, Lanham, MD: Rowman & Littlefield.

Calefato, P. (2004) *The Clothed Body,* Oxford: Berg.

Caulfield, K. (2009) *Discussion Paper: Sources of textile waste in Australia*, Melbourne: Technical Textiles Non-Woven Association. Available at: www.ttna.com.au/TEXTILE%20 WASTE%20PAPER%20March%202009.pdf (accessed 20 August 2010).

Craik, J. (1994) *The Face of Fashion: Cultural studies in fashion*, New York: Routledge.

Entwistle, J. (2009) *The Aesthetic Economy of Fashion: Markets and value in clothing and modelling*, New York: Berg.

Falk, P. (1994) *The Consuming Body (Theory, Culture and Society)*, London: Sage.

Fletcher, K. (2008) *Sustainable Fashion and Textiles: Design journeys*, Sterling: Earthscan.
From Somewhere (2011) Available at: www.fromsomewhere.co.uk (accessed 12 May 2011).
Fry, T. (2009) *Design Futuring: Sustainability, ethics and new practice*, Sydney: University of New South Wales Press.
Gregson, N. and Crewe, L. (2003) *Second-hand Cultures (Materializing Culture)*, Oxford, New York: Berg.
Gwilt, A. (2011) 'Producing sustainable fashion: the points of positive intervention by the fashion designer', in A. Gwilt and T. Rissanen (eds) *Shaping Sustainable Fashion: Changing the way we make and use clothes*, London: Earthscan.
Hawkins, G. (2006) *The Ethics of Waste: How we relate to rubbish*, Lanham, MD: Rowman & Littlefield Publishers.
Hethorn, J. (2008) 'Consideration of consumer desire', J. Hethorn and C. Ulasewicz (eds) *Sustainable Fashion: Why Now?: A conversation exploring issues, practices, and possibilities*, New York: Fairchild.
Junky Styling (2011) Available at: www.junkystyling.co.uk/about/history (accessed 12 May 2011).
Lipovetsky, G. (1994) *The Empire of Fashion: Dressing modern democracy*, Princeton, NJ: Princeton University Press.
McDonough, W. and Braungart, M. (2002) *Cradle to Cradle: Remaking the way we make things*, New York: North Point Press.
McQuillan, H. (2011) 'Zero-waste design practice: strategies and risk taking for garment design', in A. Gwilt and T. Rissanen (eds) *Shaping Sustainable Fashion: Changing the way we make and use clothes*, London: Earthscan.
Nau (2011) 'Lightbeam hoody'. Available at: www.nau.com/womens/categories/recycled_poly/lightbeam-hoody-409W01.html (accessed 12 May 2011).
Patagonia (2010) 'Introducing the Common Threads initiative'. Available at: http://www.patagonia.com/ca/patagonia.go?assetid=49139 (accessed 12 December 2010).
Polhemus, T. (1994) *Streetstyle: From sidewalk to catwalk*, New York: Thames & Hudson.
Rissanen, T. 2008. 'Creating fashion without the creation of fabric waste', in J. Hethorn and C. Ulasewicz (eds) *Sustainable Fashion: Why Now?: A conversation exploring issues, practices, and possibilities*, New York: Fairchild.
Rolston, H. (1989) *Philosophy Gone Wild: Environmental ethics*, New York: Prometheus Books.
Sandler, R. D. and Cafaro, P. (2005) *Environmental Virtue Ethics*, Lanham, MD: Rowman & Littlefield.

PART V

Epilogue

16

LOOKING BACK, FORWARD AND ELSEWHERE

An afterword

Tony Fry

Introduction

I come to this moment of statement having steered my way through the text and in so doing passing over, under and through what I discovered. It follows that there are some things that have been avoided, some stumbled over and others that I have picked up and carried into my own concerns. I read with neither the intent to be a reviewer nor a neutral commentator, but rather I want to provide the reader with a cluster of responsive reflections that prompt a return to the text with new questions to re-engage it. I hope to do this in such a way as to render much of both the said and the unsaid of the text in a constructively critical light.

Putting a collection of essays together on design and ethics is clearly a substantial challenge. The ambition could either be to build an ever-more rich and complex understanding of the relation from an enunciated position, or simply to provide a range of different points of view from which the reader draws their own conclusions. The underlying issue in making this choice is the radical difference between pluralism and plurality, a distinction that itself is generative of an ethical dilemma. I can use my own position to make this difference clearer.

I take an unequivocal position towards sustainment that is antagonistic towards those voices of pluralism that argue that sustainment is just one imperative among many. At the same time, I recognize that sustainment is plural – it cannot be reduced to just one form of acting or being. As such, it can accommodate many biophysical, social, economic, cultural and psychological imperatives. In fact, sustainment is not possible without difference.

The ethical turn: just a little spin or a full revolution?

The ethical turn to sustainment indicates both a turn to and then away from ethics as inherited from Western metaphysics. Unquestionably, the designer can be, and needs to become, an ethical subject. However, so often they are simply acting on the instructions of a client who knowingly or unknowingly has already made the very design decisions that determine the (un)ethical fate of the designed. Mostly, beyond their immediate objects of focus, designers do not know the consequences of what they are actually doing when they bring some 'thing' into being. For the most part, they simply fail to grasp how they are positioned between their designing being directed *and* the directional design of the designed (for example, the life and after-life impacts of the product).

The metaphysics of design (its underpinning knowledge) can inform the designer on how to become ethical, but in so doing the designer, via the metaphysics, has to direct, and then give way to, the ontological performance of the designed. Awareness has limited agency in a world in which unawareness is a structurally constructed and posited feature of the commodity culture of the everyday life. In such a context, directed ontological design can be an ethical counter force to the way that design is implicated in 'things' that conceal their destructive agency. So much that is rendered beautiful by design does harm to biophysical and social ecologies. It is easy to find examples that do direct environmental damage, but negation arrives in many guises. For example, in the cultural sphere, it is a primary quality of hegemonic entertainment as it covers over the serious and thereby diminished concern that motivates action – a view even more pertinent now than when it was first expressed by Carl Schmitt over three-quarters of a century ago.[1]

There is no greater ethical dilemma than the fact that actual ethical action is at odds with our being anthropocentric. Ethics, in any materialized form (which, it can be argued, is in the end the only form that counts), does not imply the transcendence of anthropocentrism. Rather, it rests on an acknowledgement of this determinate. In this respect, the need to establish our ability to sustain ourselves over time depends on an ethical turn towards an ethics materially embodied as the performative qualities of the things of the world we make. Such a turn cannot happen without recognizing how our being anthropocentric has, and continues to, undercut the very ground of our being. By implication, this means that which has to be turned is us. Design, redirected towards a full recognition of its ontological agency, and thus re-formed as a practice, has an enormous turning ability.

Ethics writ large is sustainment. Through a growing and dispersed common message of voices of difference, humanity is at the edge of recognizing that we, as a species, have no future without acquiring sustain-ability. Yet, as implied, we cannot will ourselves to acquire this ability. In fact, even though we might want to be sustain-able, the very means the vast majority of us use to sustain ourselves on a daily basis, including our disciplines, practices, knowledge and skills, currently negate the actual ground to be sustained. Here we come to confront the force of defuturing.

Unwittingly, by design and artifice, anthropocentric human beings brought an unsustainable world-within-the-world into existence. Palaeoanthropology tells us that from the coming into being of proto-humans over two million years ago, 'we' started a process of the continual modification of our actual mode of earthy habitation. Effectively, from *Anthropithecus* to *Homo sapiens*, we have always acted prefiguratively and so have been designed by the consequences of our own actions. This is to say, the actions of that animal that we were and are – an animal who picked up a stone and turned it into a tool – acted prefiguratively and in doing so caused a rift between a world that is and a world of human fabrication (the world-within-the-world). We humans have never ceased doing this; thus our trajectory towards the unsustainable was set from our very beginning. We have always been technological beings, in so far as our being has always been shaped by our being world-makers and un-makers (defuturers). Of course, when our numbers were few and our technology basic, our impacts were low and able to be accommodated by natural systems. But now the global population is so large, and still growing, and our mental and material attainments creating impacts so vast that, as already said, our very future is uncertain. So contextualized, 'defuturing' literally means taking the unknown time of our finitudinal being away.

So, framed sustainment, as an intellectual project and material practice, invites being seen as a project equal to, or greater than, the Enlightenment (as it became the intellectual and scientific 'powerhouse' of defuturing modernity). Sustainment has to provide the means to think and realize the counter force of defuturing, which, of course, is futuring. Rather than a utopian schema, futuring centres on redirecting the defuturing character of what is. As this, it can be seen as a means to transition from metaphysical to post-metaphysical design wherein the very ontological character of the agency of design, as identified, is given a form and free rein. An ethical issue needs to be acknowledged here. Design is always directional; this is its inherent essence, but now the ethical demand is that it be knowingly (re)directed towards the futural. This asserts that not only a futural ethics is ontologically bonded to design but design is made to become mono-directional (which means in all its aspects it is directed towards sustainment and massively elevated in importance).

The dialectic of sustainment

Design, all design, is unavoidably positioned within the dialectic of sustainment. This means that, as both an act of prefiguration and as the prefigured, design is always 'on the line' ethically as an agent acting towards the unsustainable or sustainment, defuturing or futuring. To grasp the implication of this positioning we need to be clear about what the 'dialectic of sustainment' tells us. Certainly, it announces that unsustainability is an increasingly dynamic event forming from the sum of all our so often unrecognized acts of negation. It also tells us that if we are to continue to be, then the creation of sustainment (as a biophysical condition, culture and economy) is the absolute creative imperative.

Writ large, whenever the natural resources of the planet are appropriated to make any element of the world-within-the-world (the world of human fabrication) there is always an act of destruction that may or may not do long-term or permanent damage to the being of beings (including us). Such action became naturalized as what human beings do from the very moment our ancient ancestors acquired and applied artifice to transform their environment in some way to meet their self-defined needs. From time immemorial, destruction, unless enacted as an overt end in itself in rage, malice or war, mostly inhabited the domain of the unconscious. But now, with overt signs of damaged natural environments and anthropogenically induced climate damage, the fact of human destructiveness of terrestrial and aquatic ecologies, and the species thereof, is becoming increasingly evident. The difference between naturally destructive events and us is that what we do is a continuous process.

Yet, at the level of the detail of our daily lives, we still fail to see the damage we do. There are two fundamental reasons why this is the case. The first is that the cultures we have created so often elevate and celebrate creation and creativity to an extraordinary degree, and in doing so overlook the material costs of what is created. Here, the second reason comes into play: aesthetics. The aesthetics of architecture and design are a force of concealment. The object, the image (and the object as image) overwhelm any ability to picture or think about the trail of destruction that led to the object in view coming into being. Beauty, elegance and style deflect the eye and mind away from the character, place, pain and time of destruction. Everything that is clean comes out of dirt. Without a moment's thought, energy that took tens of millions of years to embody in some extractable form is expended in a fraction of a moment. The issue here is not that destruction per se is bad – obviously it is unavoidable. Rather, the ethical issue is what is destroyed and for what end. Often the value of the created in no way equates with the futural value of the destroyed (as with chipping a one-thousand-year-old tree to make paper with a manufacture-to-disposal life of a few months).

Here, then, is the context that frames how we are to comprehend the dialectic of sustainment as it grounds the ethical imperative of decision on creation or destruction that is always present, but mostly overlooked, in every design act. So to say, as we have, that design is on the line ethically is to recognize that every design act that leads to some kind of designed object coming into being determines in some way which side of the line that divides the ethical from the unethical the object falls. More than this, the dialectic carries within it an essential definition of ethics that ruptures it from any association with a moral code. Morality has to be recognized as culturally relative or as ethnocentrically imposed, whereas ethics bonded to sustainment is a common good that extends over all cultural difference. As such, it is an acknowledgement that, irrespective of a concern for non-human Others, what is sought to be sustained is us, and all that we depend upon. Sustainment is anthropocentrism shifted from *habitus* to acknowledged responsibility. It tells us that we cannot be without being anthropocentric, but that equally we cannot be without taking responsibility for our being anthropocentric.

In summary, what an understanding of this dialectic exposes is the indivisible relation between creation and destruction. While one might think this relation exists in 'the domain of the absolutely obvious', what we have sought to show is that it actually exists as an ethical lacuna. Clearly, the preoccupation with creativity, as a psychology, ontology and acclaimed value of a fully formed subject, covers over our individual and collective need to make a distinction between warranted and unwarranted destruction. To recognize this condition of concealment is to learn that the creation of sustainment implies the destruction of the unsustainable. Some designers are just starting to grasp this and thus are starting to recognize that *ethics is something you do.* Such action, as said, is about making time and can be named as futuring. It is not a matter of bringing such a naming to just one industry but to all industry – bluntly, without sustainment as a condition to strive to create, we have no future.

Time

Just as the sight of destruction escapes us, so also does time. First of all, there is the misconception that time is measure, that it is duration. The clock as an instrument that measures does not tell us what time is. Rather, the clock shares a common characteristic of all things – it has a time of its own (as a speed of change), but does contain the *idea* of 'time'. That we order our lives by the measured time of our invention obstructs the plurality of the rate of change inherent to the nature of time. Time is change; as such, 'everything has its own time'.[2] Second, and even more significant to our acting in time, is the fact that human beings are kronophobic – we fear time. Drawing on Nietzsche, Bernd Magnus recognized this condition: that we seek 'permanence where and when there is none' (Magnus 1978: 190–195). Moreover, our very being is enacted via refusal of time evidenced by the pursuit of power, wealth and fame. If we wish to make time for ourselves, we have to understand time not as measure but as change, with everything having its own time.

In so far as time cannot be disaggregated from being, it exhausts thought. The last word on time will never be written or spoken. Yet one could argue that there has never been a time when the issue of time is more important to think about than now. This is because the unbroken human trajectory towards the unsustainable is unravelling the nexus between 'our being' in time and 'the time of our being'. To reiterate: as a result of our actions, what is at stake is our continuity, our time (and co-laterally the time of so many other beings). We no longer live in a moment in which our future as a species can be assumed. Even if it has always been the case that our being is inherently precarious, coming to know this in the way we do now, shifts our sense of our being finite from abstraction to reality. How we act in time is decisive of the duration of our being and will become seen as such. Unambiguously, that which is at stake is us, not the planet. Some 283 million years ago, 90 per cent of all species were wiped out. We came out of the 10 per cent. The planet will be around long after we humans have gone to dust.

Viewed in projected time, our ever-growing numbers, the destructiveness of the economy of our creation on our conditions of dependence, combined with our collective inability to deal with the consequences of the products of our creation; our illusion of power and control (not least via technology), and the negative and violent propensities of ourselves means that *we are high risk.* For all the rhetoric of sustainability, our general understanding of 'unsustainability' is abysmal, inadequate, frequently misplaced and counter-productive. There is, as yet, no general recognition that the continuity of our being cannot resemble what we currently are as uncontrollably acquisitive anthropocentric beings. An understanding of how to see and engage time in a new way recasts how ethics is enacted through ontological design and the making of things material and immaterial.

'Time is everywhere and yet nowhere and, still, it is only in the soul' (Heidegger 1988: 225). Time is the condition of change we dwell in. For us, it is the horizon of being as our being-in-the-world intersects with 'the world' (Heidegger 1988: 225). To be here in time, and thus in being, is to be both in a finite moment, world, time and to be in motion. As the ancients noted: man is the measure of all things, including time. We know we cannot hold our being in time. As François Jullien has pointed out, one cannot 'hold onto one's life' by 'clinging and grasping'; that 'in order to have a life one's life has to be risked' is a universal 'anthropological' truth that transcends time and culture (Jullien 2007: 36).

Learning how to think ethics and design 'now' cannot be divided from learning how to design in time. Such designing implies being timely in the face of the unsustainable and designing with an enhanced understanding of the medium of time as an environment of the change of things being in time. So, by developing a picture – a projection of things as they change in relation to identifiable forces of change – one can start to acquire an ability to design back from a partially comprehended future and in so doing confront directional options that invite ethical decision. There can be no claim of such a practice being able to see into the future, or deliver certainty, but it can confront the myopia that goes with thinking that design can be finished, deliver end products that end, and be managed as a linear process.

What the practice of designing in time does is to move from the observation that 'design goes on designing' to attempting to map what is actually designed in time so that the direction set in the design act can be changed, if needed, and forms of responsibility can be prefigured and projected into 'a time to act'.

Such a mapping has to be relational, aware of the need to counter the anthropocentric disposition of design (which itself implies enacted responsibility rather than transcendence). All of this implies working in an environment of complexity and ethical decision beyond simple systems. These systems have now been understood and exposited by Niklas Luhmann as second order systems theory (Luhmann 1995). Basically, it's a matter of trying to see ourselves, and what we bring into being, 'in time', but in a way that recognizes how the imperative and the medium of time should be understood.

Making things ethical

Things cannot be made ethical without design. 'Making' here can be both by the designer or the ontological designing of designed things. Either way, the designer, the act of designing and the designed object all have to change. All notions of a shift of the design agency to technology (design democracy) in the context of the existing function of design are totally misplaced and are predicated upon a simplistic and reductive notion of the designer, designing and the designed. Certainly, there has to be a massive transference to a directed ontological designing of manufactured things, including technologies with enhanced designing capability, but, and it's a huge but, only after the materialization of the ethical in the conduct of things (good design as a means of sustainment). This can only happen by the development of design expertise, which in turn requires new knowledge, a vast improvement in design education, a transformation of design practice and a new order of design leadership.

Rather than being a statement of extreme idealism, what is actually being said is absolutely pragmatic. If humanity is to have a future, it has to create the time of sustainment. There is no choice. As laid by an economy of foundational destruction and the ever-increasing material demands of an unchecked and growing global population of inequity, the defuturing path of structural unsustainability will take us to conflict, a likely massive population cull, and a dark age of species degeneration. This drift, one that we are now all on, must be countered. The situation is already beyond technological salvation – it is just not possible to engineer our way into the future. To repeat, there will be no future without directional change, and all that currently travels under the heading of sustainability is simply a therapeutic tinkering unable to come to grips with the depths of the problem to be faced.

Design and the Other

In so far as design in its ontological agency always implicates the Other (reductively and mostly inappropriately characterized as 'the user') it is always *facing* a turn towards or away from the ethical. As such, it gathers or excludes, nurtures or harms, Others – be they human or non-human. In this setting, design (con)fuses any clear distinction between designed subjects and designing objects.

Design (as the designed) is so often a covering over of otherness by the appropriative induction of the Other into an aesthetic regime of hyper-conformative difference (plurality thus becomes the same). What is identified by such action is an expedient and eclectic taking from any time, culture or place – a tendency epitomized by, but not exclusive to, fashion design. What is being recognized here is how the very possibility of a design ethics is historically and continually compromised by the already identified propensity of design to conceal. The mobilization of style – be it the architectural façade, the stylized industrially designed product, packaging or, as said, fashion – is a very clear, but not exclusive, illustration of such a process. As we shall see by considering two examples, the consequence of the propensity for design to conceal is profound.

The first example is the covering over of the critical by a seeming solution that marginalizes crisis. What this effectively does is to create a crisis of crisis. Sustainable design is deeply implicated in this problematic. Rather than making explicit the extent and complexity of the unsustainable, it trades on the assumption that solutions are on hand and are able to be delivered by an industry of replacement (via 'green, eco and sustainable' energy, architecture, technologies, products, etc). Dominantly, this approach rests on a market-centric notion of how solutions can be delivered, leaving the vast complexity of the unsustainable untrammelled and thus upholding the status quo and thereby sustaining the unsustainable. What fundamentally goes unaddressed, and so concealed, is that unsustainability cannot be resolved within the extant economic paradigm. Whether we consider the likes of natural gas, hybrid vehicles or hemp shirts, market growth continually negates impact reduction gains. Mitigation measures are just not enough, they are not solutions; they do not deliver sustainment and so easily can be used to conceal the depth of the unsustainable.

Example two is how the designed and constructed appearance of technology is deeply embedded in design as the unseen and concealment, thereby exposing the inadequacy of an aesthetic view of design and design ethics. Effectively, the history of the design of technology is a history of a covering over. Beyond the complicity of aesthetics, initially via styling and then via the presentational forms of 'black box' technologies (with retained inferences to function), there is now an ever-expanding condition of what Martin Heidegger called 'de-severance' (*entfernen*) (Heidegger 1961: 138–139). What this means is that while we may position ourselves near a technological object, we are not close to it. The engine of a motorcar or motorcycle is a case in point. Once, with a degree of mechanical knowledge, one could get near to the engine, see it, hear it and engage in minor adjustment and repairs, or major ones if one had the ability. But now, besides being stylistically encased, it and other working parts can only be reached and engaged via the interface of a diagnostic computer program (which few of us have or want). The mechanical has been coupled with the electronic and then removed into a space that we do not occupy.

A far more dramatic and ethically troubling instance of technologically induced deseverance is found in the relation between technology and war. Over an extensive period of time, and at an ever-more rapid pace, the killing of an enemy has become ever-more remote. Thus, while the ability to kill via a technology has continually increased in terms of the numbers of enemy able to be killed with accuracy, the act of killing has increasingly moved further away from the actor that kills. In many cases the killer does not even see the killed. De facto, ethical concern has become desevered as action is abstracted as a technical decision. The result is that the ethical question of war and the conduct of war appear to become more distant from each other. Put simply, the dirty gets dirtier while seemingly getting clinically cleaner by the absence of the subject that kills at the site of the surgical strike.

Here we have but one instance of just how the nature of technology is becoming more removed from a place of ethical interrogation. Calculation now marginalizes ethical concern to a new level of invisibility. The lesson of the danger of this, as it brought humanity to its lowest ebb in the Nazi era, has simply not been learned.

Any sense of a distinction between an inside and an outside of the human and technological has dissolved. The historicity of the ontological designing of technology actually suggests that the distinction was always a false one but it is only now that this is becoming apparent. To understand this remark one has to grasp that from our very coming into being as a species that made a world-within-the-world by artifice, we were equally making our selves via technics. For us, technology became naturalized. Whatever sense of the artificial we once had (as alienation from the technological) it is now rapidly eroding or has already done so. As technological beings, we are increasingly living in a condition of *autonomic technocentrism* – that is, technology is increasingly taking on a life of its own over which we have little or no control. It is not on the outside; it is not a tool simply directed from the inside. We exist in a world of technological systems that nobody (individual, corporate or national) can switch off. As, for instance, Bernard Stiegler has made very clear, we have industrialized memory and externalized the central nervous system (Stiegler 2009: 163–187). By implication, the seat of ethical judgement has been knocked beneath us. Yet to know this is to know the necessity of another way of knowing and the need for another mode of alienation. It is again to know there is a need to shift ethics out of metaphysics and into the ontological post-human domain of what 'designed things design'.

Much needs to be abandoned and eliminated. The contradiction of human-centred design (and other anthropocentrically inflected design practices) needs exposure. In the face of what threatens and challenges, there is certainly a need for the recovery and enhancement of a high order of resilience: there are skills to rediscover and to newly create, a greater capacity of endurance to be formed, a determination to be forged, a learning to endure pain and courage to be found. Unavoidably, as indicated earlier, to be futural our very being has to be refashioned (made another way as world-makers). The refashioning of our lives and living, framed by a knowledge of the dialectic of sustainment, can and has to be, a locus of sacrifice as well as the remaking of pleasure.

In the economy that has to be (for our being to be), all that is produced has to sustain, and consumption has to be predicated on that which is actually metabolically consumed. Dominantly, the production of objects for consumption is not metabolic – which is to say that the problem with consumption is that 'things' are not actually consumed. Things are just used up as sign value or they break down; thus what remains are 'things' we misname as waste. Waste, the stuff of landfill, is but a fraction of what is wasted.

Conclusion

An ethics based on the designing of the things we bring into being by design demands a number of critical reconfigurations to drive all forms of innovation. These reconfigurations would likely include:

- A confrontation, across generations and decades, with our education in error. In truth, we are taught from infancy to PhD to function within the status quo and so we are effectively learning how to be unsustainable – reformist sustainability content gets nowhere near the transformation of being and acting that sustainment actually requires.

- The building of a new foundation of 'the good' beyond any morality, theology or eudaimonia and which is centred on a commonality of difference that follows a plural pursuit of sustainment. This new foundation would, by necessity, have to overcome the existing poverty of language of ethics and the good.
- The delivery of a higher order of politically directed designing, which knows that 'we' will only get to a 'future with a future' by design. Such an elevation of design has to recognize that neither democracy (as it is), nor democratic design (as a negation of responsibility) will get us to become sustain-able (Fry 2011: 8–11).
- The imposition of a new unfreedom to secure (our) relative freedom. Just as the freedom of the modern world rested on the imposition of 'freedom under the law', all futural freedom will depend on the imposition of freedom under the plural rule of sustainment.

Finally, in the face of geopolitical and biophysical circumstances that will unfold over the next century – as they will be replete with dangers, not least of conflict (Lee 2006; Dyer 2008) and opportunities to become other than we currently are – one can say with some certainty that our species' survival and design will become (already are) indivisible. In this relation, ethics, as an ontological agency of redirection, has to be materialized as the counter-force to that unknowing, that unconsciousness, inherent in the structurally defuturing unsustainability that currently remains hegemonic.

Notes

1 These views were expressed in Leo Strauss's notes on Carl Schmitt in *The Concept of the Political*, archived in 1932 and published by Strauss in the 1960s. These notes are cited by Heinrich Meier in *Carl Schmitt and Leo Strauss: The hidden dialogue* (see editorial note, p.120 and pp. 111–12).

2 Martin Heidegger first pointed this out in 1927, *Being and Time* (H418: 471), and held to this view consistently, reiterating, including in the1967 publication *On Time and Being*, trans. Joan Stambaugh, New York, Harper & Row, 1972.

References

Dyer, G. (2008) *Climate Wars*, Melbourne: Scribe.

Fry, T. (2011) *Design as Politics*, Oxford: Berg.

Heidegger, M. (1961) *The Question Concerning Technology and Other Essays*, New York: Harper & Row.

Heidegger, M. (1988) *The Basic Problems of Phenomenology*, Bloomington, IN: Indiana University Press.

Jullien, F. (2007) *Vital Nourishment: Departing from Happiness*, New York: Zone Books.

Lee, J. R. (2006) *Climate Change and Armed Conflict*, London: Routledge.

Luhmann, N. (1995) *Social Systems*, Stanford, CA: Stanford University Press.
Magnus, B. (1978) *Nietzsche's Existential Imperative*, Bloomington, IN: Indiana University Press.
Stiegler, B. (2009) *Technics and Time 2*, Stanford, CA: Stanford University Press.

INDEX

Note: page numbers in *italic* type refer to Figures; those in **bold** type refer to Tables.